# Hamburg

# Hamburg

**Metropole an Alster und Elbe**

**Metropolis on Alster and Elbe**

**Mit einem Text von Anna Brenken**

**Fotografiert von Egbert Kossak**

Ellert & Richter Verlag

# Inhalt

# Contents

# Nonnen als Großgrundbesitzer, Poet als Ratsherr

## Nuns as big landowners, a poet as councillor

„Hamburg ick liebe Dir." Ein Berliner
Sprayer unterwegs an der Elbe. Liebeser-
klärung auf Beton am Hafenrand. In
Pink, Grün, Blau und Schwarz aus der
Dose. Die Form ist neu, die Liebe alt. In
den zwanziger Jahren schrieb der
berühmte Berliner Theaterkritiker Alfred
Kerr (1867–1948), daß Hamburg ohne
Zweifel die schönste Stadt in Deutsch-
land sei. Und im 19. Jahrhundert setzte
der Rheinländer Robert Schumann das
Hamburg-Gedicht von Heinrich Heine
„Schöne Wiege meiner Leiden ..." so
wundersam in Töne, daß diese Liebeser-
klärung heute Zuhörern in aller Welt zu
Herzen geht.

## Metropole mit Tradition und Wand-
lungsfähigkeit

Die Alster, die Elbe, die Fleete und Kanäle, der weite Himmel, der Hafen mit den
Schiffen aus aller Herren Länder machen
Hamburg zu einer Metropole, die immer
wieder zum Schwärmen verlockt. Zumal
sich die Stadt in den vergangenen Jahren
mächtig herausgeputzt hat. Die Jungen
und die Alten, die hier wohnen, wissen,
was sie an ihrem Hamburg haben. Für
alle anderen ist die Hafen-, Handels-,
Medien-, Mode-, Kultur- und neuerdings
auch Kunststadt heute ein höchst attrak-
tives Reiseziel. Seit dem Fall der Mauer
im November 1989 zieht die Metropole
am Zusammenfluß von Alster und Elbe
wieder Gäste aus allen vier Himmelsrichtungen an. In einigen Fällen von weither,
auch ungebetene, die ihr im Umfeld des
berühmten Rotlichtmilieus von St. Pauli
Ärger machen.

Straßen, die in den sechziger Jahren
noch grau vor sich hin schliefen, verräu-
cherte Schmuddelkneipen und vermuffte

"Hamburg, I love you," someone has
sprayed down by the Elbe. The dialect
makes it clear that the unknown admirer
is from Berlin. A declaration of love in
concrete down by the port. In shocking
pink, green, blue and black from a
spraycan. The form is new, the love old.
In the 1920s the famous Berlin theatre
critic Alfred Kerr (1867–1948) wrote
that Hamburg was without a doubt the
finest city in Germany. And in the nineteenth century the composer Robert
Schumann, who came from the
Rhineland, set Heinrich Heine's Hamburg poem "Lovely cradle of my suffer-
ing ..." so beautifully to music that this
declaration of love still touches audi-
ences all over the world.

## A metropolis with tradition and
versatility

The Alster, the Elbe and the canals, the
wide-open sky and the port with vessels
from all over the world make Hamburg
a metropolis which tempts one to
enthuse about it time and again. Especially as in recent years the city has gone
to great lengths to look good. Both
young and old who live here are aware
of what Hamburg offers them. For
everyone else, the city of port, commerce, media, fashion, culture and, of
late, also art is now a highly attractive
place to visit. Since the fall of the Berlin
Wall in November 1989 the metropolis
on the confluence of Alster and Elbe has
once again attracted visitors from all
points of the compass – including some
uninvited guests from far-off places who
make a nuisance of themselves in and
around the famous red-light district of St
Pauli.

Streets that in the 1960s were grey
and dreary, dingy smoke-filled pubs and
musty clothes shops have often been
rigged out so exclusively that some people find the opulence almost off-putting.
But never fear, beneath the surface something new will grow again. The conser-

Wer mit dem Schiff in Hamburg ankommt, hat die allerschönste Annäherung an die Hafenmetropole gewählt. Die Landungsbrücken mit der Grünspankuppel über dem Alten Elbtunnel sind das maritime Tor zur Stadt.

Anyone arriving in Hamburg by ship has chosen the most attractive of all approaches to the port city. The landing stages with the verdigris-covered dome atop the Old Elbe Tunnel are the maritime gateway to the city.

Modelädchen sind heute oft so nobel aufgezäumt, daß der Reichtum auf manchen fast abschreckend wirkt. Aber keine Sorge, unterm Pflaster wird wieder Neues wachsen. Der konservative hanseatische Geist war stets verschwistert mit einer großen Lust an der Veränderung. Rigoroses Handeln unter dem Primat wirtschaftlicher Nützlichkeit hat an der Elbe Tradition.

Stadt im Fluß, Metropole im Wandel, Gesellschaft im Umbruch. Den letzten großen wirtschaftlichen Schub brachte der Aufbruch nach dem Zerfall des Ostblocks seit 1989. Licht und Schatten in der Millionenstadt verändern ihr Gesicht permanent. Hamburg hat sich im Laufe der Jahrhunderte immer wieder gehäutet. Der kleine Handelsplatz am Elbstrom entpuppte sich im Mittelalter zu einer

vative Hanseatic spirit has always been twinned with a great love of change. Rigorous action with an eye to economic gain is custom and practice on the Elbe.

A city on the river. A metropolis in a state of change. A society in upheaval. The last big economic boost came with the new beginnings after the disintegra-

Im seit 1888 bestehenden Freihafengebiet Speicherstadt lagern zollfreie Waren aus aller Welt.

Duty-free goods from all over the world are stored in the free port area Speicherstadt dating back to 1888.

10

Die Brücken über die
Norderelbe faszinieren
den Ingenieur wie den
fachlich unbelasteten
Betrachter immer wie-
der. 1862–72 entstand
die erste Eisenbahn-
brücke. Es folgten zwi-
schen 1916 und 1926
die Freihafenbrücke (im
Vordergrund) und die
Neue Elbbrücke, die
das Konstruktionsprin-
zip der Freihafenbrücke
aufnahm. So entstand
für den Blick aus der
Vogelperspektive ein
irritierendes Netzwerk
von Trag- und Spann-
elementen.

The engineer and the
normal observer are
always fascinated by
the bridges over the
Norderelbe. The first
railway bridge was
constructed 1862–72.
The Freihafenbrücke in
the foreground and the
Neue Elbbrücke, using
the same principle of
the Freihafenbrücke fol-
lowed between 1916
and 1926. Thus the
bird's eye view of the
whole is an irritating
network of braces and
girders.

12

Die Außenalster als innerstädtisches Segelrevier hat nicht ihresgleichen. Gesäumt von Parkanlagen und Villengärten, bietet diese 164 Hektar große Wasserfläche Sportlern, Spaziergängern und Stadtmüden Ruhe und Entspannung.

The Outer Alster is unmatched as an inner-city sailing area. Lined by parkland and the gardens of private mansions, this 164-hectare area of water offers peace and relaxation to athletes, strollers and people weary of the city.

mächtigen Hansestadt mit einem engen Netz von Kanälen und krummen Gassen. Im 17. Jahrhundert verwandelte sich die Stadtrepublik in ein barock geprägtes Gemeinwesen, in dem wenige Patrizierfamilien Macht und Kapital besaßen. Im Industriezeitalter schließlich expandierte Hamburg zu einer der weltweit wichtigsten Hafenmetropolen und Deutschlands Tor zur Welt.

Wie sehr diese Metamorphosen im Spannungsfeld eines hamburgtypischen Konservatismus und eines ebenso unverkennbar starken Veränderungswillens standen, zeigt ein Streifzug durch die Geschichte der Stadt – von ihrer Gründung im 9. Jahrhundert bis heute.

**Hamburg: Stadt am Wasser**

Es macht Sinn, diese historische Wanderung auf der Trostbrücke zu beginnen. Dort stehen, aus Stein gehauen, die Statuen von Bischof Ansgar und Graf Adolf III. von Schauenburg, den Gründervätern der Stadt. Die Trostbrücke schlägt den Bogen über das Nikolaifleet, das zwischen bischöflicher Altstadt und herzoglicher Neustadt fließt. Altstadt und Neustadt wuchsen früh zu einem Gemeinwesen zusammen.

Bevor der Benediktinermönch Ansgar (801-865) um das Jahr 831 im Auftrag des Frankenkaisers Ludwigs des Frommen an der Elbe seine Zelte aufschlug, zum Bischof ernannt wurde und als „Apostel des Nordens" spätere Berühmtheit erlangte, hatte es im nördlichen Grenzgebiet des Frankenreichs bereits mehrere kriegerische Auseinandersetzungen mit den Sachsen gegeben. Doch zur politisch-wirtschaftlichen Region wurde die Siedlung an der Alstermündung erst mit Gründung des Bistums.

Wer heute auf der Trostbrücke steht, an Bischof Ansgar denkt und versucht, sich ein Bild von der Hammaburg zu

tion of the East Bloc in 1989. There is a permanent interplay of light and shade in this city of two million people, giving it a constantly changing appearance. Hamburg has shed its skin time and again in the course of the centuries. In the Middle Ages, the small trading-station on the River Elbe emerged as a powerful Hanseatic town with a dense network of canals and narrow, winding streets. In the seventeenth century the city republic was transformed into a Baroque-stamped community in which a few patrician families held power and capital. Finally, in the industrial age Hamburg exploded into one of the leading port cities worldwide, and into Germany's gateway to the world.

A review of the town's history from its founding in the ninth century to the present day highlights the degree to which these metamorphoses resulted from the conflict between typical Hamburg conservatism and an equally unmistakable strong will for change.

**Hamburg: city by the water**

It makes sense to begin this historic walk at Trostbrücke. On the bridge stand stone statues of Bishop Ansgar and Count Adolf III of Schauenburg, the city's founding fathers. Trostbrücke spans the Nikolaifleet, a canal which flows between the episcopal Altstadt (old town) and the ducal Neustadt (new town).

Before the Benedictine monk Ansgar (801–865), who had been sent by the Franconian emperor Ludwig the Pious, pitched his tents on the Elbe in around 831 and was appointed bishop (he later became famous as the "apostle of the north"), there had been several warlike confrontations with the Saxons in the northern border region of the Franconian empire. But the settlement on the mouth of the Alster did not become a political and economic entity until the bishopric was founded.

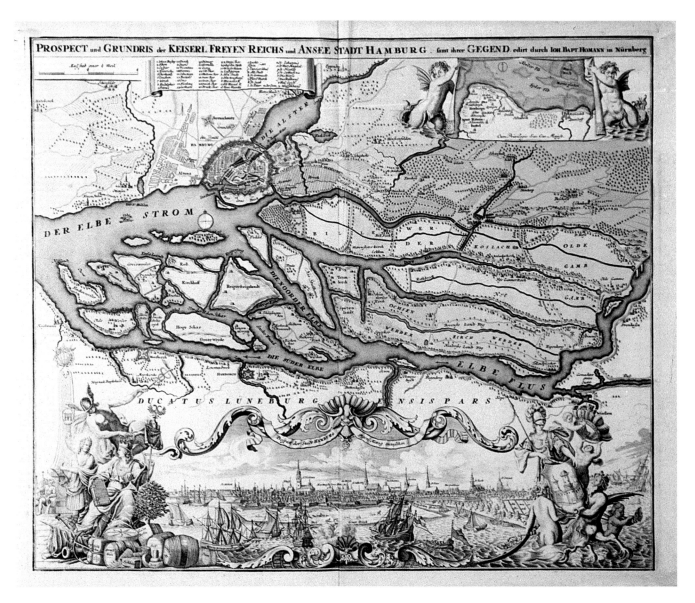

machen, die die Urzelle des heutigen Hamburg war, braucht viel Phantasie. Der Name Hammaburg (Hamm gleich Flußniederung oder Gebiet am Fluß) kam nicht von ungefähr. Ansgar siedelte in einem höchst unwegsamen Gelände. Lange vor seiner Ankunft und der ersten nachweisbaren Besiedelung überhaupt hatten Alster und Bille sich ihre kleinen und großen Wege, die letztendlich zur Elbe und somit in die 110 Kilometer entfernte Nordsee führten, gebahnt. Als

Nowadays it takes a great deal of imagination to stand on the Trostbrücke, recall Bishop Ansgar and picture what Hammaburg, the original cell of present-day Hamburg, must have looked like. The name Hammaburg (Hamm means fluvial plain or land by a river, and Burg is a castle or fort) was not accidental. Ansgar came to settle in very rough terrain. Long before his arrival and the first verifiable settlement, the rivers Alster and Bille had carved out their major and minor paths down to the Elbe and the North Sea 110 kilometres further on. The rivers were highly welcome as trade

„Prospect und Grundris" der „Keiserlichen Freyen und Anseestadt Hamburg", gezeichnet Anfang des 18. Jahrhunderts von Johann Baptist Homann.

"Prospectus and Outline of the Imperial Free and Hanseatic City of Hamburg," drawn in the early eighteenth century by Johann Baptist Homann.

Handels- und Reiserouten waren die drei Flüsse hochwillkommen. Jedoch als Siedlungsgelände war der Boden so untauglich wie das Gelände, auf dem Venedig entstand. Was damals galt, gilt auch heute noch: Hamburg profitiert vom Wasser, führt aber auch einen nie zu Ende gehenden Kampf gegen das nasse Element.

**Vom Bistum zur Handelsstadt**

Lehm, Holz und aus der Eiszeit im Urstromtal der Elbe zurückgebliebene Findlinge waren die Materialien, aus denen die ersten Siedler ihre Unterkünfte errichteten. Holz gab es genug. Denn die wildwuchernde Vegetation überzog die Landschaft mit einem Urwald, in dem die Bäume noch ungehindert in den Himmel wachsen konnten. Daß man trotzdem nicht mehr im Paradies lebte, bezeugt die Tatsache, daß Wikinger 845 die Hammaburg mit ihrem hölzernen Dom in Schutt und Asche legten. Ein neuer Dom, wieder aus Holz, wurde erst nach der Jahrtausendwende errichtet. 1248 wurde die Backsteinbasilika gebaut, der Dom, der mit allen seinen Veränderungen bis 1804 den zentralen Punkt im Herzen der Stadt bildete. Hier trafen sich die Menschen nicht nur zum Beten. Auf dem Domgelände wurden Messen und Märkte abgehalten, Beerdigungen gefeiert, und den Toten wurde auch gleich ein Dach überm Kopf gegeben. In den Weihrauchduft mischte sich der Verwesungsgeruch aus den Katakomben. Und wenige Meter weiter wurde über die jüngsten Neuerscheinungen auf dem Büchermarkt diskutiert. Denn auch Buchhändler schlugen in den Domnischen ihre Stände auf.

Köln hat seinen Dom, Hamburg hat seinen Dom nicht mehr. Er wurde in einer gewaltigen, barbarischen Kraftanstrengung abgerissen. Drei Jahre, von

and travel routes. But the ground through which they flowed into the Elbe was as unsuitable for settlement as that on which Venice grew up. So it was then, and so it remains. Hamburg benefits from the water but fights a never-ending battle against it.

**From episcopate to city of commerce**

Timber and Ice-Age boulders deposited in the glacial valley of the Elbe were the materials from which the original inhabitants built their homes. Timber was plentiful, for the landscape was covered in a jungle of rampant vegetation, in which trees could still grow skyward unhindered. Even so, this was no longer a paradise, as demonstrated by the fact that in 845 Vikings (who sailed up the Elbe from the west) reduced Hammaburg and its wooden cathedral to rubble. Not until after the millennium was a new cathedral built, this one, too, of wood. (Hamburg still had a cathedral chapter, but was no longer an episcopate, and trade flourished primarily on the other side of the Trostbrücke). In 1248 a brick basilica was built, the cathedral which with all its alterations was to remain the focal point of the city centre until 1804. People met there not just to pray. Fairs and markets were held in the cathedral precinct, funerals were celebrated and the dead given a roof over their heads. The aroma of incense mingled with the smell of decay from the catacombs. Meanwhile, a few metres away the latest books were discussed. For booksellers, too, put up their stalls in the cathedral niches.

1804 beschloß der Rat den Abbruch des mittelalterlichen Mariendoms. Bis dahin stand die stattliche Kathedralkirche an dem Platz der alten Hammaburg.

The Council decided to demolish the mediaeval St Mary's Cathedral in 1804. Until then, the imposing cathedral church stood on the site of the old Hammaburg castle.

1804 bis 1807, brauchte es, bis die Spitzhacke tabula rasa gemacht hatte. Zahlreiche Kunstschätze gingen verloren und vor allem ein Gebäudekomplex, der mit der fünfschiffigen Hallenkirche samt ihren Nebengebäuden das Stadtbild dominierte. Keine Bürgerinitiative in der sonst so petitionsfreudigen Stadt protestierte gegen den Abbruch.

Daß der Dom zu Beginn des 19. Jahrhunderts dringend einer Restaurierung bedurfte, ist Tatsache, aber kein hinreichender Grund für den Abriß einer der bedeutendsten und größten Kirchen im norddeutschen Raum. Der Hintergrund für die Beseitigung dieses einzigartigen historischen Gebäudekomplexes war finanzieller Natur, und auch politische Überlegungen der Stadtväter spielten eine Rolle. Aber aus heutiger Sicht stellt der Abriß des Doms einen großen Verlust dar. Das neue Herz von Hamburg, das gegen Ende des 19. Jahrhunderts errichtete pompöse Rathaus im Stil der Neorenaissance, macht ihn nicht wett.

Cologne has its cathedral, Hamburg no longer does. The cathedral was demolished in a mammoth, barbaric effort. It took three years, from 1804 to 1807, for the pick-axes to raze it to the ground. Numerous artistic treasures were lost, but above all a complex of buildings, including the five-section hall church and outbuildings which had dominated the townscape. No citizens' initiative in the otherwise petition-happy city protested against the demolition. True, by the beginning of the nineteenth century the cathedral was urgently in need of restoration, but this was not a sufficient reason for demolishing one of the most significant and largest churches in northern Germany. The background to the wiping out of this unique historic complex of buildings was financial, though the city fathers' political considerations also played a role. Even so,

Graf Adolf III. von Schauenburg gründete 1186 die Hamburger Neustadt. 1883 wurde ihm auf der Trostbrücke ein Denkmal gesetzt.

Count Adolf III of Schauenburg founded Hamburg's Neustadt, or New Town, in 1186. A monument to him was erected on Trostbrücke in 1883.

Da haben sicher alle Recht, die meinen, das eigentliche Herz der Stadt sei das in Binnen- und Außenalster geteilte Alsterbecken. Oder der Hafen. Auf jeden Fall ein nasses Herz.

Die Wiege dieses nassen Herzens war neben der bischöflichen Altstadt die heute vom Hamburger Wahrzeichen, dem Michel, überragte Neustadt, die an der Trostbrücke beginnt. Von der Neustadt gingen die Impulse aus, die Hamburg zu einer mächtigen Hafen- und Handelsmetropole machten. Gründer der Neustadt ist Graf Adolf III. von Schauenburg (1164–1203). Schon sein Großvater und sein Vater hatten die Burg an der Alster erweitert. Adolf III. ließ das brachliegende Gelände parzellieren und ab 1186/87 zu einer Kaufmannssiedlung mit Hafen ausbauen. Die Händler und Handwerker erhielten von ihrem Herrn wichtige Rechte zur freien Ausübung ihrer Geschäfte. Der Graf wurde der Überlieferung nach bei Kaiser Friedrich Barbarossa vorstellig und erreichte, daß der Kaiser mit Erlaß vom 7. Mai 1189 Zollfreiheit und freien Handelsverkehr auf der Niederelbe bis zur Mündung des Flusses in die Nordsee gewährte. Ein unschätzbarer Vorteil für die Hamburger Kaufleute. Eine existentiell so wichtige Zusage, daß die Hanseaten, die wohl nur im Besitz der mündlichen und nicht der schriftlichen Abmachung über dieses Privileg waren, um 1265 den kaiserlichen Freibrief heimlich selber herstellten, um Zollforderungen schwarz auf weiß begegnen zu können. Der gefälschte Freibrief wird heute im Staatsarchiv der Stadt bewahrt. Er sorgte in der Tat dafür, daß Waren, die auf Schiffen von Hamburger Kaufleuten befördert wurden, bis Mitte des 19. Jahrhunderts unverzollt die Elbe hinauf und hinunter transportiert wurden.

from the present-day point of view it remains a great loss. The new heart of Hamburg, the grandiose neo-Renaissance Rathaus (City Hall) built towards the end of the 19th century, does not fill the gap. And so those who say the real heart of the city beats in the Alster basin, divided into inner and outer Alster, or in the port, may well be right. In any case, the heart of the city is a watery one.

Alongside the episcopal old town, the cradle of this city on the water was the Neustadt, or New Town, now towered over by Hamburg's chief landmark, the Michaeliskirche (St Michael's Church), commonly known as the Michel. It was from the Neustadt, which begins at Trostbrücke, that the initiatives were launched which made Hamburg a powerful port and mercantile city. The founder of the Neustadt was Count Adolf III von Schauenburg (1164–1203). His grandfather and father before him had extended the fortified castle on the Alster. From 1186/87 onwards, Adolf III had the wasteland around it parcelled out and a mercantile settlement and harbour constructed. The traders and craftsmen were granted significant rights to enable them to ply their trades. Legend has it that the count had an audience with Emperor Frederick Barbarossa and managed to persuade the emperor to grant the city the right to duty-free trade all along the Lower Elbe to the point where it flows into the North Sea. This was granted from 7 May 1189, giving the merchants of Hamburg an inestimable advantage. It was of such crucial importance that in around 1265 the Hanseatic gentlemen, who appear to

## Streit mit Dänemark und Seeräubern

Mit Adolf III. von Schauenburg begannen aber auch die Auseinandersetzungen
mit Dänemark, die Hamburg durch die
Jahrhunderte immer wieder zusetzten.
Der tatkräftige Gründer der Neustadt
mußte selber noch miterleben, daß Hamburg von den Dänen besetzt wurde. Erst
unter seinem Sohn Graf Adolf IV. wurden die Dänen entscheidend besiegt. Wer
heute von Hamburg aus auf der Autobahn Richtung Norden fährt, kommt,
östlich von Neumünster, an Bornhöved
vorbei. Ebenda fand 1227 die Schlacht
zwischen einer Koalition norddeutscher
Fürsten mit den Städten Lübeck und
Hamburg gegen den dänischen König
statt, die Hamburg von dessen Oberho-
heit befreite. Wenn man heute hinter
dem Rathaus auf dem Adolphsplatz steht
und auf die Börse schaut, befindet man
sich an dem Ort, wo der fromme Graf
Adolf IV. aus Dank für den Sieg über die
Dänen das erste Kloster der Stadt errichten ließ. Da die Schlacht am Tag der Heiligen Maria Magdalena stattgefunden
hatte, wurde das Kloster nach ihr
benannt. Der Schriftsteller Eckart Kleß-
mann, der die „Geschichte der Stadt
Hamburg" aufgeschrieben hat, schildert
in seinem Buch, wie es mit dem dankba-
ren Hamburger Herrscher weiterging.
„Der Graf entsagte seiner politischen
Tätigkeit und trat 1239 selbst als Mönch
in das Kloster ein. Später ließ er sich
zum Priester weihen und ging in das
Franziskanerkloster nach Kiel, wo er
1261 starb." Ein frommer Herrscher
aus der Frühzeit Hamburgs, an den
heute noch der Platz vor der Börse erinnert.

Was hat die Entdeckung von Amerika
1492 durch Kolumbus mit Hamburg zu
tun? Auf den ersten Blick wenig, auf den
zweiten Blick sehr viel. Der prosperieren-
de interkontinentale Handel, der neue
Reichtum aus Übersee machten auf lange
Sicht die Kaufleute an der Elbe zu wohl-
habenden Unternehmern. Ein altes Prin-
zip bewährte sich jetzt hervorragend.

have been in possession of an oral agreement but no written charter, secretly
drew up an imperial charter themselves
to provide themselves with an aid in
black and white to counter demands for
customs duties. The forged charter is still
held in the city archive. It worked so
well that vessels operated by Hamburg
merchants sailed up and down the Elbe
without paying duty until the mid-nineteenth century.

Von dieser um 1265
entstandenen und auf
den 7. 5. 1189 rück-
datierten Urkunde wird
der Hafengeburtstag
abgeleitet.

The port's birthday
celebrations go back to
this "charter," which
dates from around
1265, and was back-
dated to 7 May 1189.

Graf Adolf IV. besiegte 1227 in der Schlacht von Bornhöved die Dänen. Er gründete das Maria Magdalenen Kloster, das auf dem Areal der heutigen Börse stand, und wurde später selber Mönch.

Count Adolf IV defeated the Danes at the Battle of Bornhöved in 1227. He founded the Mary Magdalene monastery that stood on the site of the present-day stock exchange, and later himself became a monk.

Aus den Streitigkeiten mit Dänemark hatte man gelernt, daß es klüger ist, sich aus kriegerischen Auseinandersetzungen herauszuhalten, als auf einen Sieg zu hoffen. Lieber freikaufen als kämpfen. Das war die Devise, nach der die Stadt durch die Jahrhunderte handelte. So konnte sie ihre Chance am Ende des Mittelalters wahrnehmen, dabeizusein, als die Schätze der Erde neu verteilt wurden. Gehörte Hamburg um 1400 noch zu den mittelgroßen Handelsplätzen, so konnte sich die Hansestadt im Kolonialzeitalter, als Europa durch die Ausbeutung der Kolonien reich wurde, bald rühmen, den mächtigsten, wichtigsten Hafen im Heiligen Römischen Reich Deutscher Nation zu besitzen. Ein Dokument des neuen Selbstbewußtseins ist noch heute im Hamburger Staatsarchiv zu bewundern. Die Bilderhandschrift des Stadtrechts von 1497. Ein mit 16 ganzseitigen farbigen Miniaturen auf Pergamentpapier herrlich illustriertes Buch. Ein Kunstwerk, das die Rechte und Pflichten der Menschen festschreibt, Vormundschaft und Pflegschaft regelt, Schuld und Sühne in Gesetze faßt.

Eine der 16 Miniaturen in dieser Handschrift macht die Bedeutung von Handel und Schiffahrt für die Hansestadt Hamburg besonders anschaulich. Da steht im Vordergrund des Bildes eine Gruppe ernsthaft debattierender Männer. Dahinter, an einem Tisch, werden ebenfalls wichtige Verhandlungen geführt. Würdige weiße Backenbärte stehen in gewissem Gegensatz zu dem eher munteren Outfit dieser Herrenversammlung. Blaue, rote, grüne, gelbe Überwürfe, rote Strümpfe, gezackte Kasperlekragen geben ein farbenfrohes Bild von der Männermode am Ende des 15. Jahrhunderts. Wir haben es auf dieser Illustra-

## Trouble with Denmark and pirates

However, the rule of Adolf III von Schauenburg also saw the start of the clashes with Denmark that were to plague Hamburg repeatedly through the centuries. The energetic founder of the Neustadt himself lived to see Hamburg occupied by the Danes. Not until the reign of his son Count Adolf IV was a decisive defeat inflicted on the Danes.

Nowadays, travelling north along the autobahn from Hamburg, to the east of the town of Neumünster you pass Bornhöved, the site in 1227 of the battle between an alliance of North German princes, the cities of Lübeck and Hamburg on one side and the Danish king on the other which liberated Hamburg from Danish overlordship. Standing on Adolphsplatz behind the Rathaus and facing the Stock Exchange, you are on the spot where the pious Count Adolf IV had the city's first monastery built in gratitude for his victory over the Danes. Since the battle took place on the saint's day of Mary Magdalene, the monastery was named after her. In his "Geschichte der Stadt Hamburg" (History of the City of Hamburg), Eckart Klessmann described what happened next to the grateful ruler of Hamburg: "The count renounced his political activity and in 1239 entered the convent as a monk. Later, he had himself ordained a priest and moved to the Franciscan monastery in Kiel, where he died in 1261." A pious ruler from Hamburg's early days whose name the square outside the stock exchange still bears.

What does Columbus's discovery of America in 1492 have to do with Hamburg? At first sight very little, but on closer inspection a great deal. In the long term, flourishing intercontinental trade and new riches from overseas turned the Hamburg merchants into prosperous businessmen. Now, an age-old principle was to prove its worth. As a result of the quarrels with Denmark, the Hamburgers had learnt that it was cleverer to keep

tion offensichtlich mit der Versammlung der Topmanager der Stadt zu tun. Doch wieviel bunter ist das Bild im Vergleich zu den Trägern von Nadelstreifenanzügen in den Führungsetagen von heute!

Daß sich die Gespräche dieser buntgewandeten Männergesellschaft um Handel und Schiffahrt drehen, macht die Miniatur sofort deutlich. Mit Menschen und Waren vollbeladene Hansekoggen staffeln sich vom unteren bis an den oberen Bildrand. Wie die Behausungen der Männer, denen diese Segelschiffe gehörten, im besten Falle aussahen, veranschaulicht eine propere weiße Burganlage, die wie ein Dornröschenschloß über dem Hafenbecken liegt. Daß diese Mini-

away from warlike confrontations than to hope for victory. Better to buy your way out than to fight was the motto that governed the city's actions for centuries. And so toward the end of the Middle Ages, when the treasures of the earth began to be newly distributed at the beginning of the modern age, the merchants of Hamburg were in a position to seize the opportunity to be part of this redistribution. In 1400 Hamburg had been a middle-ranking centre of trade, but in the colonial era, when Europe became rich by exploiting the colonies, it was not long before the city could boast of being the most powerful, most significant port in the Holy Roman Empire of the German Nation. One testimony to this new self-assurance that can still be admired in the Hamburg state archive is the 1497 town charter, a superbly illustrated book with 16 full-page coloured miniatures on parchment. It is a work of art that sets out people's rights and duties, regulates guardianship and tutelage and enshrines guilt and punishment in laws.

One of the 16 miniatures in this manuscript makes the significance of commerce and shipping for the Hanseatic city of Hamburg particularly clear. In the foreground of the picture stands a group of men engaged in earnest debate. Behind them, at a table, equally important negotiations are under way. Dignified white side-whiskers form a marked contrast to the somewhat jaunty attire of this gathering of gentlemen, whose blue, red, green and yellow wraps, red stockings and ruffed collars provide a colourful image of men's fashions at the end of the fifteenth century. This illustration is evidently of a meeting of the town's senior managers. They certainly make a far more colourful sight than the pin-striped executives of today!

Das prächtig illustrierte Stadtrecht von 1497. Miniaturen schmücken die einzelnen Kapitel. Hier: „Van allerhende plychten unde schulden".

The magnificently illustrated Town Charter of 1497. The chapters are decorated with miniatures. This one is headed: "Van allerhende plychten unde schulden" (About All Manner of Duties and Obligations).

The miniature also makes it perfectly clear that this multi-coloured company's conversations revolve around commerce and shipping. The edge of the picture is piled from top to bottom with Hanseatic sailing ships laden with people and goods. A pure white castle stands like a fairy-tale palace above the harbour basin, illustrating what the finest of the residences of the owners of these sailing ships looked like. Clearly, this miniature is an idealised image of the lifestyle of the Hanseatic upper class. But nowadays we also know how "the people" in Hamburg lived at that time and after. It was more the exception for an ordinary man to own his own bed. Even in around 1900 it was perfectly normal in Hamburg's working-class families for children to share a place to sleep. Nor was it unusual in the early years of the twentieth century for a young man to rent the right to a bed from a family for a few cents and share it in shifts with others. A room of one's own? In 1497, when the Hanseatic bourgeoisie so self-assuredly set down their laws, most people did not even dare to dream of such a thing.

The Museum für Hamburgische Geschichte, Hamburg's local history museum, provides a gruesome insight into how the law dealt with those poor devils who tried to come by a little wealth as pirates on the Elbe or in the North Sea and the Baltic. On display there are two staked skulls which were found during excavations on the quayside at Grasbrook. The two men had been dealt with exactly as the law of the time dictated: "their heads shall be cut off and nailed to a stake."

It is certainly just legend that these two skulls are the heads of Klaus Störtebeker and Godeke Michels. But it is a fact that in the early fifteenth century these two buccaneers and a host of companions put up a relentless fight against a Hanseatic fleet under Hamburg's command, a fight which the pirates lost. The pirates' execution at Grasbrook must

Viel läßt sich an dieser Miniatur aus dem Stadtrecht über das Leben und Treiben um 1497 ablesen. Die Illustration wurde dem Kapitel „Das Schiffsrecht" vorangestellt.

Much can be read out of this miniature from the Town Charter about life and activities in around 1497. It headed the chapter on shipping law.

atur ein Idealbild vom Lebensstil der hanseatischen Oberschicht abgibt, ist deutlich. Wie „das Volk" zu dieser Zeit, aber auch später in Hamburg lebte, wissen wir inzwischen auch. Daß der einfache Mann ein eigenes Bett besaß, war eher die Ausnahme. Noch um 1900 war es in den Hamburger Arbeiterfamilien völlig normal, daß sich die Kinder eine Schlafstelle teilten. Auch die „Kostgänger" gab es zu Beginn des 20. Jahrhunderts noch. Diese „Schlafburschen" mieteten für wenige Groschen in einer Familie das Recht auf ein Bett, das sie

manchmal schichtweise mit anderen teilten. Ein Zimmer für sich allein? Davon wagten die meisten Menschen 1497, als die hanseatischen Bürger so selbstbewußt ihr Recht festschrieben, noch nicht einmal zu träumen.

Wie es laut Gesetz den armen Teufeln erging, die als Seeräuber auf der Elbe oder in Nord- und Ostsee zu ein wenig Reichtum kommen wollten, ist im Museum für Hamburgische Geschichte heute aufs schaurigste dokumentiert. Dort werden zwei gepfählte Schädel gezeigt, die bei Erdarbeiten an den Kai-

have been a real folk festival. Even now, Störtebeker remains one of the most popular heroes of the Elbe, personifying as he does a Hamburg saga which in the course of the centuries took on a Robin Hood quality.

Everyone in Hamburg has heard of Störtebeker. Not so many know that at the same time as the pirates were making the seas unsafe two highly gifted artists in the city were producing works which are now of inestimable value. The wonderful pictorial stories related by Meister Bertram (c. 1340–1414/15) and Meister Francke (c.1385–post-1436) on their painted church altars can now be followed in the Hamburger Kunsthalle, the city's main art gallery, where the masterpieces of these two great painters are held. They represent a golden age of the fine arts in Hamburg and are unjustifiably somewhat neglected, for there a host of aspects from which they can

Auf dem Grasbrook rollen die Köpfe. Im Jahr 1400 wurden mit Störtebeker, dem Anführer der Vitalienbrüder, 30 weitere Seeräuber hingerichtet. Der kolorierte Holzschnitt wurde in späterer Zeit angefertigt.

Heads roll on Grasbrook. Claus Störtebeker, leader of the notorious Vitalienbrüder, and 30 other pirates were executed in 1400. This coloured woodcut was produced at a later date.

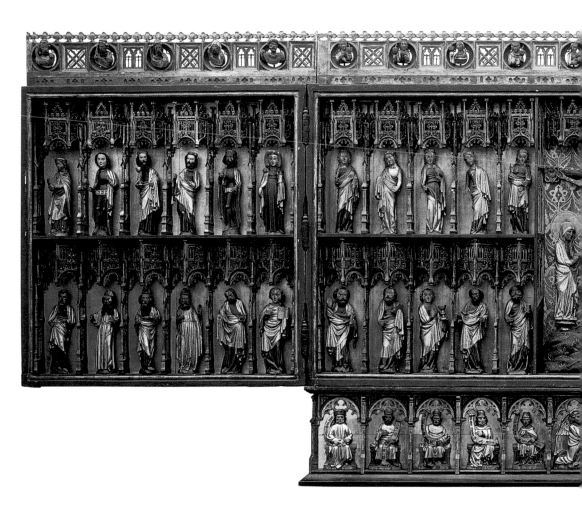

anlagen auf dem Grasbrook gefunden
wurden. Ganz so, wie es der Gesetzestext
der damaligen Zeit befahl – „men schol-
de en ere bovede (= Köpfe) afhowen und
negele se uppe den stok" –, war es bei
den beiden geschehen.

Daß es sich bei diesen beiden Schädeln
um die Köpfe von Klaus Störtebeker und
Godeke Michels handelt, ist sicher
Legende. Tatsache ist aber, daß diese beiden Freibeuter der Meere zusammen mit
einer Schar von Spießgesellen einer hanseatischen Flotte unter dem Kommando
Hamburgs zu Beginn des 15. Jahrhunderts in der Elbmündung eine erbitterte
Schlacht lieferten und verloren. Die Hin-
richtung der Seeräuber auf dem Grasbrook muß ein wahres Volksfest gewesen
sein. Störtebeker ist bis heute eine der
beliebtesten Heldenfiguren an der Elbe.

pleasurably and gainfully be viewed.
They offer as much to those interested in
early architectural fantasies as to students of historic costumes. For the art
connoisseur, the altar-pieces are in any
case a virtually inexhaustible landscape
of discovery.

That Hamburg had something like
street-lamps earlier than other cities has
to do with the Greenland voyagers, who
brought whales and thus a great deal of

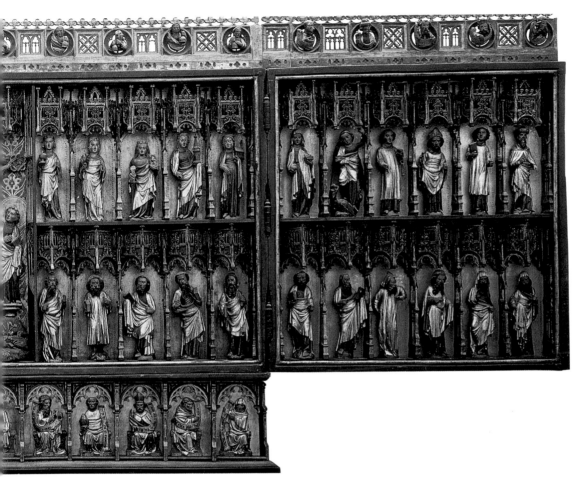

Der Petri-Altar von
Meister Bertram (geb.
um 1340, gest. um
1415) ist einer der
größten Schätze der
Hamburger Kunsthalle.
Er wurde 1903 von
Alfred Lichtwark aus
Mecklenburg in die
Hansestadt zurückge-
holt.

St Peter's Altar by Mas-
ter Bertram (born c.
1340, died c. 1415) is
one of the Hamburg
Kunsthalle's greatest
treasures. It was
brought back to Ham-
burg from Mecklenburg
by Alfred Lichtwark in
1903.

Ein Hamburger Sagenheld, der im Laufe
der Jahrhunderte die Qualität eines
Robin Hood gewann.

Von Störtebeker hat jeder in Hamburg
schon mal gehört. Daß zu derselben Zeit,
als der Seeräuber die Meere unsicher
machte, zwei hochbegabte Künstler in
der Stadt Werke schufen, die heute von
unschätzbarem Wert sind, ist nicht so
vielen bekannt. Wie wunderbar die Bil-
dergeschichten sind, die Meister Bertram
(um 1340-1414/15) und Meister Francke
(um 1385-nach 1436) auf ihren Kirchen-
altären erzählen, ist heute in der Hamburger Kunsthalle zu sehen. Dort werden
die Meisterwerke dieser beiden großen
Maler aufbewahrt. Eine Hochblüte der
bildenden Kunst an der Elbe, die zu
Unrecht etwas im Verborgenen blüht.
Dabei gibt es eine Fülle von Aspekten,
unter denen die Bilder mit Lust und
Gewinn betrachtet werden können. Wer

money to the city. The workshops where
oil was extracted from the whale blubber
stank to high heaven. But from the end
of the seventeenth century, at least in the
more major of the narrow city streets,
lanterns fuelled with whale oil ensured
that people could walk from house to
house without getting their feet wet or
injured. The terrible state of the roads
until far into the modern age beggars
imagination. Waste-water drainage and
sewage systems were non-existent or
makeshift. Pigs wallowed blissfully in the
narrow alleys, which in the lower-lying
parts of town were repeatedly flooded by
the Elbe.

sich für frühe architektonische Phantasien interessiert, kommt hier genauso auf seine Kosten, wie der, der historische Moden studiert. Für den Kunstfreund bieten die Tafeln sowieso eine nahezu unerschöpfliche Entdeckungslandschaft.

Daß Hamburg früher als andere Städte so etwas wie eine Straßenbeleuchtung erhielt, hing mit den Grönlandfahrern zusammen. Sie brachten Wale und damit Geld in die Stadt. Die Trankochereien stanken zum Himmel. Aber die mit Tran genährten Laternen sorgten seit Ende des 17. Jahrhunderts zumindest in den größeren der kleinen Gassen dafür, daß die Menschen einigermaßen trockenen und heilen Fußes von Haus zu Haus kamen. Den Zustand der Straßen kann man sich, bis weit in die Neuzeit hinein, nicht schlimm genug vorstellen. Abwassersysteme waren gar nicht oder nur notdürftig vorhanden. Mit Wonne suhlten sich Schweine in diesen Gassen, die in den tiefer gelegenen Teilen der Stadt immer wieder auch vom Hochwasser der Elbe überflutet wurden.

### Ein Schutzwall um die Stadt entsteht

Die Spuren des alten Hamburg lassen sich hervorragend noch heute an den Straßennamen ablesen. Moorweide, Bürgerweide, Weidenstieg, Weidenallee. Da grasten ehemals die Kühe, Schafe, Ziegen und Schweine. In der Gegend der heutigen Hohen und Großen Bleichen hingen auf Gestellen Stoffbahnen zum Ausbleichen in der Sonne. Der Ring der historischen Wallanlage der Stadt ist ebenfalls in den Straßennamen erhalten. Vom Klosterwall an den Deichtorhallen über Steintorwall, Glockengießerwall, Gorch-Fock-Wall bis zum Holstenwall. Genau genommen schlägt der ehemalige Schutzwall nur einen Halbkreis um die Stadt,

### The town acquires protective ramparts

Street names are still an excellent way of finding traces of old Hamburg. Names such as Moorweide, Bürgerweide, Weidenstieg and Weidenallee tell us that cows, sheep, goats and pig once grazed there – "Weide" is German for pasture. In the area around Hohe Bleichen and Grosse Bleichen, lengths of cloth were once hung on frames to bleach in the sun.

The ramparts that once encircled the city have also been preserved in street names such as Klosterwall, Gorch-Fock-Wall, Esplanade and Holstenwall. To be strictly accurate, the protective ramparts only formed a semi-circle round the city, for the southern section was formed by the somewhat less expensively fortified water's edge of Grasbrook.

The predecessor of the ring of fortifications was the Stadtgraben, or town moat, which was strengthened in 1475. One hundred and fifty years later the Dutch engineer Johan van Valckenburgh was commissioned to build the new ramparts. Deichtor, Steintor, Dammtor, Millerntor and Hafentor were the gates through the mighty wall built round the city to keep out uninvited guests. Thanks to these strong fortifications, Hamburg survived the Thirty Years' War unscathed. In any case, the city fathers had no wish to become involved in this seemingly never-ending fray, which devastated half of Europe between 1618 and 1648. As in other cities, the story has been passed down in Hamburg, too, that when peace was made the bells of the four principal churches rang out and trumpets sounded from their towers.

In the course of the eighteenth century the ramparts increasingly lost their function as a protective military installation and were transformed into parks and gardens surrounding the city on three sides. An 1825 water-colour now in the possession of the Altona Museum shows the rampart on Stintfang, now the site of

denn den südlichen Abschnitt bildete die
etwas weniger aufwendig befestigte Was-
serkante zum nördlich gelegenen Grasbrook.

Vorläufer des Wallrings war der 1475
verstärkte Stadtgraben. 150 Jahre später
wurde der niederländische Ingenieur
Johan van Valckenburgh mit dem Bau
der neuen Wallanlage beauftragt. Deichtor, Steintor, Dammtor, Millerntor und
Hafentor hießen die Durchlässe durch
den gewaltigen Wall der Stadt gegen
ungebetene Gäste. Dank dieser starken
Befestigungsanlage überstand Hamburg
ungeschoren den Dreißigjährigen Krieg.
Mitmischen mochten die Stadtväter bei
diesem nicht enden wollenden Schlach-
tengetümmel, das zwischen 1618 und
1648 halb Europa verwüstete, ohnehin
nicht. Wie überall im Reich ist auch in
Hamburg überliefert, daß bei Friedens-
schluß die Glocken der vier Hamburger
Hauptkirchen geläutet wurden und
Trompeten von den Kirchtürmen er-
schallten.

Der Wall, der im Verlauf des 18. Jahrhunderts seine militärische Schutzfunk-
tion mehr und mehr verloren hatte,
wurde in eine die Stadt in drei Himmelsrichtungen umfassende Parkanlage
umgewandelt. Ein Aquarell von 1825,
das heute im Besitz des Altonaer
Museums ist, zeigt den Wall am Stintfang (heute Standort der Jugendherber-
ge) als Gartenanlage. Eine biedermeier-
lich gekleidete Familie, der Vater in Geh-
rock und mit einem Zylinder, die Mutter
mit Strohhut in ein bis auf den Boden
reichendes Sommerkleid gewandet, die
Kinder erscheinen wie eine Miniaturaus-

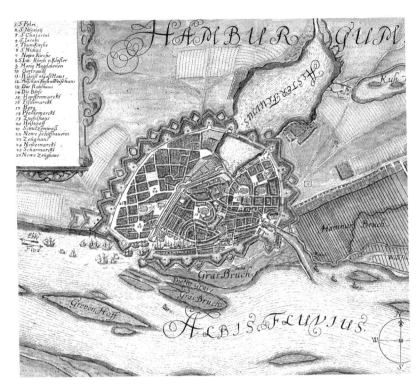

a youth hostel, as a public garden. The
picture portrays a family attractively
attired in Biedermeier style, the father in
frock coat and top hat, the mother wearing a straw hat and a floor-length summer dress, the children looking like a
miniature version of their elders. This
small company is doing what Hamburgers liked doing best on Sundays in the
early nineteenth century - going for a
walk to look at the port and the ships.
All this is taking place against the dignified backdrop of the famous skyline with
the church towers of St Michael's, St
Peter's, St Nicholas's, St James's and St
Katharine's.

And what has happened to the ring of
ramparts now? The historian and Hamburg expert Hermann Hipp has aptly described it as an "educational landscape."
Dotted around the ring are a large number of cultural institutions. They make
an impressive list: the Museum für Hamburgische Geschichte on Holstenwall,
the Hamburger Musikhalle (concert hall)
on Johannes-Brahms-Platz, the university

Der kolorierte Kupfer-
stich zeigt die Stadt, die
ab 1620 durch eine
erweiterte Wallanlage
gesichert wurde. Der
Verlauf des Befesti-
gungsrings ist noch
heute an den Straßen-
namen nachzuvoll-
ziehen.

This coloured copper
etching shows the city
as it looked from 1620
on, when it was pro-
tected by an extended
system of ramparts.
The pattern of the ring
of fortifications can still
be traced from the
street names.

Das Millerntor, das
auch Altonaer Tor
genannt wurde und die
Westseite der Stadt
begrenzte, um 1810. Es
bestand aus zwei größe-
ren Gebäuden und zwei
Torhäuschen, von
denen eines noch erhal-
ten ist.

Millerntor, also known
as the Altona Gate,
which marked the city's
western boundary, in
around 1810. It used to
consist of two larger
buildings, one of which
is still standing.

gabe der Erwachsenen – diese kleine
Gesellschaft tut das, was Hamburger zu
Beginn des 19. Jahrhunderts sonntags
am liebsten taten: spazierengehen, Hafen
und Schiffe gucken. Und das alles vor
der ehrwürdigen Kulisse des berühmten
Stadtbildes mit seinen Kirchtürmen:
St. Michaelis, St. Petri, St. Nikolai,
St. Jacobi und St. Katharinen.

Und der Wallring heute? Der Kunsthistoriker und Hamburgexperte Hermann
Hipp bezeichnet ihn zu Recht als „Bil-
dungslandschaft". An diesem Ring liegt
heute eine imponierende Fülle von Kulturinstitutionen. Ihre Anzahl ist beein-
druckend: das Museum für Hamburgische Geschichte am Holstenwall, die
Hamburger Musikhalle am Johannes-
Brahms-Platz, die Universität nördlich
des Dammtorbahnhofs, die Staatsoper
südlich des Dammtorbahnhofs, die
Hamburger Kunsthalle mit ihren drei
Gebäuden am Glockengießerwall, wenige Meter davon entfernt das Deutsche
Schauspielhaus und das Museum für
Kunst und Gewerbe, am Klosterwall das
Veranstaltungszentrum Markthalle, das

to the north of Dammtor station, the
State Opera to its south, the three buildings of the Hamburger Kunsthalle on
Glockengiesserwall, a few metres further
on the Deutsches Schauspielhaus (theatre) and the Museum für Kunst und
Gewerbe (arts and crafts museum), on
Klosterwall the Markthalle events venue,
the Kunsthaus galleries, the Kunstverein
(art society), the Freie Akademie der
Künste (academy of arts) and finally the
large and small Deichtor halls where art
exhibitions are held. All in all, a most
fortunate metamorphosis from military
ramparts to ring of culture.

Galeriengebäude, das Kunsthaus, der
Kunstverein, die Freie Akademie der
Künste und schließlich die große und die
kleine Deichtorhalle für Kunst-Ausstel-
lungen. Also eine durchaus geglückte
Metamorphose vom militärischen
Schutzwall zum Ring der Kultur.

Street names also lead us on the trail
of a chapter when Hamburg nuns
became big landowners. Names such as
Klosterallee, Klosterstern, Nonnenstieg,
Abteistrasse and Heilwigstrasse are hints
of a past which began in 1295 when a
Cistercian convent moved from the village of Herwardeshuthe to a site by the
Alster outside the gates of Hamburg.
The daughters of good families who
became nuns there often brought a considerable fortune with them. Since the

Das Dammtor, hier eine
Darstellung vom Ende
des 17. Jahrhunderts.
Im Jahr 1817 wurde die
Befestigungsanlage
geschleift.

Dammtor gate, seen
here in a picture dating
from the late seven-
teenth century. The for-
tification was razed to
the ground in 1817.

Straßennamen führen auch auf die Spur eines Kapitels, in dem sich Hamburger Nonnen als Großgrundbesitzerinnen entpuppen. Klosterallee, Klosterstern, Klosterstieg, Nonnenstieg, Abteistraße, Heilwigstraße. Hinweise auf eine Vergangenheit, die 1295 mit dem Umzug eines Zisterzienserinnenklosters aus dem elbnahen Dörfchen „Herwardeshuthe" auf das Gelände an der Alster vor den Toren Hamburgs begann. Die Töchter aus guter Familie, die hier Nonnen wurden, brachten oft ein ansehnliches Vermögen mit. Da der Orden zu einem Leben in Armut verpflichtete, wurde das Geld in Grundbesitz umgemünzt. Den Nonnen gehörten alsbald ganze Dörfer: Eppendorf, Winterhude, Eimsbüttel, Bahrenfeld, Alsterdorf, Niendorf, Groß Borstel, Lokstedt, Ohlsdorf, Ottensen, Othmarschen und Rissen. Ein Blick auf den Stadtplan genügt, um zu sehen, daß ein großer Teil des heutigen Hamburg ehemals Klosterland war. Geblieben sind davon nur die Namen, vor allem im vornehmen Harvestehude, in dessen Stadtteilnamen das Kloster „Herwardeshuthe" bis heute fortlebt. 1530 wurden die Klostergebäude abgerissen. Ein Jahr nachdem die von dem Reformator Johannes Bugenhagen ausgearbeitete neue Kirchenordnung im Sinne der Lehre Luthers von Rat und Bürgerschaft der Stadt verabschiedet worden war. Bugenhagen muß ein den Musen wohlgesonnener Reformator gewesen sein. In seiner Schulordnung legte er Wert darauf, „daß die Kinder in Musik lustig und wohl unterwiesen werden". In der neugegründeten Lateinschule, dem Johanneum, das heute noch Hamburgs renommiertestes Gymnasium ist und damals in das Gebäude des aufgehobenen Johannisklosters am heutigen Rathausmarkt einzog, wurde ganz im Sinne Bugenhagens die Musik sehr gepflegt. Die reiche Tradition der Kirchenmusik in Hamburg hat ihre

order committed them to a life of poverty, the money was used to buy land. Soon the nuns owned whole villages - Eppendorf, Winterhuthe, Eimsbüttel, Bahrenfeld, Alsterdorf, Niendorf, Gross-Borstel, Lokstedt, Ohlsdorf, Ottensen, Othmarschen and Rissen, now all districts of Hamburg. A glance at a map of the city is enough to see that a large part of present-day Hamburg was once convent land. All that remain now are the names, particularly in the up-market district of Harvestehude, its very name derived from the convent of Herwardeshude. The convent building was demolished in 1530, one year after the town council and house of burgesses had adopted new church rules drawn up by the reformer Johannes Bugenhagen in keeping with Luther's doctrine. As a reformer, Bugenhagen must have been kindly disposed towards the arts. In his new regulations for schools he stressed that children should be "enjoyably and well instructed in music." Certainly, in the newly founded Johanneum, a Latin school which moved into the building of the dissolved Johanniskloster monastery on Rathausmarkt, a great deal of attention was paid to music. The Johanneum is still Hamburg's best-known high school. The city's rich tradition of church music also has its roots in the fact that the reformer had a heart for the arts.

## Foreigners bring new impetus

A fine location on Ice Age slopes rising above the north bank of the Elbe, reaching their highest point in Blankenese's

Wurzeln fraglos darin, daß der Reformator ein Herz für diese Kunst hatte.

## Fremde bringen neuen Aufschwung

Die schöne Lage am Wasser mit dem
Geesthang aus der Eiszeit, der am Nordufer der Elbe in Blankenese mit dem Süllberg (75 m) seine höchst Erhebung aufweist. Ein in Jahrhunderten gewachsener
Reichtum, der Wohnquartiere der nobel-
sten Art entstehen ließ. Ein bürgerliches
Kulturverständnis, das ohne himmelstür-
mende Visionen auskam, aber viel mehr
leistete, als den „Pfeffersäcken" in der
Regel nachgesagt wird. Eine Weltoffenheit, die der Handel und die Seefahrt mit
sich brachten. Das alles prägte Hamburg. Aber was wäre Hamburg ohne die
Zuwanderer, denen immer wieder die
Tore geöffnet wurden!
Woanders sagt man „Päpstlicher als der
Papst". Das heißt, etwas 150prozentig
gut machen zu wollen. In Hamburg ist
man gern britischer als die Engländer.
Die Anglophilie hat an der Elbe eine
lange Tradition. Im 16. Jahrhundert
erwarb die englische Kaufmannsvereini-
gung der Merchants Adventurers eine
feste Niederlassung in der Stadt. Die
Engländer brachten feines Tuch, und die
hanseatischen Kaufleute lieferten ihnen
Holz, Wein und Leinen. Ein gutes
Geschäft für beide Seiten.

Noch einflußreicher in der Stadt wurden zur selben Zeit die vor den katholischen Truppen Philipps II. geflüchteten
Niederländer calvinistischen Glaubens.
Unter ihnen z. B. auch die Amsincks, die
zu einer höchst angesehenen Familie in
Hamburg wurden. Die Kaufleute und
Handwerker aus Antwerpen, Brabant
und Flandern brachten Samt und Seide
in die Stadt. Die niederländischen Han-
delsherren waren so tüchtig, daß Im- und
Export an der Elbe bald überwiegend
von ihnen beherrscht wurden. Dem
Hamburger Rat war es recht, denn die
Stadt prosperierte. Und die sonst gegen
„fremde Religionsverwandte" so gestren-
ge lutherische Geistlichkeit mußte

Johannes Bugenhagen
(1485–1558) setzte in
Hamburg die Luther-
sche Reformation
durch.

Johannes Bugenhagen
(1485–1558) carried
through the Lutheran
Reformation in Ham-
burg.

75-metre Süllberg; wealth that accumulated through centuries, leading to the
building of palatial residences; a bourgeois understanding of culture which
shunned high-flying visions but achieved
much more than the "pepper sacks," as
rich Hamburgers are nicknamed, are
normally credited with; cosmopolitan
attitudes which brought trade and shipping in their tow. All these things shaped
Hamburg. But where would the city
have been without the immigrants to
whom its gates were opened time and
again?

Elsewhere, they say "more Catholic
than the Pope" to describe someone who
goes all out to be something he is not. In
Hamburg, they like to be more British
than the British. Anglophilia on the Elbe
goes back a long time. In the sixteenth
century the Merchant Adventurers Company established a permanent office in
Hamburg. The English merchants
brought fine cloth, and their Hanseatic
counterparts supplied them with timber,
wine and linen. A good business for both
parties.

Der Jüdische Friedhof in Altona, gegründet 1613, ist die älteste Begräbnisstätte der Glaubensgemeinschaft in Hamburg.

The Jewish cemetery in Altona, founded in 1613, is Hamburg's oldest Jewish burial ground.

Der Bankier Salomon Heine (1767–1844), Onkel des Dichters Heinrich Heine, unterstützte entscheidend den Wiederaufbau der Stadt nach dem Großen Brand von 1842.

Banker Salomon Heine (1767–1844), uncle of the writer Heinrich Heine, played a crucial role in funding the city's rebuilding after the Great Fire of 1842.

schließlich die Vereinbarungen der Stadtväter mit den Zugewanderten zähneknirschend hinnehmen.

Die Geschichte der Juden in Hamburg besteht aus vielen dunklen und einigen hellen Seiten. Im Museum für Hamburgische Geschichte ist die Bedeutung dieses historischen Kapitels heute gut dokumentiert. Sephardische Juden aus Portugal und Spanien kamen im 17. Jahrhundert an die Elbe. Die jüdischen Händler und Ärzte wurden hier zwar nicht in ein Ghetto gezwungen wie anderswo, aber wie überall galten auch in Hamburg die strengsten Restriktionen für diese Gruppe von Zuwanderern. Wieder wurde nach dem Opportunitätsprinzip gehandelt. Die Kenntnisse und die wirtschaftlichen Verbindungen der Juden kamen den Hanseaten zupaß, während ihnen ansonsten die bürgerlichen Rechte und die öffentliche Ausübung ihrer Religion verweigert wurden. Der Erwerb von Grundbesitz wurde für Juden offiziell erst möglich, als 1842 der Große Brand von Hamburg die Stadt in Schutt und

Even more influential in the city at that time were Dutch Calvinists who had fled from the Catholic troops of Philip II. Among them were the Amsincks, who were to become one of Hamburg's leading families. The merchants and craftsmen from Antwerp, Brabant and Flanders brought velvet and silk to the city. The Dutch merchants were so industrious that they soon came to dominate much of the import and export trade on the Elbe. The Hamburg city council had no objections, because the city was flourishing. And the Lutheran clergy, otherwise so hard on "foreigners of related religion," had grudgingly to accept the city fathers' agreements with the newcomers.

The history of the Jews in Hamburg consists of many dark and a few bright chapters. It is well documented in the

Asche legte und man dringend Investoren zur Beseitigung der Trümmerwüste
benötigte. Zu dieser Zeit trat der jüdische Bankier Salomon Heine, Onkel des
Dichters Heinrich Heine, als einer der
ersten in Erscheinung, als es darum ging,
Hamburg mit großzügiger finanzieller
Hilfe ohne entsprechende Gegenleistun-
gen beim Wiederaufbau zu unterstützen.
Als der Rat ihn zum Dank mit der
Ehrenbürgerwürde auszeichnen wollte,
geriet er in die paradoxe Situation, einen
Mann ausgewählt zu haben, der nicht
das Bürgerrecht besaß. Und weil er es als
Jude vor 1849 nicht besitzen durfte,
mußte ihm auch die Auszeichnung ver-
wehrt bleiben.

Liberaler verhielt man sich gegenüber
den Zuwanderern, die die Französische
Revolution von 1789 nach Hamburg
verschlug. Der kulturelle Einfluß der
Franzosen wurde wie in weiten Teilen
der europäischen Adelsgesellschaft nun
auch an Alster und Elbe bald unübersehbar. Die feine Gesellschaft speiste um
1800 französisch, konnte französisch
parlieren, kleidete sich französisch und
las französisch.

Daß im 20. Jahrhundert Chinesen, Italiener, Jugoslawen, Türken (gegen Jahr-
tausendende die größte nichtdeutsche
Gruppe), Polen, Afrikaner und Zuge-
wanderte aus vielen anderen Ländern
das Bild der Bevölkerung an Alster und
Elbe noch bunter gemacht haben, ist
bekannt. Die zugereisten Bayern, Schwa-
ben oder Sachsen, die manchem hartge-
sottenen Hamburger fremder erscheinen
mögen als die Briten, sind dabei noch
außer acht gelassen. Die immer noch
gern kolportierten Abgrenzungen zwischen geborenen, gebürtigen und zugewanderten Hamburgern sind also längst
hinfällig geworden. Eigentlich haben
diese Eingrenzungen auch nicht zu der
Stadt gepaßt, die durch ihren Handel
und Wandel seit jeher zur Weltoffenheit
gezwungen wurde. Zwei Exempel – die
unorthodoxe Person des Dichters und
Ratsherrn Barthold Hinrich Brockes und
die wunderbare Institution der Patrioti-

Museum für Hamburgische Geschichte
(Museum of Hamburg History).
Sephardic Jews from Portugal and Spain
arrived in Hamburg in the seventeenth
century. The Jewish traders and doctors
were not forced into a ghetto as they
were elsewhere, but in Hamburg, as in
other cities, they were subjected to
extremely tough restrictions. Again, the
city fathers acted opportunistically. They
were quite happy to take advantage of
the Jews' knowledge and trading contacts, but denied them civic rights or per-
mission for them openly to practise their
religion. Jews were not officially allowed
to own land or property until, in 1842,
the Great Fire of Hamburg left the city
in ruins and investors were urgently
needed to get rid of the devastation. One
of the first to step forward at this time
with generous financial support to aid
reconstruction – without the promise of
anything in return – was the Jewish
banker Salomon Heine, uncle of the
writer and poet Heinrich Heine. In
return, the city council planned to make
him an honorary citizen, but found itself
in the paradoxical situation of having
chosen someone who did not enjoy citi-
zenship rights. And because as a Jew he
was not allowed to have them until
1849, he was forced to forgo the honour.

The city was more liberal towards the
immigrants whom the French Revolution
drove to Hamburg from 1789 onwards.
The cultural influence of the French on
the city was soon evident, as it was
among the nobility in much of Europe.
In around 1800 high society ate French
food, spoke French, dressed in the
French style and read French books.

It is well known that in the twentieth
century Chinese, Italians, Yugoslavs,
Turks (the largest non-German minority
towards the end of the millennium),
Poles, Africans and immigrants from

Der Dichter Heinrich
Heine (1797–1856)
lebte sechs Jahre lang in
Hamburg, seiner „schö-
nen Wiege meiner Lei-
den", wo er liebte, an
ewigem Geldmangel litt
und seinen Verleger
Julius Campe fand.

Writer Heinrich Heine
(1797–1856) spent six
years in Hamburg,
which he called the
"beautiful cradle of my
sorrows." He fell in
love, was always short
of money, and found
his publisher Julius
Campe in the city.

Das Haus der Patriotischen Gesellschaft von 1765 an der Trostbrücke, die damals als „Hamburgische Gesellschaft zur Beförderung der Künste und Gewerbe" gegründet wurde, wurde 1925 aufgestockt, behielt aber seinen gotisierenden Stil.

The Patriotic Society of 1765's building on Trostbrücke. The society was founded as the Hamburg Society for the Promotion of the Arts and Crafts. An additional storey was added in 1925, but the building retained its neo-Gothic style.

schen Gesellschaft – sollen am Ende des historischen Streifzugs Beispiel geben für die Tugenden, die echt „hamburgisch" sind.

### Geist, Kultur und Patrioten

Wie der vorbildliche Dichter, Diplomat, Ratsherr und Aufklärer Barthold Hinrich Brockes (1680–1747) aussah, zeigt uns ein von Dominicus van der Smissen gemaltes Porträt, das sich heute im Besitz der Hamburger Kunsthalle befindet. Ein zuversichtlich und freundlich blickender Herr mit vollem Gesicht, kräftiger Nase und starken Augenbrauen. Pelzmütze und Pelzkragen geben Zeugnis davon, daß der Porträtierte durchaus zur besseren Gesellschaft zählte. Der Kaufmannssohn hatte das Johanneum und das Akademische Gymnasium absolviert und

many other countries have made the city's population profile more colourful than ever. Not forgetting people from other parts of Germany, for example Bavarians, Swabians and Saxons, all of whom some dyed-in-the-wool Hamburgers tend to regard as more foreign than the British. So the reputed divisions between original Hamburgers, people born in Hamburg and immigrants to Hamburg have long ceased to exist. And in fact such barriers do not befit a city whose trade and history have always forced it to have an international outlook. At the end of this historical review two examples, the unorthodox figure of the writer and councillor Barthold Hinrich Brockes and the wonderful institution of the Patriotische Gesellschaft (Patriotic Society), will serve to illustrate some genuinely "Hamburg" virtues.

### Intellect, culture and patriots

We know what the exemplary poet, diplomat, councillor and man of the Enlightenment Barthold Hinrich Brockes (1680–1747) looked like from a portrait painted by Domenicus van der Smissen which now hangs in the Hamburger Kunsthalle: a confident, likeablelooking man with a roundish face, large nose and thick eyebrows. His fur cap and collar testify to the fact that he came from a prosperous social background. Brockes, the son of a merchant, attended the Johanneum and the Akademisches Gymnasium before studying at the University of Leiden in Holland, where he gained his doctorate. He had inherited a considerable fortune from his father and increased it handsomely by marrying into a rich family. This provided a secure financial cushion for a life dedicated to the welfare of his fellow human beings and to the arts. This fortunate combination of intellect and money is more common in Hamburg than is generally assumed.

nach dem Studium der Rechtswissenschaft an der Universität Leiden den Doktortitel erworben. Vom Vater hatte er ein beträchtliches Vermögen geerbt, das er durch eine reiche Heirat noch wesentlich vermehren konnte. Ein finanzielles Polster für sein dem Gemeinwohl und den Musen gewidmetes Leben. In Brockes Person tritt uns eine glückliche Paarung von Geist und Geld entgegen, wie sie in Hamburg häufiger vorkommt, als im allgemeinen angenommen wird.

Neben vielen anonym Bleibenden bieten sich als Beispiel aus der Gegenwart der Millionenerbe Jan Philipp Reemtsma und das von ihm gegründete Hamburger Institut für Sozialforschung am Mittelweg an, zumal es ein schönes geistiges Band zwischen Reemtsma und Brockes gibt. Reemtsma unterstützte den 1914 in Hamburg geborenen Schriftsteller Arno Schmidt („Zettels Traum") und fördert seit vielen Jahren sein Werk. Schmidt wiederum widmete dem Barockdichter in Verehrung einen Essay mit dem Titel „Barthold Hinrich Brockes oder Nichts ist mir zu klein". Überdies wuchs Schmidt im Stadtteil Hamm auf und ging nicht weit von der Stelle zur Schule, wo Brockes einst sein Landhaus errichtet hatte.

Der Dichter Brockes war ein frommer Naturliebhaber, der in Tausenden von Versen Gottes schöne Schöpfung besang. Wobei ihm jede Blume, jeder Schmetterling – „Nichts ist mir zu klein" – als gelungene Miniatur eines großen Plans willkommen war. In seinem Barockgarten vor dem Steintor am Besenbinderhof (in der Nähe des Gewerkschaftshauses) fand er die nötige Inspiration für seine Naturlyrik. Und häufig schickten ihm

A good present-day example, alongside many who remain anonymous, is the wealthy tobacco heir Jan Philipp Reemtsma and the Hamburg Institute of Social Research which he founded – particularly as there is a neat intellectual link between Reemtsma and Brockes. Reemtsma sponsored the writer Arno Schmidt, born in Hamburg in 1914, and funded his work for many years. Schmidt in turn dedicated to Brockes an essay entitled, "Barthold Hinrich Brockes or nothing is too small for me." Not only that, Arno Schmidt grew up in the Hamm district of Hamburg, and went to school not far from where Brockes built his country house.

The Baroque poet Brockes was a deeply religious lover of nature, and wrote thousands of verses singing the praises of God's wonderful creation. He saw every flower, every butterfly – "Nothing is too small for me" – as a perfect miniature of a grand design. In his Baroque garden outside the Steintor gate to the city, close to where the trade union headquarters now stands, he found the necessary inspiration for his nature lyrics. Often, strangers sent him flowers with the request to write poems about them too. His first volume of poetry was a bestseller . It sold 3,500 copies, an unbelievable success in those days. By the time he died his output of verse had grown to nine volumes, which were published under the title "Irdisches Vergnügen in Gott" (Earthly Pleasure in God).

But the poet in him was only one aspect of this exemplary Hanseatic citizen. As a councillor and senator, Brockes was also a man of the world, and on more than one occasion conducted successful diplomatic missions on behalf of his home town. In 1721 in Vienna he wrote a poem to pacify the emperor, whose legation in Hamburg had been destroyed by religious fanatics. "Your Hamburg lies here in us at your feet/ To make amends for that which it did, and did not do." The emperor, enchanted,

Der Sozialwissenschaftler Jan Philipp Reemtsma (geb. 1952) gründete das Hamburger Institut für Sozialforschung am Mittelweg und war ein früher Förderer des Hamburger Schriftstellers Arno Schmidt (1914–79). Seine Entführung 1996 gehört zu den spektakulärsten Kriminalfällen der Bundesrepublik.

Social scientist Jan Philipp Reemtsma (born in 1952) founded the Hamburg Institute for Social Research in Mittelweg and was an early patron of the Hamburg writer Arno Schmidt (1914–79). Reemtsma's kidnapping in 1996 was one of Germany's most spectacular crimes.

wildfremde Menschen Blumen mit der Bitte, auch diese noch zu besingen. Sein erster Gedichtband wurde zum Bestseller. Mit 3500 verkauften Exemplaren für die damalige Zeit ein unglaublicher Erfolg. Am Ende seines Lebens war seine Lyrik auf neun Bände angewachsen, die unter dem Titel „Irdisches Vergnügen in Gott" erschienen.

Der Dichter in ihm war aber nur die eine Seite dieses vorbildlichen Hanseaten. Als Ratsherr und Senator agierte Brockes als Mann von Welt mehr als einmal mit Erfolg in diplomatischer Mission für seine Heimatstadt. Mit einem Gedicht besänftigte er 1721 in Wien den Kaiser, dessen Hamburger Gesandtschaftsgebäude von religiösen Fanatikern zerstört worden war: „Dein Hamburg lieget hier in uns zu Deinen Füßen/Das was es teils gethan, teils nicht gethan, zu büßen". Der Kaiser wurde versöhnlicher und milderte die Geldstrafe etwa um die Hälfte. Seine Gesandtschaft zog 1722 in das Görtz-Palais am Neuen Wall 86 ein. Ein Gebäude, dessen historische Fassade heute den noblen Schlußpunkt von Hamburgs teuerster Einkaufsmeile bildet.

Ganz in der Nähe des Görtz-Palais wohnte zu des Dichters Zeiten Hamburgs prominenter Musikdirektor Georg Philipp Telemann. Daß der Komponist, der damals in ganz Europa großes Ansehen genoß, der Hansestadt erhalten blieb, war ebenfalls der Überredungskunst von Brockes zu verdanken. Telemann und Georg Friedrich Händel waren nur zwei von insgesamt elf Komponisten, die die 1712 verfaßte Passionsdichtung des Lyrikers vom Besenbinderhof in Töne setzten.

Daß die Beerdigung des Dichters und Aufklärers 1747 in der Nikolaikirche zu einem Stadtereignis wurde, hat aber noch einen weiteren guten Grund. Als Mitherausgeber der richtungweisenden Hamburger Zeitschrift „Der Patriot" vertrat Brockes ungewöhnlich fort-

reduced the fine on the city by approximately half. In 1722 his legation moved into Görtz Palace at Neuer Wall 86, a building whose historic facade now elegantly rounds off Hamburg's most expensive shopping street.

Close to Görtz Palace in Brockes' day lived Hamburg's celebrated director of music, the composer Georg Philipp Telemann. Telemann was held in high regard throughout Europe, and it was thanks to Brockes' powers of persuasion that he remained in Hamburg. Telemann and Georg Friedrich Händel were just two of no fewer than eleven composers who set Brockes' Passion, written in 1712, to music.

However, there is yet another good reason why the poet and man of the Enlightenment's burial in St Nicholas' Church in 1747 was a state event. As co-publisher of the trailblazing Hamburg magazine "Der Patriot" (The Patriot), Brockes promulgated unusually progressive ideas. He argued for a women's academy, since he found that women's education was criminally neglected. Moreover, he suggested establishing factories where destitutes shut up in poorhouses could find work. Towards the end of 1723 he was a co-founder of the Patriotische Gesellschaft (Patriotic Society), which was inspired by the world-improving ideas of the Enlightenment.

Brockes' charitable organisation was the forerunner of an institution which still plays an exemplary role in Hamburg today. The Hamburg Society for the Promotion of Manufacture, the Arts and Useful Trades was founded in 1765 by progressively-minded pillars of Hanseatic society. For more than 200 years the society, known for short as the Patriotic Society, has combined the useful with the

Der Ratsherr und Dichter Barthold Heinrich Brockes (1680–1747) war ein maßgeblicher Förderer der frühen Aufklärungsbewegung an der Elbe.

City councillor and writer Barthold Heinrich Brockes (1680–1747) was an influential patron of the early Enlightenment in Hamburg.

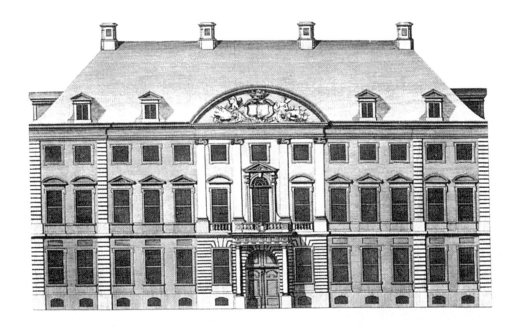

Das barocke Görtz-Palais am Neuen Wall hatte im 18. Jahrhundert als repräsentativer Adelssitz kaum seinesgleichen in der Stadt der Kaufleute.

As a prestigious aristocratic seat, in the eighteenth century the Baroque-style Görtz Palace on Neuer Wall was almost without equal in a city of merchants.

schrittliche Ideen. Er plädierte für eine Frauenakademie, da er das Bildungswesen für Frauen sträflich vernachlässigt fand. Ferner schlug er vor, Fabriken zu gründen, in denen die in Armenhäusern kasernierten Erwerbslosen Arbeit fänden. Ende 1723 war er Mitbegründer der „Patriotischen Gesellschaft", die von den Weltverbesserungsideen der Aufklärung getragen wurde.

Brockes' gemeinnütziger Verein wurde zum Vorläufer der Institution, die der Freien und Hansestadt bis heute beispielhaft Ehre macht. Die „Hamburgische Gesellschaft zur Beförderung der Manufacturen, Künste und Nützlichen Gewerbe" wurde 1765 von den fortschrittlich gesinnten Stützen der hanseatischen Gesellschaft gegründet. Der Verein, kurz „Patriotische Gesellschaft" genannt, verbindet seit über 200 Jahren das Nützliche mit dem Schönen. Eine ebenso traditionsreiche wie vorbildliche Bürgerinitiative, deren soziales Engagement mit einem pädagogischen und ästhetischen Impetus Hand in Hand geht.

Das Haus, in dem die Patriotische Gesellschaft noch heute ihren Sitz hat, wurde Mitte des 19. Jahrhunderts an der

aesthetically pleasing. An exemplary citizens' initiative with a rich tradition, in which social commitment goes hand in hand with an educational and aesthetic impetus.

The building which is still the Patriotic Society's headquarters was built close to Trostbrücke in the mid-nineteenth century. It was erected on the site of the Hamburg town hall, which had been destroyed in the 1842 fire – a fitting location of which the institution was thoroughly deserving. After all, through its numerous private initiatives it intervened so successfully in the life of the town that its role as a kind of "voluntary ministry of culture which simultaneously fulfils the functions of a parliament" (as Alfred Lichtwark, the first director of the Kunsthalle, described it), above all in the first 150 years of its existence, cannot be stressed highly enough.

Der Komponist Georg Philipp Telemann (1681–1767) war Hamburgs berühmtester Musikdirektor.

Composer Georg Philipp Telemann (1681– 1767) was Hamburg's most famous director of music.

Das 1847 eingeweihte
Gebäude der Patrio-
tischen Gesellschaft,
das am Platz des 1842
zerstörten Rathauses
errichtet wurde

The Patriotic Society
building, inaugurated in
1847, was built on the
site of the Town Hall
that had been destroyed
in 1842.

Trostbrücke gebaut. Bauplatz war das
Grundstück des während des Großen
Brandes 1842 zerstörten Hamburger
Rathauses. Ein würdiger Platz, der dieser
Institution durchaus zustand. Griff doch
die Gesellschaft mit zahlreichen Privat-
initiativen so erfolgreich in das Leben
der Stadt ein, daß ihre Rolle als eine Art
„freiwilliges Kultusministerium, das
zugleich die Funktionen eines Parlaments
ausübt" (so der erste Kunsthallendirek-
tor Alfred Lichtwark) vor allem in den
ersten 150 Jahren ihrer Existenz nicht
hoch genug eingeschätzt werden kann.

Eine Gewerbeschule und eine Zeichen-
schule für Bauhandwerker unter dem
Dach der Patriotischen Gesellschaft
demonstrierten den praktisch orientierten Ehrgeiz des Vereins. In seiner Frühzeit kümmerte er sich um eine Verbesse-
rung der Armenfürsorge und setzte sich
für bessere Bepflasterung der Straßen
und deren Beleuchtung ein. Auch die
Einführung von Blitzableitern in Hamburg war von der Gesellschaft unterstützt worden. Mit der Aktivierung der

A trade school and a draftsmen's
school for building craftsmen under the
Patriotic Society's roof demonstrated the
society's practically-oriented ambition.
In the early days it concerned itself with
ameliorating the lot of the poor and with
improving road surfaces and lighting.
The introduction of lightning-conductors
in Hamburg was sponsored by the society, which also established Hamburg's
first fire insurance company, the Hamburger Feuerkasse – which still exists
today – to make sure that fires no longer
inevitably led to destitution. The Patriotic Society library soon acquired an excellent reputation, and was the forerunner
of the city's present-day public lending
libraries. Germany's first savings bank
and riverside bathing-pool, both established towards the end of the eighteenth
century, were two more of the society's

Das Alte Rathaus mit
Niederngericht um
1700. Sein Grundstein
wurde 1290 gelegt.
Beim Großen Brand
wurde das mehrfach
erweiterte Gebäude völ-
lig zerstört.

The Old Town Hall
and courthouse in
around 1700. Its found-
ation stone was laid in
1290. The building,
which had been extend-
ed several times, was
completely destroyed in
the Great Fire.

ersten deutschen Feuerversicherung, der
heute noch existierenden „Hamburger
Feuerkasse", wurde dafür gesorgt, daß
ein Brand die Menschen nicht mehr an
den Bettelstab bringen mußte. Die
Bibliothek der Patriotischen Gesellschaft
genoß bald großes Ansehen und wurde
Vorreiter für die Öffentlichen Bücherhal-
len von heute. Auch Deutschlands erste
Sparkasse und Flußbadeanstalt, beide
gegen Ende des 18. Jahrhunderts gegründet, waren Verdienste der Gesellschaft.
Als sinniges Emblem für ihre Arbeit hatten sich die Mitglieder den Bienenkorb
gewählt. Sich mit Fleiß und Witz für das
Gemeinwohl einzusetzen, das war und
ist das Ziel dieser bürgerlichen Privatinitiative, die ihre guten Taten nie an die
große Glocke hängte. Der Dichter und
Politiker Barthold Hinrich Brockes und
die gemeinnützige Patriotische Gesellschaft vereinen in sich eine Fülle der
besonders positiven, besonders hamburgischen Züge, die den Menschen dieser
Stadt – neben den besonders negativen –
nachgesagt werden.

achievements. The society's members fit-
tingly chose the beehive as the emblem
to symoblise their work. The aim of this
private citizens' initiative was and
remains to work with industry and creativity on behalf of the common good. It
has never made a lot of noise about its
good works. The poet and politician
Barthold Hinrich Brockes and the charitable Patriotische Gesellschaft unite a
large number of the particularly positive,
particularly Hamburgian features which
the people of this city are credited with –
alongside some particularly negative
ones, of course.

Das Hamburger Wap-
pen im Signet der Ham-
burger Feuerkasse von
1676, der ersten deut-
schen Feuerversiche-
rung. Reproduktion
eines Emailschildes

The Hamburg coat of
arms in the logo of the
Hamburger Feuerkasse
von 1676, the first Ger-
man fire insurance.
Reproduction of an
enamel nameplate

# Medien, Modemacher und Mäzene
## Media, fashion leaders and patrons

Gibt es den typischen Hamburger? Auf jeden Fall gibt es ein typisches Schimpfwort für ihn, nämlich „Pfeffersack". Überaus tüchtige Kaufleute mit Hang zur Leibesfülle und zu zugeknöpften Taschen werden als Pfeffersäcke bezeichnet. Ein Wort aus dem Ursumpf des Kapitalismus, als der Import von Pfeffer (altindisch: pippali) aus Indien blühte und die europäischen Gewürzhändler sich eine goldene Nase mit diesen scharfen Früchten verdienten. Übrigens dienten Pfefferkörner im Mittelalter vereinzelt auch als Zahlungsmittel, und ein Sack voller Pfeffer konnte ein kleines Vermögen darstellen.

Also Pfeffersäcke sollen die Hamburger sein. Das Schimpfwort ist so oldfashioned, daß die Betroffenen es schon fast wieder mögen. Und wie in jedem anständigen Vorurteil steckt natürlich auch in diesem ein Körnchen Wahrheit. Genauso wie eine gewisse Vorliebe für die Farbe Dunkelblau an Alster und Elbe unverkennbar ist. Bei den Damen ist das Blau aufgeputzt durch eine schlichte Perle als Ohrschmuck und eine ganze Kette dieser Preziosen um den Hals, bei den Herren taucht es bei den Schlipsen mit dem Wappen des jeweiligen Segelclubs auf. Konservativ mit Anzeichen von Arroganz, liberal, hilfsbereit und freundlich, solange die Distanz gewahrt bleibt. Soweit das Klischee vom typischen Hamburger aus der „besseren Gesellschaft". Wie er hat auch der „gemeine Mann" kein semmelweißes Haar, wie die Nordfriesen, sondern dunkelblondes, das natürlich von einem Elbsegler auf dem Kopf verdeckt wird. Daneben ruht auf der Schulter ein Seesack, der noch aus der guten alten Zeit von Hein und Fiete stammt, als jeder echte Hanseat einen Onkel hatte, der in einem mit englischen Brocken angereicherten Plattdeutsch abendfüllend von seinen Segelabenteuern auf Drei-, Vier und Fünfmastern erzählte.

Is there such a thing as a typical Hamburger? Well, there is at least a typical derogatory nickname for one – "Pfeffersack" (pepper sack). It is used to describe thoroughly industrious businessmen with a tendency to corpulence who keep a tight grip on their money. The word originates from the early days of capitalism when the import trade in pepper (old Indian: pippali) from India was booming and the European spice dealers earned themselves a pretty penny from these hot fruits. Incidentally, in the Middle Ages peppercorns were occasionally used as a means of payment, and a sack full of pepper could represent a small fortune.

So, the Hamburgers are said to be pepper sacks. The term is so quaintly old-fashioned that the people it is applied to have quite come to like it. And, as with every decent prejudice, there is a grain of truth in this one, too. Just as a certain predilection for navy-blue is unmistakable in Hamburg. The ladies relieve it with plain pearl earrings and a string of pearls around their necks, while the gentlemen lash ties with their sailing-club emblems round theirs. Conservative with a streak of arrogance, liberal, helpful and friendly provided they can keep their distance. So much for the stereotype of the typical Hamburger from the "upper echelons" of society. Like them, the "common man" does not have the snow-white mane of the North Frisians but dark blonde hair, covered of course by a navy-blue "Elbsegler" (Elbe sailor) peaked cap. Across his shoulder is slung a sailor's kitbag dating from the good old days when every genuine Hamburger had an uncle who whiled away many an evening telling old salt's tales in Low German enriched with broken English.

You see this typical Hamburger about as often as the yodelling Municher in leather shorts, the typical Berlin money-grubber, the true happy-go-lucky Cologner or the genuine Frankfurt apple-wine drinker – namely, rather seldom in reality. It is true that Hamburg-

Diesen typischen Hamburger gibt es etwa genauso oft wie den jodelnden Münchner im Trachtenlook, den typischen Berliner Raffke, die wahre Kölner Frohnatur oder den waschechten Frankfurter Äbbelwoitrinker: nämlich in Wahrheit ziemlich selten. Sicher ist, daß die Hamburger – anders als die Düsseldorfer, Münchner oder Berliner – mit Bedacht ein traditionelles Understatement pflegen. Über Geld redet man nicht, man hat es. Immerhin 6000 Millionäre schweigen sich hier am liebsten über ihre finanziellen Verhältnisse aus. Damit steht die Stadt in Deutschland an der Spitze dieser Statistik.

Hamburgs Prominenz ist vielschichtig und bunt: wie es sich gehört für diese selbstbewußte Weltstadt, in der die meisten Menschen überzeugt davon sind, daß ihr schönes Hamburg der Nabel der Welt sei. Wolf Biermann und Udo Lindenberg sind hier musikalisches Urgestein. Die Elbe gehört zu dem Dichter und Sänger Biermann („Mit Marx- und Engelszungen") wie die Alster zu dem Rockmusiker Lindenberg, der in den siebziger Jahren im Eppendorfer „Onkel Pö" seine Karriere startete, der Musikkneipe, in der damals der „Mississippi in die Alster floß". Heute findet sich vor

ers – unlike people from Düsseldorf, Munich or Berlin – deliberately cultivate a traditional understatement. You don't talk about money in Hamburg, you just have it. No fewer than 6,000 millionaires prefer to keep quiet about their financial circumstances – putting Hamburg at the top of Germany's millionaires' league table.

Hamburg's VIPs are multi-layered and colourful, as befits this self-assured cosmopolitan city, where most people are firmly convinced that their beautiful Hamburg is the centre of the world. Wolf Biermann and Udo Lindenberg are its homespun musicians. The Elbe is as much a part of the poet and singer Biermann, well-known as a dissident in communist East Germany, as the Alster is of rock musician Lindenberg, who began his career in the 1970s in "Onkel Pö," a live-music pub in the Eppendorf district. Outside former Cafe Keese on the Reeperbahn, where the women ask the men to dance, a large star in Lindenberg's honour is set into the much-trodden pavement.

But what is a VIP? Heidi Kabel must surely surpass them all in this respect. To many people, the aging, eternally young popular actress with her heart in the right place is the Hamburger par excellence. When her home – a rather plain suburban residence and not a mansion on Elbchaussee – was ransacked by burglars, the whole city was up in arms. Incidentally, Germany's former chancellor Helmut Schmidt, a keen ambassador for his home town, and his wife Loki live not in a white villa with a view of the Elbe but in a simple brick terrace house on the northern outskirts of the city. When the former chancellor climbs into the pulpit in one of the city's principal churches – as he is fond of doing – there is not an empty seat in the place. A sign of the authority which the Hamburg politician still enjoys.

„Onkel Pö's Carnegie Hall" in Eppendorf war von 1971 bis zu ihrer Schließung 1985 Treffpunkt der Hamburger Musik-Szene mit internationalem Renommee. Hier singt Otto Waalkes, am Schlagzeug begleitet von Udo Lindenberg.

From 1971 until it was closed in 1985, Onkel Pö's Carnegie Hall in Eppendorf was an internationally known rendezvous of the Hamburg music scene. Otto Waalkes is here seen singing, accompanied by Udo Lindenberg on percussion.

Der Elbsegler, die einst traditionelle Kopfbedeckung der Hamburger Arbeiterwelt, ist mittlerweile aus dem Straßenbild verschwunden.

The Elbsegler cap, once the traditional headgear of Hamburg workers, has now disappeared from the streets.

Wie in alten Zeiten:
Akrobaten auf dem
Spielbudenplatz an der
Reeperbahn begeistern
ihr Publikum.

As in bygone days,
acrobats are here seen
on the Reeperbahn's
Spielbudenplatz per-
forming to a delighted
audience.

dem ehemaligen Café Keese an der Reeperbahn, wo Damenwahl obligat ist, im
vielbegangenen Pflaster ein Ehrenstern
für Udo Lindenberg.

Aber was heißt schon prominent?
Wahrscheinlich schießt in dieser Hinsicht
Heidi Kabel sowieso den Vogel ab. Die
betagte, ewig junge Volksschauspielerin
mit dem Herzen auf dem rechten Fleck
gilt vielen als die Hamburgerin schlecht-
hin. Wenn ihre Wohnung – ein eher
schlichtes Vorortdomizil und keine Elb-
chausseevilla – von Einbrechern verwü-
stet wird, empört sich die ganze Stadt.
Übrigens: auch Altbundeskanzler Helmut Schmidt, ein überzeugter Botschaf-
ter seiner Heimatstadt, wohnt mit seiner
Frau Loki nicht in einer weißen Villa mit
Elbblick, sondern in einem einfachen
Backsteinreihenhaus am Nordrand der
Stadt. Wenn der Altbundeskanzler in
einer der Hauptkirchen der Stadt auf die
Kanzel steigt – was er gerne tut –, ist das
Gotteshaus bis auf den letzten Platz
gefüllt. Ein Zeichen für die Autorität, die
der Politiker an der Elbe nach wie vor
genießt.

But where would Hamburg be without "our Uwe"? When the outstanding
footballer Uwe Seeler celebrated his 60th
birthday in November 1996, his fans ser-
enaded him in the great hall of the
Rathaus. Standing in the balcony high
above the crowd waving HSV (Hamburg
Sports Club) scarves, "our Uwe" shout-
ed "Keep well, all of you," and followed
the mayor to a breakfast with the Senate
which had been organised in his honour.
The occasion was crowned with a massive ice cream for the legendary footballer.

What bridge leads from Uwe Seeler
and the Hamburg Sports Club to Jil
Sander and the Hamburg fashion scene?
Actually none. Or at most the fact that
both are front-runners as media
favourites. The soccer king and the fashion queen are a totally unmatched cou-
ple, which illustrates the fact that the different social circles in Hamburg do not
come into contact with each other, and
that their leading members dance at
completely different weddings. The
Hamburg high society of former times is
a thing of the past and no longer exists.
The homogeneity has dissolved into
many different circles which together
make up a colourful social mosaic.

Germany's most successful fashion
designer, who lives in a thirty-roomed
white mansion on Harvestehuder Weg, is
a cool North German beauty. With her
stunning looks, Jil Sander was the best
model for her own products. Her photograph was on display worldwide advertising the style whose easy cut and fine-
quality fabrics, in short whose very puri-
ty appeals to wealthy women from
Berlin to Paris, New York and Tokyo.
And, more recently, to men too. For
since she launched her new men's collection in Milan in 1997, Jil Sander's
clothes and accessories have been all the
rage with fashion-conscious men. Jil
Sander opened her boutique in Milchstrasse in 1968, at the age of 25. In those
days the Pöseldorf district was a sleepy,
slightly shabby, area of villas. Now it is a

Und was wäre Hamburg ohne „uns Uwe"? Als der verdiente Fußballspieler Uwe Seeler im November 1996 seinen 60. Geburtstag feierte, brachte ihm seine Fangemeinde in der großen Rathausdiele ein Ständchen. „Uns Uwe" stand auf dem Balkon hoch über der HSV-Schals schwenkenden Menge und rief: „Bleibt alle schön gesund." Dann folgte er dem Bürgermeister zum Senatsfrühstück, das ihm zu Ehren angerichtet worden war. Bekrönt war es mit einem „Bomber-Eis" für den erfolgreichen Fußballer.

Welche Brücke führt von Uwe Seeler und dem Hamburger Sportverein zu Jil Sander und der Hamburger Modeszene? Eigentlich keine. Oder höchstens die Tatsache, daß beide als Lieblinge der Medien ganz vorne im Rennen liegen. Der Fußballkönig und die Modekönigin geben ein herzlich ungleiches Paar ab, das exemplarisch dafür ist, wie sich die diversen gesellschaftlichen Kreise an Elbe und Alster durchaus nicht berühren und ihre Spitzen auf sehr verschiedenen Hochzeiten tanzen. Die feine Hamburger Gesellschaft früherer Tage ist Vergangenheit, sie gibt es nicht mehr. Die Homogenität hat sich aufgelöst in viele unterschiedliche Zirkel, die ein buntes gesellschaftliches Mosaik bilden.

Deutschlands erfolgreichste Modedesignerin, die in einer weißen 30-Zimmer-Villa am Harvestehuder Weg residiert, ist eine kühle norddeutsche Schönheit. Jil Sander mit ihrem blendenden Aussehen gab für ihre Produkte selber das beste Model ab. Ihr Bild warb weltweit für die

synonym for the Alster smart set. And Jil Sander's empire includes shops in the most up-market districts of the metropolises of the world, since 1999 as part of the Prada Group. In 1989 her company was floated on the stock exchange. Nine years previously, she had launched her first perfume, "Woman Pur."

The only fashion designer on the Alster to match up to Jil Sander's success is Wolfgang Joop, whose collections are also known worldwide. Representing medium-sized companies is Iris von Arnim, who has established herself with her high-class knitwear in a 800-square-metre art nouveau villa in Harvestehude.

The figures alone indicate that it is the media which set the tone in Hamburg. More than 6,000 companies vie with each other in the print media, film, TV, advertising, music, radio and new media industries. Hamburg has more advertising agencies than any other German city, and with the ten biggest model agencies tops the field in that business, too. There are 3,200 advertising industry firms, followed by the print media with 1,600 publishers and printers, and in third place by 700 film companies. Favourite

Uwe Seeler, die Hamburger Fußball-Legende, 1961 beim Spiel gegen den FC Burnley. Der HSV gewann 4:1.

Hamburg soccer legend Uwe Seeler playing against Burnley FC in 1961. Hamburg's HSV won 4–1.

Mode, die wegen ihres lässigen Schnitts, ihrer qualitätvollen Stoffe, kurz: wegen ihres Purismus, zahlungskräftige Käuferinnen von Berlin, Paris, New York bis Tokio findet. Und neuerdings auch Käufer. Denn seit die Designerin 1997 in Mailand ihre neue Herrenkollektion präsentierte, macht auch ihre Kleidung nebst Accessoires für den modisch bewußten Mann Furore. Mit 25 Jahren hatte Jil Sander 1968 in der Pöseldorfer Milchstraße ihre Boutique eröffnet. Damals war Pöseldorf ein verschlafenes, leicht heruntergekommenes Villenquartier. Heute steht es synonym für Alster-Schickimicki. Zum Imperium der Boutiquenbesitzerin, seit 1999 Teil der Prada-Group, zählen Geschäfte mit vornehmsten Adressen in den Metropolen der Welt. 1989 ging die Designerin mit ihrem Unternehmen an die Börse, neun Jahre vorher hatte sie ihr erstes Parfüm auf den Markt gebracht: „Woman Pur".

Vergleichbar erfolgreich wie Jil Sander ist in der Modebranche an der Alster nur noch Wolfgang Joop, dessen Kollektionen ebenfalls weltweit getragen werden. Iris von Arnim hat ihr mittelständisches Unternehmen mit hochfeiner Strickmode in einer 800 Quadratmeter großen Jugendstilvilla in Harvestehude etabliert.

Wie die Medienszene in Hamburg den Ton angibt, lassen allein einige Zahlen erahnen. Über 6000 Unternehmen tummeln sich in den Bereichen Printmedien, Film, TV, Werbewirtschaft, Musik, Hörfunk und Neue Medien. Hamburg ist in Deutschland die Stadt mit den meisten Werbeagenturen. Auch mit den zehn größten Model-Agenturen liegt Hamburg an der Spitze der Bundesrepublik. Die Werbewirtschaft zählt 3200 Firmen, gefolgt von den Printmedien mit 1600 Verlagen und Druckereien sowie von 700 Filmunternehmen, die damit an dritter Stelle in der Medienbranche rangieren. Als „locations" für Dreharbeiten stehen an erster Stelle: Hafen, Flughafen,

film locations include the port, the airport, Hagenbeck Zoo, the Warehouse City, St Pauli and the up-market residential suburbs. But much of what looks like genuine Hamburg in the cinema or on TV is only a painted backdrop. The Hanseatic city's dream factory is in Tonndorf, where more than 2,000 television programmes are produced each year. Studio Hamburg with its 20 subsidiaries is Germany's largest audiovisual service provider. The father of this Hanseatic leader is Hungarian-born entrepreneur Gyula Trebitsch. Born in 1914, his career reads like a miracle. After being liberated from the concentration camp in Wöbbelin, near Ludwigslust in Mecklenburg, eastern Germany, Trebitsch made his way to Hamburg, where in 1947 he and film distributor Walter Koppel founded Real Film GmbH, the embryo of present-day Studio Hamburg. The founder's children, Katharina and Markus Trebitsch, have long played a role in the film and television history that has been written on the premises for over half a century, and run the business as brilliantly as their father.

Hamburg's celebrity scene is rich in outsiders who have made it their home, popularly known as "Quiddjes." Sometimes they turn out to be as passionate Hamburgers as the "Pfeffersäcke" themselves ever were. Take, for example, Kurt A. Körber (1909–92). Born in Berlin, he came to Hamburg after World War II with a suitcase full of inventions. He founded the Hanseatische Universelle (Hauni) works, which went on to gain a monopoly position in filter cigarette-making machines, securing a 90 per cent

Die Abteistraße ist eine der typischen feinen Wohnstraßen in Harvestehude. Ihr Name erinnert an das Zisterzienserkloster Herwardeshuthe, dem einst weitläufige Ländereien am Westufer der Alster gehörten.

Abteistrasse is a typical up-market residential street in Harvestehude. Its name, which means Abbey Street, recalls the Cistercian monastery that once owned extensive lands on the west bank of the Alster.

Hagenbecks Tierpark, Speicherstadt, St. Pauli und die noblen Villenvororte. Aber manches, was im Kino oder im Fernsehen wie echt Hamburg aussieht, ist in Wirklichkeit gemalte Kulisse. Die Traumfabrik der Hansestadt liegt in Tonndorf. Das 80 000 Quadratmeter große Ateliergelände von Studio Hamburg ist ein Klein-Hollywood, ausgerüstet mit allen technischen Raffinessen. Hier werden jährlich mehr als 2000 Fernsehsendungen produziert. Studio Hamburg mit 20 Tochterfirmen ist der größte audiovisuelle Dienstleister in Deutschland. Vater dieses hanseatischen Superlativs ist der gebürtige Ungar Gyula Trebitsch. Die Karriere des 1914 geborenen Unternehmers klingt wie ein Wunder. Nach der Befreiung aus dem Konzentrationslager Wöbbelin bei Ludwigslust geriet Trebitsch nach Hamburg und gründete hier 1947 zusammen mit dem Filmverleiher Walter Koppel die Real Film GmbH, die Keimzelle des heutigen Studio Hamburg. An der Film- und Fernsehgeschichte, die seit über einem halben Jahrhundert auf dem Gelände geschrieben wird, sind seit langem schon die Sprößlinge des Firmengründers beteiligt,

market share. Körber was rich, and through his Körber Foundation became one of Europe's outstanding patrons. He founded the influential Bergedorfer Gesprächskreis (Bergedorf Discussion Circle), which holds international conferences in different venues around the

Die Häuser der Deichstraße – hier brach 1842 der Große Brand aus – vom Nikolaifleet aus gesehen, sind Zeugen des alten Hamburg.

The houses on Deichstrasse – the Great Fire of 1842 broke out here –, seen from the Nikolaifleet, are testimony to old Hamburg.

Der Hafen ist ohne
Frage der aufregendste
Schauplatz der Stadt.
Die lange Promenade
zwischen Deichtor-
hallen und Fischerei-
hafen bietet immer
wieder atemberaubend
großartige Blicke. Der
Bug der RICKMER RICK-
MERS und die neuen
Dächer der Landungs-
brücken rahmen einen
Ausblick auf Contain-
erterminals und Eng-
landfähre.

The port is without
question one of the
city's most exciting
scenes. The long prom-
enade between the
Deichtorhallen and the
fishing port offers many
a breathtakingly mag-
nificent view. The bow
of the RICKMER RICK-
MERS and the new roofs
of the landing stages
frame a view of con-
tainer terminals and the
terminal for ferries to
and from England.

Der Blick von der
Alsterpromenade in
Harvestehude über die
Außenalsterufer ist
immer wieder faszi-
nierend. Hamburg ohne
diesen großzügigen
Wasserspiegel?
Undenkbar. Man macht
sich kaum noch klar,
daß sowohl Binnen- als
auch Außenalster
künstlich aufgestaute
Seen sind.

The view from Alster-
promenade in Harveste-
hude across the bank of
the Outer Alster is
always fascinating.
Hamburg without this
extensive stretch of
water? Unthinkable.
Nowadays, people
hardly recall that both
Inner and Outer Alster
are artificially dammed
lakes.

Die Studio Hamburg GmbH entstand 1960 im Stadtteil Tonndorf. Ihr Gründer, Gyula Trebitsch, gilt als einer der erfolgreichsten Film- und Fernsehproduzenten der Nachkriegszeit. Seine Villa war die Keimzelle des heutigen Studiogeländes.

Studio Hamburg GmbH was founded in the district of Tonndorf in 1960. Its founder, Gyula Trebitsch, is regarded as one of the most successful film and television producers of the post-war era. His villa was the germ cell of the present studio complex.

Klein Erna hat das sprichwörtliche Hamburger Mundwerk. Die Geschichten von dieser Hamburger Deern sammelte Vera Möller (1911–98).

Klein Erna has the proverbial Hamburg quick wit. Vera Möller (1911–98) collected tales about this typical Hamburg girl.

Katharina und Markus Trebitsch, die das Geschäft ebenso glänzend betreiben wie der Vater.

Hamburgs Prominentenszene ist reich an Zugereisten, die Quiddjes genannt werden. Manchmal entpuppen gerade sie sich in ihrer Wahlheimat an der Elbe als leidenschaftlichere Hamburger als es die „Pfeffersäcke" je waren. Zum Beispiel Kurt A. Körber (1909–92). Der gebürtige Berliner kam nach dem Zweiten Weltkrieg mit einem Köfferchen voller Erfindungen an die Elbe. Er gründete die Hauni-Werke (Hanseatische Universelle), die eine Monopolstellung für Maschinen zur Filterzigarettenherstellung mit einem Weltmarktanteil von 90 Prozent erlangten. Kurt Körber war reich und wurde mit seiner Körber-Stiftung einer der herausragenden Mäzene Europas. Er rief den einflußreichen „Bergedorfer Gesprächskreis" ins Leben, der weltweit an wechselnden Orten internationale Tagungen zu Kernproblemen der Gesellschaft und zur Völkerverständigung durchführt. Seine gut ausgestattete Stiftung unterstützt kulturelle Unternehmungen, fördert Wissenschaft, Forschung, Bildung und Erziehung. Sie hilft alten und kranken Menschen und vergibt eine Vielzahl an Preisen, darunter den Rolf-Liebermann-Preis für Komponisten, den Boy-Gobert-Preis für Schauspieler. Ohne Kurt Körber gäbe es sie nicht mehr, die herrlichen Deichtorhallen, in denen seit 1989 internationale Kunst gezeigt wird. Körber stiftete 25 Millionen Mark für die Restaurierung des nördlichen dreischiffigen Langbaus und der südlichen Zentralhalle. Schande über den, der darüber lästert, daß der Mäzen sein Firmenzeichen, zwei Ringe, unübersehbar auf den Platz pflanzte. Ein weiterer bekannter Mäzen war Alfred Toepfer (1894–1993). Der gebürtige Altonaer erwirtschaftete als Getreidekaufmann ein

world on fundamental problems of society and on international understanding. His wealthy foundation supports cultural undertakings, and promotes science, research and education. It helps the old and the sick and awards a large number of prizes, including the Rolf Liebermann Prize for composers and the Boy Gobert Prize for actors.

Were it not for Kurt Körber, Hamburg would no longer have its splendid Deichtor halls, which have been used for international art exhibitions since 1989. Körber donated 25 million marks for the restoration of the elongated, three-section northern building and the southern central hall. Shame upon those who made nasty remarks about Körber for having his company logo, two rings, displayed prominently on the site.

Another well-known patron was Alfred Toepfer (1894–1993). Born in Altona, he earned a fortune as a grain merchant, and set up a number of foundations. The present-day Alfred Toepfer Stiftung F.V.S. awards a large number of prizes. Among other things, its founder rendered outstanding services to nature conservation, and the programme to develop nature parks in Germany was established on his initiative. Heading the list of Hamburg's private foundations is the Zeit-Foundation Ebelin and Gerd Bucerius. It was founded in 1971 by publisher Gerd Bucerius, 1906–1995. With its support the private Bucerius Law School was set up in Hamburg in 2000.

Turning to the lighter side of the Hamburg mentality, we must not forget

Vermögen und rief mehrere Stiftungen ins Leben. Die heutige Alfred Toepfer Stiftung F.V.S. verleiht eine Vielzahl von Preisen. Besondere Verdienste erwarb sich ihr Gründer auch im Naturschutz, und auf seine Initiative entstand das Programm zur Entwicklung von Naturparks in Deutschland. Den Spitzenplatz bei den Hamburgischen Privatstiftungen nimmt die ZEIT-Stiftung Ebelin und Gerd Bucerius ein. Sie wurde 1971 von dem Verleger Gerd Bucerius (1906– 1995) ins Leben gerufen. Mit ihrer Unterstützung entstand im Jahr 2000 in Hamburg die private Bucerius Law School für Studenten der Rechtswissenschaften.

Wenn es um hanseatische Mentalität in Form von Frohnaturen geht, darf „Klein Erna" nicht fehlen. Die Witze rund um diese Hamburger Deern sammelte Vera Möller (1911–98). Sie paaren hanseatischen Sinn für Bodenständigkeit aufs schönste mit einem ziemlich absurden Mutterwitz. Zum Beispiel: „Mamma sitzt auf ne Bank an der Alster und Klein Erna geht in die Anlagen spazieren. Mamma strickt zwei schlicht zwei kraus und will gaanich gestört werden. Und wie da mit 'n mal 'n großer Schwan angeschwommen kommt, da ruft Klein Erna: ‚Mamma, Mamma, kuck mal den Schwan, der hat aber 'n langen Hals!' Mamma: ‚Den laß man, Klein Erna, der soll ja wohl.'"

"Klein Erna" ("Little Erna"). Vera Möller (1911–98) compiled a collection of jokes centring on this Hamburg lass. They beautifully combine Hanseatic down-to-earthness with a somewhat absurd native wit. For example: Mummy is sitting on a bench by the Alster and Klein Erna goes off for a walk in the gardens. Mummy is knitting two plain, two purl and doesn't want to be disturbed. All at once, a big swan comes swimming up, and Klein Erna shouts, "Mummy, mummy, look at the swan, what a long neck it's got!" Mummy: "Leave it alone, Klein Erna, it's probably meant to have one."

Das Alte Botanische Institut beherbergt seit Januar 2000 die private Bucerius Law School (Hochschule für Rechtswissenschaft), die die ZEIT-Stiftung Ebelin und Gerd Bucerius als alleinige Gesellschafterin unterhält.

The Old Botanical Institute has since January 2000 housed the private Bucerius Law School, run by its sole shareholder, the ZEIT Foundation Ebelin and Gerd Bucerius.

# Rund um Binnenalster und Jungfernstieg

## Around the Inner Alster and Jungfernstieg

Die wunderschöne Kombination eines Uferspaziergangs mit der Möglichkeit des Promenierens auf einem gediegenen Boulevard bietet der Jungfernstieg. Der Wasserspiegel der Binnenalster, der den Himmel so großzügig mitten in die Stadt holt, gibt Hamburgs prominentester Straße ihr weites Gepräge. Die noch nicht einmal einen Kilometer lange Strecke zwischen Gänsemarkt und Ballindamm etablierte sich als Flaniermeile für vornehme und weniger vornehme Jungfern, nachdem 1665 der Staudamm an der Binnenalster aufgeschüttet und das dadurch entstandene Uferstück mit Linden bepflanzt worden war. Der Jungfernstieg ist die prominenteste Straße der Hafenstadt. Die bekannteste oder gar populärste ist sie jedoch nicht. Dieser Rang ist und bleibt der Reeperbahn vorbehalten, die auf eine internationale Berühmtheit verweisen kann – doch das ist ein anderes Kapitel.

Wie Maulwürfe haben die Ingenieure Ende der 1960er Jahre die Erde unter Jungfernstieg und Binnenalster durchwühlt. Auf drei Etagen bringen U- und S-Bahnen Menschen in die Innenstadt und wieder hinaus. In der guten alten Droschkenzeit, als die Kutscher auf dem Bock einnickten, wenn sich die Herrschaften im Alsterpavillon oder in der Austernstube verplauderten, ging es ruhiger zu am Jungfernstieg. Meistens jedenfalls, denn wie es sich für einen anständigen, wenn auch etwas kurz geratenen Boulevard gehört, spiegelte die Straße immer auch jede Unruhe oder Katastrophe wider, die die Stadt heimsuchten.

Eine friedliche kleine Menschenschar versammelte sich am 21. Januar 1815 vor dem Haus Nr. 22. Man trauerte um den 1740 geborenen Dichter Matthias Claudius. Der „Wandsbecker Bote", Ver-

The Jungfernstieg offers the delightful combination of a walk along the bank of the Alster with the opportunity to promenade on a high-class boulevard. The surface of the Inner Alster, which so generously opens the city centre to the sky, gives Hamburg's most celebrated street its wide-open character. Less than a kilometre long, the stretch between Gänsemarkt and Ballindamm established itself as a place where respectable and not-so-respectable young ladies went for a stroll after the Inner Alster was dammed in 1665 and the resulting embankment planted with linden trees. The Jungfernstieg is the port city's most celebrated street, but not its best-known or most popular. That rank is and will remain reserved for the world-famous Reeperbahn. But that is another chapter.

Towards the end of the 1960s, engineers burrowed through the earth under Jungfernstieg like moles. A three-storeyed underground and suburban train station pours visitors into the city centre and out again. In the good old days of carriages, when the coachmen nodded off on their boxes as the ladies and gentlemen whiled the time away in the Alster Pavilion or the oyster bar, things were quieter on Jungfernstieg. Usually, that is. For as befits a respectable, if somewhat short, boulevard, the street also reflected every disturbance or disaster that struck the city.

On 21 January 1815, a small, quiet group of people gathered outside No. 22. They were mourning the death of the poet Matthias Claudius, born in 1740. Claudius, known as the "Wandsbek Messenger" and author of one of Germany's best-loved poems "Der Mond ist aufgegangen" (The moon has risen), had breathed his last in the house of his son-in-law, the well-known bookseller Friedrich Christoph Perthes (1772–1843). In those days the city centre was still residential and Jungfernstieg was a highly desirable place to reside. It remains a top location for shops and offices.

Matthias Claudius (1740–1815), der „Wandsbecker Bote", starb in einem Haus am Jungfernstieg. Sein Abendlied „Der Mond ist aufgegangen ..." ist unvergessen.

Matthias Claudius (1740–1815), the "Wandsbeck Messenger," died in a house on Jungfernstieg. His evening song "Der Mond ist aufgegangen ..." (The Moon Has Risen) is unforgotten.

Der Jungfernstieg vor dem Großen Brand von 1842. Der Dichter Heinrich Heine hat das Leben auf dieser Flaniermeile zu eben der Zeit ebenso schön wie unnachahmlich böse beschrieben.

Jungfernstieg before the Great Fire of 1842. The writer Heinrich Heine described life on this promenade in those days in an attractive yet inimitably sarcastic style.

fasser des wunderbaren Poems „Der Mond ist aufgegangen, die goldnen Sternlein prangen ...", hatte im Haus seines Schwiegersohns, des berühmten Buchhändlers Friedrich Christoph Perthes (1772–1843) den letzten Atemzug getan. Damals war die Innenstadt noch Wohnquartier, und der Jungfernstieg galt als feine Adresse. Bis heute ist er eine Toplage für Geschäfte und Büros geblieben.

Politisch brisant war dagegen ein Fackelzug, der am 5. Oktober 1841 vor Streit's Hotel, 16 Hausnummern von Matthias Claudius' Sterbehaus entfernt, ankam. Man demonstrierte für ein einiges Deutschland und sang ein noch druckfrisches Lied aus dem Haus des Hamburger Verlegers Johann Julius Campe (1792–1867), von dem niemand

In contrast, a torchlight procession that arrived outside Streit's Hotel, 16 doors along from the house where Matthias Claudius died, on 5 October 1841, was politically explosive. The marchers were demonstrating for a united Germany and singing a song hot off the press of the Hamburg publisher Johann Julius Campe (1792–1867)

Der Jungfernstieg im Jahr 1899. Die Alsterschiffe erhielten damals einen 175 Meter langen neuen Anleger.

Jungfernstieg in 1899. At that time the Alster ships were given a new, 175-metre-long jetty.

Die Binnenalster vom Wall bei der Lombardsbrücke aus gesehen. Die Lithographie zeigt die Szenerie am 5. Mai 1842, als der Große Brand ein Drittel der Stadt in Schutt und Asche legte.

View of the Inner Alster from the Lombardsbrücke embankment. This lithograph shows the scene on 5 May 1842 when the Great Fire reduced one third of the city to ruins.

Julius Campe

Julius Campe (1792–1867) war der Verleger des Dichters Heinrich Heine. Sein Mut und seine Geschäftstüchtigkeit machten den Hoffmann und Campe Verlag zu einem der wichtigsten deutschen Verlage.

Julius Campe (1792–1867) was Heinrich Heine's publisher. His courage and business acumen made Hoffmann und Campe one of Germany's leading publishers.

ahnte, daß es einmal die deutsche Nationalhymne werden sollte. August Heinrich Hoffmann von Fallersleben (1798–1874) hatte sein „Deutschlandlied" („Deutschland, Deutschland über alles …") auf der damals englischen Insel Helgoland gedichtet. Campe versah die markigen Verse mit der Haydn-Melodie zu „Gott erhalte Franz den Kaiser …"

Campe hatte als Verleger eine geniale Spürnase. 1826 veröffentlichte er Heinrich Heines „Reisebilder" und verhalf damit dem jungen Dichter zum Durchbruch. Der Poet aus Düsseldorf schrieb zu seiner Zeit die bissigsten und elegantesten Anmerkungen zur hanseatischen Society. Er war ein häufiger und schwieriger Gast im Hause seines Onkels, Salomon Heine, der sich als erfolgreicher Bankier an Hamburgs Nobelboulevard ein Haus leisten konnte.

Wer heute vor dem 1903 in anmutigem Jugendstil errichteten Heine-Haus am Jungfernstieg steht, befindet sich an dem Platz, wo eine der größten Katastrophen, die die Stadt jemals erschütterten, ihr Ende fand. Der Große Brand von

which was one day to become the German national anthem. August Heinrich Hoffmann von Fallersleben (1798–1874) had composed his "Deutschlandlied" ("Deutschland, Deutschland über alles …") while staying on the island of Heligoland, at that time British territory. Campe furnished the poet's grandiloquent words with Haydn's tune to "God save Kaiser Franz …"

Campe had a brilliant instinct as a publisher. In 1826 he published Heinrich Heine's "Reisebilder" (Pictures of a Journey), thus helping the young writer to make his breakthrough. In his day Heine, who came from Düsseldorf, wrote the most vicious and elegant remarks on Hanseatic society. He was a frequent, and difficult, guest in the house of his uncle, Salomon Heine, who as a successful banker was able to afford a house on Hamburg's exclusive boulevard.

1842, dem nahezu die gesamte Altstadt zum Opfer fiel, wurde durch die Sprengung von Salomon Heines Haus und einigen Nachbargebäuden gestoppt. Die Flammen, die sich vom 5. bis 8. Mai von der Deichstraße am Nikolaifleet bis zur Alster durchgefressen hatten, vernichteten das Rathaus, die Börse, die Nikolaikirche, die Petrikirche sowie unzählige Wohnungen und Kontorhäuser. Marodierende Plünderer zogen über den Jungfernstieg und verschonten auch den Alsterpavillon nicht, der als Treffpunkt der feinen Gesellschaft über erstklassige Weinvorräte verfügte.

## Vom Alsterpavillon zum Gänsemarkt

Der Alsterpavillon ist heute wieder Hamburgs berühmteste Kuchenstation. Dieses so wunderbar an der Binnenalster gelegene Gebäude, von dem aus der Blick beim Kaffeetrinken genüßlich über das Wasser bis zur Lombardsbrücke schweifen kann, ist wie ein Kristallisationspunkt der Geschichte des Jungfernstiegs. Wobei die Historie des Jungfernstiegs auch immer partiell ein Exempel liefert für die Entwicklung der ganzen Stadt. Wohl und Wehe, Aufstieg und Niedergang dieser Metropole am Wasser spiegeln sich im Schicksal ihres Boulevards, erweitert um das Netz der Straßen, die den Jungfernstieg erschließen: Alsterarkaden, Ballindamm, Neuer Jungfernstieg, Colonnaden, Große Bleichen, Neuer Wall, Esplanade und die Bergstraße als Verlängerung zur Mönckebergstraße.

Das erste Gebäude des Alsterpavillons, 1799 eingeweiht, war von biedermeierlicher Bescheidenheit. Auch der zweite, bis 1874 bestehende Bau genügte den neureichen Ansprüchen der Hanseaten in der zweiten Hälfte des 19. Jahrhunderts nicht mehr. Der Boulevard hatte sich nach der Feuerkatastrophe von 1842 zu einer Meile der Nobelhotels gemausert, in denen die Welt zu Gast war. Wie ein

Standing today outside the Heine building on Jungfernstieg, built in 1903 in graceful art nouveau style, one is on the very spot where one of the greatest disasters ever to shake the city came to a halt. The Great Fire of 1842, to which virtually the whole historic city centre fell victim, was halted by blowing up Salomon Heine's house and several adjacent buildings. The flames, which between 5 and 8 May had eaten their way from Deichstrasse by the Nikolaifleet to the Alster, destroyed the town hall, the stock exchange, St Nicholas' Church, St Peter's Church and innumerable homes and office buildings. Plunderers marauded along Jungfernstieg, not sparing the Alster Pavilion, which as a meeting-place for high society had a first-class wine cellar.

## From Alster Pavilion to Gänsemarkt

Nowadays, the Alster Pavilion is once more Hamburg's most famous cafe. In its wonderful location by the Alster, where you can drink a cup of coffee as your gaze roams across the water to Lombardsbrücke, the building is like a crystallisation point of Jungfernstieg's history. At the same time, the history of Jungfernstieg is partly a model for the development of the whole town. The ups and downs, rise and fall of this metropolis by the water are reflected in the fate of its boulevard and the network of streets around it – Alsterarkaden, Ballindamm, Neuer Jungfernstieg, Colonnaden, Grosse Bleichen, Neuer Wall, Espanade and Mönckebergstrasse.

The first Alster Pavilion building, opened in 1799, was a respectably modest affair. Even the second, which

Der Jungfernstieg mit dem Alsterpavillon ist Hamburgs klassische Flaniermeile. Der erste Alsterpavillon wurde 1799 errichtet. Der 1953 fertiggestellte Bau ist die siebte Fassung dieser berühmten Kaffee- und Kuchenstation.

Jungfernstieg, complete with Alster Pavilion, is Hamburg's traditional promenade. The first Alster Pavilion was built in 1799. This 1953 building is the seventh version of this famous coffee and cake stop.

prächtiger Phönix aus der Asche war die Straße wiedererstanden, und dem neuen Repräsentationsbedürfnis entsprach auch der Neubau des Alsterpavillons von 1875. 25 Jahre später wurde der nächste noch aufwendiger gestaltete Entwurf verwirklicht, und nun sah das Kaffeehaus fast so pompös aus wie das neue Schauspielhaus, mit dem sich die Stadt zur selben Zeit schmückte. Nur 14 Jahre später war dann wieder hanseatische Gediegenheit Trumpf, und es gehört zu den schönen Geschichten aus der Zeit dieser vierten Variante des Alsterpavillons, daß während der Nazizeit die Anhänger der Swingmusik hier einen ihrer Treffs hatten und zu den verbotenen Jazzklängen tanzten. Wie ein Großteil des Jungfernstiegs wurde auch der heimliche Tanzpalast im Zweiten Weltkrieg von Bomben vernichtet.

Der heutige Alsterpavillon, 1953 von dem Architekten Ferdinand Streb errichtet, ist in seiner klaren, sachlichen und großzügigen Form eines der besten Markenzeichen für die Architektur des Wiederaufbaus im Hamburg der fünfziger Jahre. Vor dem Haus rauscht der Autoverkehr. An seiner Rückseite, unweit der geschwungenen Café-Terrasse am Wasser, starten die Boote von Hamburgs Weißer Flotte zu Fleet- und Kanalfahrten.

Anders als auf anderen Großstadtboulevards, wo ein gleichmäßiger Schnellschritt den Takt angibt, mischen sich auf dem Jungfernstieg traditionell der Bummeltritt der Müßiggänger und der Eilgang der Geschäftsleute. An der Ampel Jungfernstieg/Große Bleichen kommt es manchmal zu kleinen Kollisionen von Einkaufstüten mit Aktentaschen. Die Zuschauer bei diesen ungewollten Rempeleien sitzen auf dem Boden an den Häuserwänden und hoffen auf die Mildtätigkeit der Passanten. Der Jungfernstieg ist heute auch ein spannungsreiches Pflaster zwischen Hoffnung und Hoff-

remained until 1874, no longer fulfilled the nouveau riche aspirations of the Hanseatics in the second half of the nineteenth century. After the disastrous fire of 1842, the boulevard had blossomed into a street of exclusive hotels for visitors from all over the world. Jungfernstieg had emerged like a splendid Phoenix from the ashes, and the new Alster Pavilion of 1875 reflected this new craving for show. Twenty-five years later followed the next, even more extravagant design. The coffee-house now looked almost as grand as the new theatre the city adorned itself with at the same time. Just 14 years later, Hanseatic tastefulness took over again, and one of the nice stories from the days of this fourth Alster Pavilion is that during the Nazi era it was a meeting-place for adherents of swing music, who danced here to the strains of the forbidden jazz. The secret palais de dance, like a large proportion of Jungfernstieg, was destroyed by World War II bombs.

With its clear, functional and spacious lines, the present Alster Pavilion, built in 1953 by architect Ferdinand Streb, is one of the finest trademarks of the architecture of reconstruction in 1950s Hamburg. At the front of the building, road traffic roars by. At the back, not far from the curved cafe terrace, the boats of Hamburg's "White Fleet" leave for trips along the canals.

Unlike on other big-city boulevards, where a uniform rush sets the pace, Jungfernstieg is traditionally a combination of idlers strolling along and businesspeople in a hurry. At the Jungfernstieg/Grosse Bleichen traffic lights there

nungslosigkeit. An der Schar von Bett-
lern kann niemand mehr vorbeischauen.
Hamburgs reiche Straße macht deutlich,
wie sehr sich die Gesellschaft in Arm und
Reich gespalten hat.

Auf dem Gänsemarkt, wo der Boulevard in einem Dreieck endet, sitzt, in
Bronze gegossen, der Dichter und Aufklärer Gotthold Ephraim Lessing
(1729–81), der noch die Hoffnung hatte,
mit seinen Gedanken um das Wohl der
Menschheit die Welt glücklicher machen
zu können. Zu Lessings Zirkel in der
Hansestadt gehörten nicht nur seine
Schriftstellerkollegen, sondern auch
Kaufleute und Wissenschaftler.

Seitdem sind mehr als 200 Jahre vergangen. Die hohen Gedanken des Dra-
matikers Lessing, der einige glückliche
Jahre als Dramaturg am Hamburgischen
Nationaltheater neben dem Gänsemarkt
verbrachte, sind nüchterner Skepsis und
wirtschaftlichem Kalkül gewichen. Als

are sometimes minor collisions between
shopping-bags and briefcases. The wit-
nesses to this inadvertent jostling sit on
the ground outside the buildings, hoping
for the generosity of passers-by. Nowadays, the Jungfernstieg is also a field of
tension between hope and hopelessness.
It is impossible to overlook the large
number of beggars. Hamburg's wealthy
street makes clear the degree to which
society has split into poor and rich.

On Gänsemarkt, where the boulevard
ends in a triangle, sits, cast in bronze, the
writer and dramatist of the Enlightenment, Gotthold Ephraim Lessing
(1729–81), who hoped his ideas about
the good of humanity would help to
make the world a happier place. Less-

Die Reedereiflaggen an
der Binnenalster signa-
lisieren, worauf die
Stadt stolz ist: Ham-
burgs Weltgeltung in
der internationalen
Schiffahrt.

Shipping line flags by
the Inner Alster signal
what the city is proud
of: Hamburg's world
rank in international
shipping.

Das Foto zeigt die Ent-
hüllung des Lessing-
Denkmals auf dem
Gänsemarkt im Septem-
ber 1881, einhundert
Jahre nach dem Tod des
großen Schriftstellers
und Aufklärers.

This photograph shows
the unveiling of the
Lessing monument on
Gänsemarkt in Septem-
ber 1881, the centenary
of the death of the great
writer and Enlighten-
ment figure.

ing's circle in Hamburg included not just
his fellow-writers, but also merchants
and scientists. More than 200 years have
passed since then. The elevated ideas of
Lessing the dramatist, who spend a few
happy years as literary manager of the
Hamburg national theatre next to
Gänsemarkt, have given way to sheer
scepticism and economic calculation.
The members of a club which has its elegant headquarters just a short walk
away from Lessing's monument now ful-
fil the role of enlightened thinkers in the
city.

### Neuer Jungfernstieg, five famous broth-
### ers and a shipping company director

The Übersee-Club (Overseas Club) building at Neuer Jungfernstieg 19 is a listed
monument. The classical-style urban
mansion, named the Amsinckpalais after
one of its subsequent owners, was built
in 1834 by the architect Franz Gustav
Forsmann. The splendid Übersee-Club
meeting-place is aptly in the same row of
buildings as the Vier Jahreszeiten Hotel,
an exclusive establishment with an international reputation. Both buildings are
high-society reserves.

  Those invited to speak to the closed
society of the Übersee-Club as a rule
have plenty to say. In 1948, the year of
currency reform, Ludwig Erhard, later to
be "father of the Economic Miracle," ex-
pounded his ideas about the social market economy to the club's members. Federal presidents and chancellors are regular guests at the highly regarded club on
Neuer Jungfernstieg. The prestige of the
club, which has set itself the aims of promoting democracy, international understanding and Germany's reputation
abroad, is international. Not for nothing
have past speakers included people such
as Charles de Gaulle, Bruno Kreisky,
François Mitterrand and Boutros
Boutros-Ghali during his term of office
as United Nations secretary-general.

ein Kreis von Vordenkern fungiert heute
ein Club, der nur einen kurzen Fußweg
vom Lessing-Denkmal entfernt sein
nobles Domizil hat.

### Neuer Jungfernstieg, fünf berühmte
### Brüder und ein Reedereidirektor

Das Haus des Übersee-Clubs am Neuen
Jungfernstieg 19 steht unter Denkmalschutz. Die klassizistische Stadtvilla,
nach einem der späteren Besitzer
Amsinck-Palais genannt, wurde 1834
von dem Architekten Franz Gustav Forsmann fertiggestellt. Das prächtige Ver-
einslokal des Übersee-Clubs steht sinnig
in einer Reihe mit dem Vier Jahreszeiten
Hotel, einer Nobelherberge von Weltgeltung. Beide Häuser sind Reservate der
High-Society.

  Wer vor der geschlossenen Gesellschaft des Übersee-Clubs sprechen darf,
hat in der Regel auch viel zu sagen. Im
Jahr der Währungsreform 1948 legte
Ludwig Erhard, der spätere „Vater des
Wirtschaftswunders", den Mitgliedern
des Übersee-Clubs seine Vorstellungen

The Übersee-Club, which now has 1,800 members, including – despite rumours to the contrary – several female members, was founded in 1922 in the Patriotic Society building. Its founding father was the leading Jewish banker Max M. Warburg, who was born in Hamburg in 1867.

The Warburgs are one of the internationally most influential Jewish families in the twentieth century. Their destiny is still closely linked with the Hanseatic city of Hamburg. The story of this Hamburg dynasty is a good example of the rise and fall of the Jewish bourgeoisie in Germany. Max Warburg and his four brothers, known as the "Famous Five," were a truly outstanding quintet. Max, Paul and Felix forged brilliant careers in the financial world. Paul and Felix successfully founded banks in New York, to which they had emigrated back in 1900. Aby M. Warburg (1866–1929) is now regarded as one of the most influential art historians of the twentieth century. He, the eldest son, passed his right of primogeniture with delightful chutzpah to his younger brother Max, in return for which his brothers had to promise to buy him any book he wanted. This deal turned out to be expensive for the brothers, but gave a fantastic library to science. In 1933, the Warburg library of cultural history was transferred to London because of the threat that it would be destroyed by the Nazis. Today, as the Warburg Institute, it is a separate department of London University. The building with the famous elliptical reading-room at Heilwigstrasse 116 in Hamburg, which was designed for the library by the self-taught scholar and bibliophile himself, has been owned by the city since 1993 and is now open once more for scientific events. Since recently, it has

von der sozialen Marktwirtschaft dar. Bundespräsidenten und Bundeskanzler sind regelmäßige Gäste des angesehenen Vereins am Neuen Jungfernstieg. Das Prestige des Clubs, der sich die Förderung der Demokratie, der Völkerverständigung und des deutschen Ansehens im Ausland zum Ziel gesetzt hat, gilt international. Nicht umsonst traten hier in der Vergangenheit Redner auf wie Charles de Gaulle, Bruno Kreisky, François Mitterand, der UN-Generalsekretär Boutros Boutros-Ghali.

Der Übersee-Club, der heute 1800 Mitglieder zählt, entgegen anderslautenden Meldungen darunter auch mehrere weibliche, wurde im Jahr 1922 im Haus der Patriotischen Gesellschaft gegründet. Gründungsvater war der bedeutende jüdische Bankier Max M. Warburg, der 1867 in Hamburg geboren worden war.

Die Warburgs zählen zu den international einflußreichen jüdischen Familien des 20. Jahrhunderts. Ihr Schicksal ist bis heute eng mit der Hansestadt Hamburg verknüpft. Die Geschichte dieser Dynastie von der Alster zeigt beispielhaft den

Wo kann man so schön ausruhen wie an der von Ballindamm, Lombardsbrücke, Neuem Jungfernstieg und Jungfernstieg eingerahmten Binnenalster?

What better place to take a rest than by the Inner Alster, framed by Ballindamm, the Lombardsbrücke, Neuer Jungfernstieg and Jungfernstieg?

Der Kulturwissenschaftler Aby M. Warburg (1866–1929) ist heute berühmter als sein Bruder Max, der das 1798 gegründete Bankhaus am Ballindamm groß machte.

Nowadays, humanities scholar Aby M. Warburg (1866–1929) is better known than his brother Max, who built up the banking house on Ballindamm, founded in 1798.

Der ellipsenförmige Lesesaal in der Kulturwissenschaftlichen Bibliothek Warburg in der Heilwigstraße wird heute wieder für wissenschaftliche Veranstaltungen genutzt.

The elliptical reading-room in the Warburg humanities library in Heilwigstrasse is now back in use for academic events.

Aufstieg und Fall des jüdischen Bürgertums in Deutschland. Max M. Warburg und seine vier Brüder, die „Famous Five", die „berühmten Fünf", waren ein wahrhaft herausragendes Quintett. Max, Paul und Felix machten großartige Karrieren in der Finanzwelt. Paul und Felix gründeten erfolgreich Banken in New York, wohin sie schon um 1900 ausgewandert waren. Aby M. Warburg (1866–1929) gilt heute als einer der einflußreichsten Kunstwissenschaftler des 20. Jahrhunderts. Er, der Älteste, vermachte sein Erstgeburtsrecht mit hinreißender Chuzpe dem jüngeren Bruder Max und nahm im Gegenzug den Brüdern das Versprechen ab, daß sie ihm jedes Buch seiner Wahl bezahlen müßten. Dieser Deal kam die Brüder teuer zu stehen und schenkte der Wissenschaft eine grandiose Bibliothek. Die Kulturwissenschaftliche Bibliothek Warburg wurde 1933 vor der drohenden Zerstörung durch die Nazis nach London gebracht und ist dort bis heute eine eigene Abteilung der London University. Das für sie von dem Privatgelehrten und Bücherfreund selbst entworfene Gebäude mit dem berühmten ellipsenförmigen Lese-

housed a collection on political iconography.

The successful financier Max M. Warburg, Aby's younger brother, took a passionate and active interest in politics. In 1919 he was a member of the German delegation at the peace negotiations in Versailles. The influence he had exercised in the Kaiser's Reich continued in the 1920s. The Hamburg banker's good contacts with important politicians such as Gustav Stresemann and Walther Rathenau forged a successful link between Berlin and Hamburg.

But the first indications of the downfall that began in 1933 were already there. The capable idealist was unable to attend the founding meeting of the Übersee-Club he had got up and running. Five days previously, on 22 June 1922, the German foreign minister Walther Rathenau had been murdered by right-wing extremists. For security reasons, Warburg had to stay at home, because he too had received murder threats. When his banking-house was expropriated in 1938, he emigrated to New York, where he died eight years later. The Übersee-Club had been dissolved in 1934, and was re-founded in 1948.

The story of a friendship forms the link between the Amsinckpalais on Neuer Jungfernstieg and the opposite bank of the Inner Alster. Since 1947 the street, raised from the ruins after the Great Fire of 1842, has been called Ballindamm. In the good times, the shipowner Albert Ballin (1857–1918)

saal in der Hamburger Heilwigstraße 116 gehört seit 1993 der Stadt und steht wieder für wissenschaftliche Veranstaltungen offen. Seit jüngstem beherbergt es eine Sammlung zur politischen Ikonographie.

Der erfolgreiche Finanzier Max M. Warburg, Abys jüngerer Bruder, mischte sich mit leidenschaftlichem Interesse immer wieder auch in die Politik ein. 1919 war er Mitglied der deutschen Delegation bei den Versailler Friedensverhandlungen. Der Einfluß, den er im Kaiserreich gehabt hatte, setzte sich in den zwanziger Jahren fort. Die guten Kontakte des Hamburger Bankiers zu so wichtigen Politikern wie Gustav Stresemann und Walther Rathenau bildeten eine erfolgreiche Verbindung zwischen Berlin und der Hansestadt.

Doch es gab auch erste Anzeichen für den Untergang, der 1933 begann. An der Gründungssitzung des von ihm initiierten Übersee-Clubs konnte der tüchtige Idealist nicht teilnehmen. Fünf Tage zuvor, am 22. Juni 1922, war der deutsche Außenminister Walther Rathenau von Rechtsextremisten ermordet worden. Warburg mußte aus Sicherheitsgründen zu Hause bleiben, weil auch er Morddrohungen erhalten hatte. Als sein Bankhaus 1938 enteignet wurde, emigrierte er nach New York, wo er acht Jahre später starb. Der Übersee-Club hatte sich 1934 aufgelöst und wurde 1948 wiedergegründet.

Die Geschichte einer Freundschaft schlägt den Bogen vom Amsinck-Palais am Neuen Jungfernstieg über die Binnenalster zum Gegenufer. Seit 1947 heißt die Straße, aufgeschüttet aus den Trümmern nach dem Großen Brand von 1842, Ballindamm. In guten Zeiten unternahmen der Reeder Albert Ballin (1857–1918) und der Bankier Max M. Warburg regelmäßig gemeinsame Spaziergänge um die Alster. Die Freunde, beide aus jüdischem Haus, waren treue Anhänger des Kaisers.

and the banker Max M. Warburg regularly took a walk round the Alster together. The two friends, both from Jewish families, were loyal supporters of the Kaiser. When Wilhelm II visited Hamburg he usually stayed at the house of the shipowner, who as a confidant of the Kaiser possessed great influence.

Ballin could boast a picture-book career. The son of a lower middle-class family, just four years after joining the HAPAG shipping company he became a member of the board. In 1899 he became chairman of Germany's largest shipping company. With the fall of the Reich, he saw the end of his shipping company too. Unable to come to terms with this collapse, he committed suicide.

Ballin was HAPAG's outstanding personality. HAPAG, the Hamburg-Amerikanische Packetfahrt-Actien-Gesellschaft, had been founded in 1847. The company flourished in the second half of the nineteenth century, when millions of people left Germany to seek their fortunes overseas. In 1890, the first cruises for rich idlers were offered. In summer 1997 HAPAG, which in 1970

Der Übersee-Club am Neuen Jungfernstieg ist der noble Ort für Begegnungen von Wirtschaft, Wissenschaft und Politik.

The Übersee-Club on Neuer Jungfernstieg is the elegant venue for meetings of business people, academics and politicians.

Schwimmendes Status-
symbol: Der IMPERA-
TOR wird zum ersten
Mal elbabwärts ge-
schleppt. Am Ufer
drängen sich Tausende,
um den Stolz Ham-
burgs zu bewundern.

A floating status sym-
bol: the IMPERATOR is
towed down the Elbe
for the first time. Thou-
sands throng the bank
to admire the pride of
Hamburg.

Wenn Wilhelm II. Hamburg besuchte,
war er meist auch Gast im Hause des
Reeders, der als sein Vertrauter großen
Einfluß besaß.

Ballin hatte eine Bilderbuchkarriere
vorzuweisen. Aus einer kleinbürgerlichen
Familie stammend, brachte er es schon
vier Jahre nach seinem Eintritt in die
HAPAG-Reederei zum Vorstandsmit-
glied. 1899 wurde er Generaldirektor
von Deutschlands größtem Seefahrtsunternehmen. Mit dem Niedergang des
Reiches sah er auch das Ende seiner Reederei gekommen. Er konnte diesen
Zusammenbruch nicht verkraften und
nahm sich das Leben.

Ballin war die herausragende Füh-
rungspersönlichkeit der HAPAG. Die
Hamburg-Amerikanische Packetfahrt-
Actien-Gesellschaft war 1847 gegründet
worden. Das Unternehmen florierte, als
in der zweiten Hälfte des 19. Jahrhunderts Millionen von Menschen Deutsch-

merged with the Bremen company Norddeutscher Lloyd to become Hapag-
Lloyd, celebrated its 150th anniversary
at its splendid head office on Ballindamm. Ballin would have been dumb-
founded by the balance-sheet in this
jubilee year. With its fleet of high-tech
container vessels, the company now
transports more than a million containers round the world each year. Twenty-
five aircraft carry around 4.8 million
passengers to holiday destinations – not
forgetting the cruise liners for those who
prefer a slower pace of travel.

land verließen, um in Übersee ihr Glück zu machen. 1890 wurden zum ersten Mal Kreuzfahrten für reiche Müßiggänger angeboten. Im Sommer 1997 feierte HAPAG, die 1970 mit dem Bremer Lloyd zur heutigen Hapag-Lloyd AG fusionierte, im prächtigen Verwaltungsgebäude am Ballindamm 150jähriges Bestehen. Ballin hätte über die Bilanz im Jubiläumsjahr nur staunen können. Das Unternehmen transportiert heute mit seiner Flotte von High-Tech-Containerschiffen jährlich über eine Million Container rund um den Globus. 25 Flugzeuge nehmen jedes Jahr rund 4,8 Millionen Passagiere an Bord, um sie an ihre Ferienziele zu bringen. Hinzu kommen die Kreuzfahrtschiffe für alle, die gern etwas langsamer reisen.

„Mein Feld ist die Welt." Das war Albert Ballins Wahlspruch. Heute nennt man jemanden wie ihn einen „Global Player". Und es gibt mehr als einen davon am Ballindamm. Einer verkauft und vermietet zum Beispiel in aller Welt Privatinseln. Das Abenteuer des „Big business" findet am Ballindamm hinter den streng repräsentativen Fassaden von Kontorhäusern statt, die im Wirtschaftsboom von 1900 errichtet wurden.

## Shopping und Flanieren: die Passagen

Ein geradezu südliches Flair verbreiten dagegen die dem Jungfernstieg benachbarten Alsterarkaden, die sich nach dem Überqueren der Reesendammbrücke, der Trennung zwischen Binnenalster und Kleiner Alster, zum Flanieren anbieten. Die hellen Arkaden sind der anmutigste Teil des nach dem Großen Brand neugeschaffenen Herzens von Hamburg. Ihr Architekt, der 1799 in Hamburg als Sprößling einer französischen Emigrantenfamilie geborene Alexis Chateauneuf, hatte unter anderem in Paris und Rom studiert. Die 1846 eingeweihten Arkaden lassen deutlich die südlichen Vorbilder ahnen. Genauso wie die dahinter liegende Alte Post, die ebenfalls von Chateau-

"My field is the world" was Albert Ballin's motto. Nowadays he would be called a global player. And there is more than one of this species on Ballindamm. One, for example, sells and rents out private islands all over the world. On Ballindamm, the big business adventure takes place behind the strictly image-conscious facades of office buildings built during the economic boom around 1900.

## Shopping and strolling: the arcades

In contrast, the Alster arcades close to Jungfernstieg exude a serene, almost Mediterranean air. Reached by crossing Reesendammbrücke, which separates the Inner Alster from the Little Alster, they are an inviting place to stroll. The light arcades are the most graceful part of the city centre rebuilt after the Great Fire. Their architect Alexis de Chateauneuf, born in Hamburg in 1799 to French emigré parents, had studied in Paris and Rome among other places. The arcades, which were formally opened in 1846, are clearly inspired by models from further south. As is the Alte Post (Old Post Office) behind them, which was also designed by Chateauneuf and completed in 1847. At the time, the building was used by four different postal services, the Royal Swedish Mail, the Hanover Mail,

Das Verwaltungsgebäude der HAPAG-Lloyd, Hamburgs und Europas bedeutendste Reederei sowie erfolgreiches Logistikunternehmen, gehört zu den imposantesten Kontorhäusern am Ballindamm (links). Sein Feld war die Welt. Albert Ballin (1857–1918) wurde 1899 Generaldirektor von Deutschlands damals größtem Seefahrtsunternehmen, der Hamburg-Amerikanischen Packetfahrt-Actien-Gesellschaft (HAPAG)-Reederei (oben).

The administrative headquarters of HAPAG-Lloyd, Hamburg's and Europe's leading shipping line and a successful logistics company, is one of the most imposing office buildings on Ballindamm (left). His field was the world. In 1899 Albert Ballin (1857–1918) became managing director of Germany's largest shipping business at the time, the Hamburg-Amerikanische Packetfahrt-Actien-Gesellschaft (HAPAG) shipping line (above).

Der Architekt Alexis de Chateauneuf entwarf nach dem Großen Brand 1842 in Hamburg die Alsterarkaden. Damit verband er die Häuser an der Kleinen Alster zu einem harmonischen Ensemble.

Architect Alexis de Chateauneuf designed the Alster arcades after the Great Fire of Hamburg in 1842, thus uniting the buildings on the Little Alster into a harmonious ensemble.

neuf entworfen und 1847 fertiggestellt wurde. Das Gebäude diente damals vier Postanstalten (Königlich Schwedische Post, Hannoversche Post, Thurn und Taxis'sche und Hamburgische Stadtpost). Es fällt durch seinen achteckigen Turm auf, der in Anlehnung an den Brügger Belfried entstand.

Die Alsterarkaden und die Alte Post mit ihren feinen Geschäften sind frühe Vorreiter der ausufernden Passagenlust, die heute in der Einkaufsstadt Hamburg herrscht. Die Durchgänge, die von den Alsterarkaden zum Neuen Wall führen, sind die historischen Kleinode unter den Passagen. Alle jüngeren Passagen haben jeweils ihre speziellen Liebhaber: Galleria, Kaufmannshaus mit Commercie, Gänsemarktpassage, Hamburger Hof, Hanseviertel, Kleiner Gänsemarkt, Bleichenhofpassage.

the Thurn and Taxis Mail and the Hamburg City Mail. Its most striking feature is an octagonal tower, which was inspired by the keep in Bruges.

The Alster arcades and the Alte Post with their exclusive shops were the forerunners of a host of arcades which dominate Hamburg's shopping areas. The passages leading from the Alster arcades to Neuer Wall are the historic gems among them. The more recent ones – Galleria, Kaufmannshaus and Commercie, Gänsemarktpassage, Hamburger Hof, Hanseviertel, Kleiner Gänsemarkt, Bleichenhofpassage – all have their particular adherents.

Der Abstecher vom Jungfernstieg in die Großen Bleichen führt in eine seit Jahren äußerst belebte Einkaufsstraße für Besitzer gut gefüllter Portemonnaies. Die östliche Parallele zu den Großen Bleichen, Neuer Wall, hat sich erst neuerdings zu einer erstklassigen Adresse für hochkarätiges Mode- und Möbeldesign entwickelt. Poststraße, ABC-Straße und Hohe Bleichen sind ruhigere Reviere für Stadtbummler. Mit gutem Blick lassen sich neben der auch hier angebotenen reichen Auswahl an modernem Design in zahlreichen Antiquariaten und Antiquitätenläden alte Kostbarkeiten entdecken. Was man nicht kaufen kann, was umsonst zu genießen ist, das sind hier, in Hamburgs teurem Karree hinter dem Jungfernstieg, die herrlich aufgeputzten alten und neuen Fassaden der Häuser. Daß sich dahinter oft prächtige alte Treppenhäuser verbergen, wissen viele erst durch Bildbände, die in den vergangenen Jahren diese Kunstwerke ins Licht rückten.

## Zwei Bahnhöfe

In der historischen Bausubstanz der Innenstadt Hamburgs nicht zu übersehen sind dagegen zwei besonders schöne Bahnhöfe. Der Dammtorbahnhof mit seinen geschwungenen Triumphbogenfassaden, die mit Jugendstil- und Historismusornamenten geschmückt sind, markiert den hochgemuten Übergang des Eisenbahnzeitalters in das 20. Jahrhundert. 1903 eingeweiht und um die Jahrhundertwende restauriert, gilt der am nördlichen Rand des Innenstadtgür-

Turning from Jungfernstieg into Grosse Bleichen, you find yourself in a bustling shopping street that has long been a favourite with well-padded wallets. Neuer Wall, the next parallel street to the east, has only more recently grown into a centre of exclusive fashion and furniture design. Poststrasse, ABC-Strasse and Hohe Bleichen are quieter places to stroll or window-shop. Apart from a wide selection of modern designer goods, those with an eye for them can also discover antique treasures in numerous antique shops and antiquarian bookshops. Something you cannot buy, but which can be enjoyed for free, are the superb ornamental facades of the buildings here in the exclusive grid of streets

Hamburg als attraktive Einkaufsstadt: Edle Geschäfte und Boutiquen prägen die Mellin-Passage (o.l.), das Hanseviertel (o.r.) und die Galleria (u.), deren Angebote fast keine Wünsche offenlassen.

Hamburg is an attractive city for shopping. High-class shops and boutiques characterise the Mellin arcade (top left), the Hanseviertel (top right) and the Galleria (below). The wares they offer leave scarcely any wish unfulfilled.

Seit einem guten Jahrzehnt haben die Hamburger den Reiz ihrer Fleete in der City wiederentdeckt wie hier das Bleichenfleet zwischen Neuer Wall und Große Bleichen.

A decade or so ago, Hamburg people rediscovered the charm of their downtown canals, or Fleete. This picture is of the Bleichenfleet between Neuer Wall and Grosse Bleichen.

behind Jungfernstieg. Often they conceal wonderful old entrance halls and staircases, a fact which many people have only come to realise through picture-books published in recent years revealing the existence of these works of art.

## Two railway stations

Not to be overlooked in the historic architecture of Hamburg's city centre are two particularly fine railway stations. Dammtorbahnhof with its attractively curved triumphal arch adorned with art nouveau and historicist elements, symbolises the cheerful transition of the age of the railway into the twentieth century. Opened in 1903 and restored in the

Ein neuer Platz (l.), gesäumt von modernen Backsteinfassaden, die Fleetinsel. Gelungene Architektur prägt das Bild der ABC-Straße.

A new square lined by modern brick facades, the Fleetinsel (left). Successful architecture shape ABC-Strasse's image.

tels nahe der Universität gelegene Bahnhof noch heute als Hamburgs nobelste Station. Nach dem Vorbild des Bahnhofs Berlin-Alexanderplatz liegt die Eingangshalle unter den Gleisen.

Der Hauptbahnhof mit seiner eindrucksvollen Stahlkonstruktion, der gewaltigen dreischiffigen Bahnsteighalle,

Das Levante-Haus an der Mönckebergstraße war ein großes Kontorhaus, um 1912 gebaut. Heute residiert dort ein komfortables Hotel, und eine Ladenpassage bietet großstädtisches Flair.

The Levante-Haus on Mönckebergstrasse was a large office building erected in around 1912. It now houses a luxury hotel and a shopping arcade that gives it a metropolitan air.

wurde 1906 fertiggestellt. Die Umnutzung der Wandelhalle zu einer Kette kleiner Geschäfte hat ihm nicht geschadet. Die Halle ist der logische Abschluß der betriebsamen Mönckebergstraße mit ihren großen Kaufhäusern. Die von 1908 bis 1911 angelegte Durchfahrtstraße zwischen Rathausmarkt und dem Hauptbahnhof, benannt nach dem Hamburger

2000s, the station on the northern outskirts of the inner-city belt close to the university is regarded as Hamburg's finest railway station. The concourse is under the railway tracks, on the model of Berlin's Alexanderplatz station.

The Hauptbahnhof, or main station, with its impressive steel structure and immense three-section platform hall was

Blick auf die Bahnsteighalle (l.) des Hauptbahnhofs.
Die Mönckebergstraße ist Hamburgs populäre Einkaufsmeile.

The spacious concourse (left) of the main railway station.
Mönckebergstrasse is Hamburg's popular

Bürgermeister Johann Georg Mönckeberg (1839–1908) hat in den neunziger
Jahren entscheidend an Attraktivität
gewonnen. Jüngste Errungenschaft: die
neue Laden- und Restaurantpassage im
Levante-Haus, einem Kontorgebäude aus
der Entstehungszeit der Mönckebergstraße, das die Verwaltung der Deutschen
Levante-Schiffahrtslinie beherbergte, die
die östlichen Mittelmeerländer (Levante
bedeutet Sonnenaufgang) belieferte. Wo
in den siebziger Jahren noch eine
unsichtbare gesellschaftliche Trennungslinie zwischen dem feinen Jungfernstieg
und der deutlich weniger vornehmen
Mönckebergstraße bestand, fluten heute
die Stadtbummler, Käufer, Passanten,
Müßiggänger, alles, was den berühmten
Jungfernstieg und sein Ambiente lebendig macht, ungebremst durch die feinen
Abstufungen des Kaufrauschmilieus.

## Hamburgs Bürgerpalast, das Rathaus

Das Hamburger Rathaus liegt tatsächlich
am geographischen Mittelpunkt des 755
Quadratkilometer umfassenden Stadtstaates. Das politische und verwaltungs-
technische Herz der Stadt schlägt in
einem Gebäude, welches ganz unübertrefflich das bürgerliche Selbstbewußtsein repräsentiert, das sich weitgehend
ohne die von außen kommende Bevor-
mundung durch einen Landesherrn in
der Republik an Elbe und Alster durch
die Jahrhunderte entwickeln konnte.

„Sieht ja aus wie ein Königsschloß!"
Vielen unter den 200 000 Gästen und
Touristen, die das Rathaus jährlich
besichtigen, mag dieser Vergleich in den
Sinn kommen. Doch das ist ein Fehl-
schluß, denn hinter der aufwendigen
Prachtentfaltung an der Fassade funktio-
niert das Rathaus ganz praktisch als Sitz
der Hamburger Bürgerschaft und des
Senats. Alle Fäden des Stadtstaates mit
seinen sieben Bezirken und 104 Stadtteilen laufen hier zusammen.

completed in 1906. The transformation
of the concourse into a series of small
shops has not done it any harm. In fact,
it is the logical complement to bustling
Mönckebergstrasse with its large department stores. Mönckebergstrasse, built
between 1908 and 1911 and named after
a mayor of Hamburg, Johann Georg
Mönckeberg (1839–1908), runs straight
from Rathausmarkt (the town hall
square) to the main station. In the 1990s,
it was made markedly more attractive.
The latest achievement is the new arcade
of shops and restaurants in the Levante
building, an early twentieth-century
office block that was once the headquarters of the Deutsche Levante-Schiffahrtslinie, a shipping line that served the eastern Mediterranean. Whereas in the
1970s there was a clear social divide
between up-market Jungfernstieg and far
less exclusive Mönckebergstrasse,
nowadays sightseers, shoppers, passers-
by, idlers, indeed the whole gamut of
people who lend the famous Jungfernstieg its vitality, flock uninhibitedly
through all the finely differentiated layers of the city-centre shoppers' paradise.

## Hamburg's citizens' palace,
the Rathaus

The Hamburg Rathaus, or city hall,
stands plumb in the geographical centre
of the 755-square-kilometre city-state.
The political and administrative heart of
the city beats in a building which is an
unbeatable symbol of the bourgeois self-
assurance that developed during the
course of the centuries in the republic on
Elbe and Alster, largely without having
to obey orders from an external ruler.

"Looks like a royal palace!" This com-
parison may occur to many of the
200,000 guests and tourists who visit the
Rathaus each year. But they have jumped
to the wrong conclusion, for behind its
magnificently extravagant facade the
Rathaus functions quite practically as the
seat of Hamburg's House of Burgesses
and Senate, which together form the city

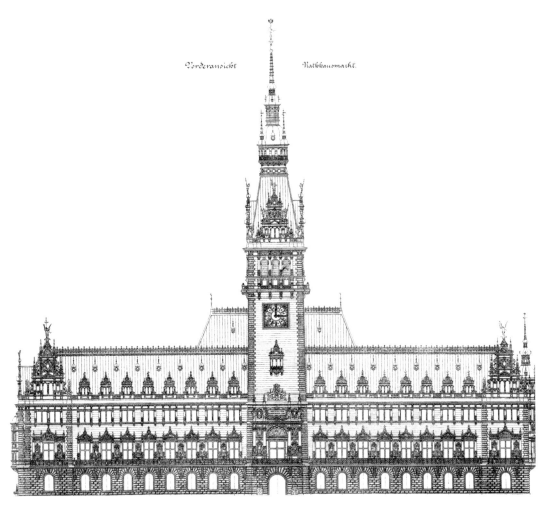

Original-Aufriß der Rathausfassade 1890 von Martin Haller und Kollegen

Original elevation of the City Hall facade in 1890, by Martin Haller and colleagues

Als zum hundertjährigen Bestehen des Bürgerpalastes im Jahr 1997 insgesamt 75 Millionen Mark für seine Sanierung bereitgestellt wurden, war dabei nicht nur an die Restaurierung der 20 überlebensgroßen Kaiser- und Königsfiguren aus Bronze gedacht worden, die die Ehre haben, die Rathausfassade zu schmükken. Viel Geld floß auch in die elektronische Ausrüstung der einzelnen Säle, damit zum Beispiel die hier veranstalteten Konferenzen von Ministerpräsiden-

parliament. All the threads of the city-state with its seven boroughs and 104 administrative districts run together here.

When the sum of 75 million marks was spent on restoring this bourgeois palace to mark its centenary in 1997, the restorers did not only think of restoring the twenty outsize bronze statues of emperors and kings which have the honour of adorning its facade. A great deal of money was spent on electronically equipping the individual rooms, so that, for example, conferences held by the prime minister, who in Hamburg is still known as the mayor, or receptions held for foreign guests benefit from up-to-date technology.

Just as the building was equipped with what was then state-of-the-art steam heating when it was first built, during its restoration a hundred years later a great deal of money was spent on air-condi-

Martin Haller (1835–1925) leitete den zur Errichtung des Rathauses (1886–97) gebildeten Baumeisterbund.

Martin Haller (1835–1925) headed the federation of master builders that was formed to build the City Hall (1886–97).

Das Rathaus von den Alsterarkaden aus gesehen, noch ohne Flaggenmasten auf dem Rathausmarkt. Foto von 1898

View of the City Hall from the Alster Arcades, with the square in front still devoid of flagstaffs. This photograph dates from 1898.

ten oder Empfänge auswärtiger Staatsgäste technisch auf dem Stand der Zeit durchgeführt werden können.

Wie das Gebäude bei seiner Errichtung mit einer für die damalige Zeit äußerst modernen Dampfheizung ausgerüstet worden war, so wurde auch im Rahmen seiner Restaurierung einhundert Jahre später wieder viel Geld auf eine neue Klimaanlage verwandt. Hamburg ist stolz darauf, mit über 90 akkreditierten konsularischen Vertretungen heute der größte Konsularplatz der Welt zu sein. Selbst New York kann nicht so viele diplomatische Vertretungen aufweisen. Da sollen die Herrschaften beim traditionellen Neujahrsempfang des diplomatischen Corps im Rathaus auf keinen Fall frieren. Wohltemperiert wollen es natürlich auch die haben, die täglich ihren Arbeitsplatz im repräsentativen Bau am Rathausmarkt ansteuern. Vom Bürgermeister bis zum Ratsdiener.

Wer sich dem Rathaus nähert, der hat mit Gewißheit schon eine Reihe der 2453 Brücken von Hamburg überquert. Die Stadt hat mehr Brücken als Venedig oder Amsterdam. Daß das neue Rathaus so zu Alsterfleet, Börse und Rathausmarkt liegend errichtet wurde, daß es noch heute seine wunderbare Wirkung entfalten kann, war nur eine Antwort auf die vielen Fragen, die sich gleich nach der Zerstörung seines Vorgängers um den Neubau rankten. Nur über zwei Voraussetzungen war man sich einig gewesen: Es sollte ungefähr an seiner heutigen Stelle stehen und ebenso groß wie repräsentativ gestaltet werden. Alles andere wurde lange und heiß debattiert, und ob Venedig mit seinem unübertrefflich schönen Markusplatz als Vorbild damals schon durch die Köpfe spukte, ist heute immer noch ein Thema für Experten.

Jedenfalls reiften die Pläne für den Rathausneubau nach 1842 unglaublich langsam. Obwohl der in Altona geborene Architekt Gottfried Semper (1803–1879) und sein Hamburger Kollege Chateauneuf schon im Brandjahr erste

tioning. Hamburg is proud of having more consulates than any other city in the world – it has more than 90 accredited consuls. Even New York cannot boast so many diplomatic offices. And you would not want the ladies and gentlemen to freeze during the traditional New Year's reception for the diplomatic corps in the Rathaus. Not forgetting, of course that those who go about their daily work in the Rathaus – from mayor to doorman – like a comfortable temperature too.

Anyone approaching the Rathaus must have crossed at least a few of Hamburg's 2,453 bridges. The city has more bridges than Venice or Amsterdam. The new Rathaus's location between Alsterfleet, the stock exchange and Rathausmarkt – a site which still enables it to be seen to full advantage – was only one reply to the many questions which were discussed after the destruction of its predecessor. Agreement was reached on just two points – it was to be built on roughly its present site and to be large and suitably prestigious. Everything else was long and fiercely debated, and experts are still undecided as to whether Venice with its unsurpassably beautiful St Mark's Square was considered as a model or not.

What we do know is that plans for the new Rathaus after 1842 developed unbelievably slowly, even though the Altona-born architect Gottfried Semper (1803–1879) and his Hamburg colleague Alexis de Chateauneuf put forward initial proposals in the year of the fire itself. But more than four decades – decades in which there was one good excuse after another for postponing the project – were to pass before the ceremonial laying of the foundation stone on 6 May

Vorschläge machten. Bis zur feierlichen Grundsteinlegung am 6. Mai 1886 vergingen jedoch noch über vier Jahrzehnte, in denen es immer wieder Gründe für eine Verschiebung des Projektes gab. So unterbrachen politische Spannungen und Wirtschaftskrisen die Planungen oder sorgten Streiks der organisierten Arbeiterschaft für Verzögerungen bei der Fertigstellung des neuen Rathauses. Eine tiefgreifende Lähmung der Stadt hatte auch die furchtbare Choleraepidemie zur Folge, der im Spätsommer 1892 in der Hansestadt mehr als 8000 Menschen zum Opfer fielen.

Das reiche Hamburg, das nach der Reichsgründung und dem Zollanschluß im ausgehenden 19. Jahrhundert einen Wirtschaftsboom sondergleichen erlebte, mußte sich vorwerfen lassen, die völlig unzureichenden hygienischen Verhältnisse in den Wohnquartieren der ärmeren Bevölkerung durch zu lange Untätigkeit heraufbeschworen zu haben. Die seit jeher in der Stadt tonangebende Kaufmannschaft wurde gezwungen, in Anlagen zur Kanalisation zu investieren. Während der ebenfalls von ihnen finanzierte Prachtbau des Rathauses langsam seiner Vollendung entgegenging, begann unter der Erde die Erneuerung der Wasserver- und -entsorgung. Ein mindestens ebenso teures Projekt.

Die Gestalt, in der das neue Rathaus entstand, wurde seit Beginn der achtziger Jahre entscheidend von einem Mann bestimmt, der im Jubiläumsjahr 1997 in der Hansestadt als Lichtgestalt der Hamburger Architektur wiederentdeckt wurde. Der Bürgermeistersohn Martin Haller (1835–1925) war nach Studienjahren in Potsdam, Berlin und vor allem in Paris 1881 in seine Heimatstadt zurückgekehrt. „Mein Spezialfach ist:

1886. While political tensions and economic crises interrupted the planning, organised labour strikes caused delays in completing the new Rathaus. The terrible cholera epidemic to which more than 8,000 people in Hamburg fell victim in the late summer of 1892 had a crippling effect on the city. Wealthy Hamburg, which after the founding of the Reich and customs union experienced an unprecedented economic boom in the closing years of the nineteenth century, was reproached for causing the totally inadequate hygienic conditions in the living-quarters of the poor, through its prolonged inactivity. The merchants, who had always set the tone in the town, were forced to invest. As the magnificent Rathaus building, which they also financed, slowly neared completion, beneath the ground another, equally expensive, project was beginning – the renewal of the city's water-supply, sewage and drainage system.

From the 1880s, the shape the new Rathaus was to take was decisively influenced by one man, a man who in the centenary year of 1997 was rediscovered as a shining light of Hamburg architecture. Martin Haller (1835–1925), the son of a mayor of Hamburg, returned to his home town in 1881 after studying in Potsdam, Berlin and most importantly Paris. "My speciality is private and luxury architecture. That befits my character and my taste." This quotation from one of Haller's letters alludes to only some of his gifts. The man who was to become Hamburg's outstanding historicist architect, also possessed a keen curiosity about technical innovations. The Haller and Geissler partnership's Renaissance- and Baroque-influenced buildings stamp the city to this day. They include banks and office buildings, the Musikhalle and private mansions. Haller was inundated with work in this field, because his grand historicist buildings perfectly matched

## Bekanntmachung.

Vor dem Genuß ungekochter Speisen, namentlich ungekochten Elb- und Leitungs-Wassers sowie ungekochter Milch wird dringend gewarnt.

Hamburg, den 1. September 1892.

### Die Cholera-Commission des Senats.

Privat- und Luxusarchitektur. Das entspricht meinem Charakter, meinem Geschmack." Das Briefzitat Hallers trifft nur einen Teil seiner Begabung. Dieser Baumeister, der an der Elbe zum herausragenden Architekten des Historismus wurde, besaß auch eine starke Neugier für technische Neuerungen. Das Büro Haller & Geißler prägt die Stadt bis heute mit seinen an der Renaissance und am Barock orientierten Bauten: Bank- und Kontorhäuser, die Musikhalle und besonders Privatvillen, ein Aufgabenbereich, der Haller zahlreiche Aufträge verschaffte, denn seine historisierenden Prachtbauten trafen genau den Geschmack der Zeit. Haller baute und baute. Und alle seine Gebäude waren technisch ganz auf der Höhe der Zeit und mit modernen Heizungen, Fahrstühlen und elektrischem Licht ausgestattet.

Zugunsten seines Großprojektes Rathaus versammelte Haller die Architekten-Intelligenz der Stadt in einem Baumeisterbund. Das Gebäude wurde das Werk von vielen. Seine überbordende Ausschmückung, bei der an nichts gespart wurde, war damals auch gedacht als Beförderung der deutschen Handwerkskunst. Anders als z. B. der absolutistische Barockfürst August der Starke,

the taste of the day. Haller built and built. All his buildings were technically state-of-the-art and equipped with modern heating systems, lifts and electric light.

For his Rathaus project, Haller enlisted the cooperation of Hamburg's leading architects. The building that ensued was the work of many. Its rich ornamentation, with no expense spared, was designed with an eye to promoting German craftsmanship. Unlike, for example, the autocratic Baroque ruler Augustus the Strong, who in the eighteenth century commissioned an international artistic

Die Cholera-Epidemie von 1892 kostete über 8000 Menschen das Leben. Enge Bebauung prägte das Bild des Gängeviertels. Foto vom Anfang des 20. Jahrhunderts.

The 1892 cholera epidemic cost more than 8,000 people their lives. Buildings crowded together were characteristic features of the passages and alleyways of the "Gängeviertel".

Der Große Festsaal des Rathauses mit den gewaltigen Wandgemälden zur Entwicklung der Weltstadt (oben). Der Rathausturm mit seinen 112 Meter Höhe hat sich Ende des 19. Jahrhunderts würdig in die Silhouette der Kirchtürme von Hamburg eingereiht.

The City Hall's great ceremonial hall with its massive wall-paintings depicting the development of a cosmopolitan city (above).
The 112-metre tower of the City Hall was a dignified addition to the skyline of Hamburg church towers in the late nineteenth century.

der im 18. Jahrhundert eine internationale Künstlerelite für die Gestaltung seiner Stadt Dresden engagierte, herrschte in Hamburg republikanisches Augenmaß. Bei aller Prachtentfaltung hieß das beim Rathausneubau, daß auch ein gewisses Mittelmaß gewahrt blieb.

Die Botschaft des Hauses, in dem die Freie und Hansestadt seit 1897 regiert und repräsentiert wird, steht in Gold über dem Eingang: „Libertaten quam peperere maiores digne studeat servare posteritas." Die Freiheit, die die Väter erwarben, möge die Nachwelt würdig erhalten. Die Hanseaten und ihre Gäste tun heute nichts lieber – abgesehen von einem Bummel über die Reeperbahn –, als bei einem Bummel durchs Rathaus schauend Besitz zu ergreifen von den Prachträumen, der Flut der Bilder und kostbaren Materialien, die hier unterm Kupferdach in Fülle versammelt sind. Rathausdiele, Kaisersaal, Saal der Republiken, Bürgermeistersaal, Phönixsaal, Großer Festsaal sowie das Senatsgehege mit der Ratsstube und der Plenarsaal der Bürgerschaft sind die Höhepunkte des Raumprogramms. Doch wer weiß, daß das Rathaus insgesamt 647 Räume hat, dem wird sogleich bewußt, daß bei aller

elite to fashion the city of Dresden, in Hamburg it was a republican eye that prevailed. In the case of the Rathaus, this meant that despite all the show, a happy medium was maintained.

The motto of the building from which the Free and Hanseatic City has been officially represented and governed since 1897 is emblazoned in gold over the entrance: "Libertatem quam peperere maiores digne studeat servare posteritas." The liberty which was earned by the fathers, may posterity worthily preserve. Hamburgers and their guests like nothing better – apart from a stroll along the Reeperbahn – than to tour the Rathaus, taking stock of its magnificent rooms, the vast number of paintings and precious materials assembled beneath its

Pracht selbstverständlich die Repräsentation hinter dem Tagesgeschäft in den Hunderten von Büros und Sitzungszimmern weit zurücksteht.

Ruhe herrscht im schönen Innenhof, wo am 1895/96 geschaffenen Hygieia-Brunnen nur das Wasser rauscht. Die für Gesundheit zuständige Göttin Hygieia erhebt sich als schöne weibliche Figur über die allegorischen Darstellungen des Wassers. Der Drache, den die Göttin im Brunnenbild besiegt, symbolisiert die überwundene Choleraepidemie.

Eine Seite des Innenhofes gehört der Börse. Diese räumliche Verknüpfung von Rathaus und Börse ist in einer Kaufmannsrepublik wie Hamburg logische Konsequenz des inneren Zusammenhangs. Die 1558 gegründete hanseatische Börse ist die älteste unter den heute noch bestehenden acht deutschen Wertpapierbörsen. 1841 bezog sie das von Franz Gustav Forsmann und Carl Ludwig Wimmel errichtete klassizistische Gebäude. Die Halle im Erdgeschoß ist als einer der schönsten Säle Norddeutschlands gar nicht genug zu rühmen.

copper roof. The entrance hall, Emperor's Hall, Hall of the Republics, Mayor's Hall, Phoenix Hall, Great Banqueting Hall and the Senate enclosure with the Ratsstube restaurant and the plenary chamber of the House of Burgesses are the highlights of the tour. But anyone told that the Rathaus has 647 rooms in all immediately becomes aware that, despite all the magnificence, outward show takes a back seat to the daily work that goes on in the hundreds of offices and meeting-rooms.

In the attractive inner courtyard, peace and quiet prevails, with only the splashing of water in the Hygieia fountain, built in 1895/96, to break the silence. A shapely statue of Hygieia, the Greek goddess of health, rises above allegorical portrayals of the benefits of water, such as fishing and shipping. The goddess is depicted overcoming a dragon, a symbol of the cholera epidemic.

One facade of the courtyard belongs to the Börse, or stock exchange. In a mercantile republic like Hamburg, this spatial link between town hall and stock exchange is the logical consequence of their inner connection. The Hanseatic

Der Hygieia-Brunnen im Innenhof des Rathauses ist der Göttin der Gesundheit gewidmet.
Die Halle der Börse im Stil der italienischen Renaissance gehört zu den schönsten Innenräumen der Stadt.

The Hygieia Fountain in the City Hall courtyard is dedicated to the goddess of health.
The Stock Exchange's Italian Renaissance-style hall is one of the city's most beautiful interiors.

Auch die Handelskammer, die unter dem Dach des klassizistischen Börsengebäudes ihr Domizil hat, kann mit Superlativen aufwarten. Sie war die erste Handelskammer der Bundesrepublik Deutschland. Die Kammer, deren Vorläufereinrichtung die 1665 gegründete Commerzdeputation war, betreut heute rund 90 000 Mitgliedsfirmen. Kein Wunder, daß auch die Bankhäuser im Schatten von Rathaus und Börse in die Breite gegangen sind. In den Himmel geschossen, wie in Frankfurt am Main, sind sie nicht und haben somit Hamburgs nach wie vor von alten Türmen geprägte Silhouette bewahrt. Aber auch zum Thema Geldinstitut kann die Hansestadt mit einem Superlativ aufwarten: Die Hamburger Sparkasse, genannt Haspa und mit ihrer Hauptverwaltung gegenüber der Börse am Adolphsplatz gelegen, ist die größte Sparkasse der Bundesrepublik.

Bei soviel Geld und Glanz am Rathausmarkt und Adolphsplatz verkriecht sich die Kultur leise in die Ecken. Am Rande des Rathausmarktes steht der Dichter Heinrich Heine auf einem kleinen Sockel (Waldemar Otto, 1982) und sinniert mit schräg geneigtem Kopf. Ebenso eindrucksvoll ist in ihrer Bescheidenheit die Stelle an der Treppenanlage zur Kleinen Alster, die der Architekt Claus Hoffmann Anfang der dreißiger Jahre als Mahnmal gegen den Krieg schuf. Das Relief „Trauernde mit Kind" stammte ursprünglich von Ernst Barlach. In der NS-Zeit wurde es zerstört und ist seit 1949 wieder in einer Rekonstruktion zu sehen. Obwohl auf dem Platz vor dem Rathaus niemals Handel getrieben wurde, erscheint der Name Rathausmarkt dennoch stimmig. Buntes Treiben ist auf dem weiten Platz beinahe die Regel, denn hier wird viel gefeiert. Kuli-

Stock Exchange, founded in 1558, is the oldest of Germany's eight surviving securities exchanges. It moved into the neoclassical building designed by Franz Gustav Forsmann and Carl Ludwig Wimmel in 1841. The ground-floor hall, one of the finest in northern Germany, cannot be praised too highly.

The Chamber of Trade, which has its headquarters beneath the roof of the Stock Exchange, can boast some impressive statistics, too. It was the first chamber of trade in the Federal Republic of Germany, its predecessor, the Commerzdeputation, having been founded in 1665. Nowadays, it looks after around 90,000 member-companies. No wonder that banks have spread out in the shadow of the Rathaus and Stock Exchange. Unlike in Frankfurt, they have not shot skywards, thus preserving Hamburg's traditional townscape, which is marked by ancient church towers. However, the Hanseatic city does have one record to boast as far as money institutes are concerned: the Hamburger Sparkasse, or savings bank, commonly known as Haspa, which has its headquarters opposite the Stock Exchange on Adolphsplatz, is the biggest in Germany.

With so much money and pomp on Rathausmarkt and Adolphsplatz, the arts disappear quietly into corners. At the edge of Rathausmarkt, the poet Heinrich Heine stands, his head inclined deep in thought, on a small pedestal (Waldemar Otto, 1982). Equally impressive in its modesty is the stone slab designed by the architect Claus Hoffmann in the early 1930s as an anti-war memorial. The original relief, "Mourning Woman with Child," was by Ernst Barlach. It was destroyed in the Nazi era, and the present one is a 1949 reconstruction.

Although the Rathausmarkt was never a market square, it still seems appropriate to call it a market. It is regularly the venue for lively events and festivals, especially of the culinary kind, and a stage is often erected there for ballet,

Das historische Foto zeigt die Einweihung des Ehrenmals an der Kleinen Alster im Jahr 1931. Das Barlach-Relief auf der Rückseite wurde 1939 von den Nationalsozialisten entfernt und 1948 rekonstruiert.

This historic photograph shows the opening of the monument on the Little Alster in 1931. On the back was a relief by Ernst Barlach which was removed by the National Socialists in 1939 and reconstructed in 1948.

narische Feste haben Vorrang. Aber vor der Rathausfassade wurde oft auch die Bühne aufgebaut für Ballett-, Musik- und Theaterveranstaltungen. Unter dem Motto „Kino im Fluß" wurde in den achtziger Jahren eine schwimmende Riesenleinwand in die Binnenalster gesetzt. 1986 wanderte das Kino auf den Rathausmarkt, und die Filmfans träumen schon im Winter von einer lauen Sommernacht auf dem weiten Platz, wo bei dem Kultfilm „Wem die Stunde schlägt" die Rathausuhr für Ingrid Bergmann die Minuten zählt.

musical and theatrical performances. The 1980s saw the start of "Cinema in the River," and the erection of a gigantic floating screen in the Inner Alster. In 1986 the open-air screenings were transferred to Rathausmarkt. In winter, film fans can dream of a balmy summer night on the spacious square, with the Rathaus clock counting down the minutes for Ingrid Bergman at a showing of the cult movie "For Whom the Bell Tolls."

# Der Hafen: Hamburgs Tor zur Welt

## The Port: Hamburg's gateway to the world

Die St. Pauli-Landungs-
brücken sind Hamburgs
grandiosester Laufsteg.

The St. Pauli-Landungs-
brücken, or landing
stages, are Hamburg's
most magnificent
catwalk.

Der Hafen, das ist ein wichtiges wirt-
schaftliches Standbein der Stadt, die
Drehscheibe für Waren aus aller Herren
Länder, der größte Arbeitgeber der
Metropole (mit 140 000 direkt oder
indirekt vom Hafen abhängigen
Erwerbstätigen), Hamburgs Tor zur
Welt. Der Hafen ist aber nicht nur ein
Ort des großen Geldes, sondern auch ein
grandioser Schauplatz für starke Gefühle
und Sinneseindrücke – für Fernweh und
Heimweh.

Die Herzen der Schaulustigen auf den
Pontons der Landungsbrücken schlagen
höher, wenn die Barkassen das graue
Elbwasser durchpflügen, der Boden
unter ihren Füßen sich hebt und senkt,
wenn eine Katamaranfähre von Stade
kommend ihr Anlegemanöver exerziert
und das Wasser weiß aufschäumen läßt,
altmodische Schuten vorbeigeschoben
werden, ein Binnenschiff mit im Winde
flatternder Wäsche an Deck vorbeizieht,
ein Segelboot mutig durchs Kabbelwas-
ser steuert, am Horizont ein hochbelade-
nes Containerschiff auftaucht oder ein
Kran auf schwimmendem Untersatz des
Weges kommt.

Viele Generationen von Hafenkränen
längs der Kaimauer des insgesamt 63
Quadratkilometer großen Hafengeländes
(ein Zehntel der Gesamtfläche Hamburgs) erzählen Industriegeschichte.
Mehr als 100 Kräne markieren die fili-

The port is an economic mainstay of the
city, a turntable for goods from all over
the world, Hamburg's biggest employer
(with 140,000 jobs directly or indirectly
dependent on it) and its gateway to the
world. However, the port is not just a
place for large-scale money-making, but
a grand showplace for strong emotions
and sensory impressions. The port is a
place where wanderlust and homesick-
ness meet.

The hearts of the spectators on the
Landungsbrücken pontoons beat faster
as the launches plough through the grey
waters of the Elbe, as the ground
beneath their feet rises and falls when a
catamaran ferry from Stade ties up in a
flurry of white foam, as old-fashioned
lighters are pushed past, an inland vessel
chugs by with washing hung out to dry
on its deck, a yacht valiantly steers
through the choppy water, a vessel piled
high with containers looms into view on
the horizon or a floating crane swims
along.

Generations of cranes lined up on the
quayside of the 63 square kilometres of
dock (one tenth of the total area of
Hamburg) tell industrial history. More
than a hundred cranes shape the intri-
cate, photogenic port skyline. Many
have long since been overtaken by technological progress. The future is on the
container wharves, where a gigantic vessel carrying up to 3,000 multi-coloured
crates is unloaded in the space of a few
hours, giving its crew just six hours of
shore leave. Then tugs pull the vessel
away from the quayside so that it
embarks punctually on its scheduled
voyage to Asia, Africa, Australia or
America.

grane, fotogene Silhouette des Hafens.
Über viele ist die technische Entwicklung
längst hinweggegangen. Die Zukunft
liegt an den Containerbrücken, wo die
Ladung der Schiffsriesen mit bis zu 3000
bunten Kisten im Bauch innerhalb von
wenigen Stunden gelöscht wird und die
Mannschaft mal eben sechs Stunden Zeit
für einen Landgang hat. Dann ziehen die
Schlepper das Containerschiff wieder
vom Kai ab, damit es pünktlich nach
vorgegebenem Stundenplan die Reise
nach Asien, Afrika, Australien oder
Amerika antritt.

### Die bunten Kisten am Kai

Der Siegeszug des Containers begann
Anfang der siebziger Jahre. Über 80 Prozent des Stückguts im Hamburger Hafen
werden heute verladefreundlich in den
genormten Kisten befördert. Nur Mas-
sengut wie Kohle, Getreide, Erz entzieht
sich diesem inzwischen weltweit einge-
führten Transportsystem, das die Verla-
dung vom Schiff auf die Schiene oder
Straße und umgekehrt erheblich verein-
facht hat. Der Standardcontainer mißt
zwanzig Fuß (TEU = Twenty Foot Equivalent Unit). Die größten Containerschif-
fe, die länger sind als zwei aneinanderge-
reihte Fußballfelder, können bis zu 4000
dieser genormten Behälter in ihrem
Bauch fassen. Mit den bis zu zehn Etagen in die Tiefe und fünf Etagen in die
Höhe gestapelten bunten Kisten sehen
die Schiffe aus wie schwimmende Bau-
klotzkästen für Riesen. Transportiert
wird alles, was in den Normbehälter hin-
einpaßt, von Antibabypillen für Thailand, Filzpantoffeln für Finnland, Näh-
maschinen für Nigeria bis zu Glühbirnen
für Grönland, Stapelmöbeln für Südafri-
ka, Kuckucksuhren für die USA und für
Kanada.
　Hamburg steht heute im weltweiten
Wettbewerb der Containerhäfen an
neunter Stelle. Nach Hongkong, Singa-

### Multi-coloured boxes on the quayside

The triumphal progress of the container
began in the early 1970s. Now, more
than 80 per cent of the mixed cargoes in
the port of Hamburg are transported in
these convenient, standardised crates.
Only bulk commodities such as coal,
grains and ores escape this worldwide
transportation system, which has consid-
erably simplified the transfer of goods
from ship to rail or road and vice versa.
A standard container is twenty feet long
(TEU, or twenty-foot equivalent unit).
The largest container vessels, each longer
than two soccer pitches laid end to end,
can carry up to 4,000 of these standardised containers in their hold. With their
many-coloured boxes stacked up to ten
layers below deck and five above, the
vessels look like floating sets of building-
blocks for giants. Their cargo is anything
that will fit into a standard container,
from contraceptive pills for Thailand,

Der Container-Terminal
Toller Ort wirkt wie ein
Spielplatz für Riesen.

Toller Ort container
terminal looks like a
giants' playground.

Das Anlegen der Con-
tainerschiffe am Atha-
baskakai ist jedesmal
ein beeindruckendes
Schauspiel. Logenplätze
bietet der Strand in
Övelgönne.

Ships berthing at the
Athabaska quay are
always an impressive
sight. On the beach in
Övelgönne you have a
privileged view of the
proceedings.

Das Panorama der
St. Pauli-Landungs-
brücken, vom Wasser
aus gesehen, wird über-
ragt vom Turm der
Michaeliskirche (l.),
Hamburgs bekann-
testem Wahrzeichen.

This panoramic view of
the St. Pauli landing
stages seen from the
water is dominated by
the tower of St Micha-
el's Church (left),
Hamburg's best-known
landmark.

Die Docks der Werft
Blohm + Voss gegen-
über den Landungs-
brücken dienen heute
fast nur noch dem
Umbau und der
Reparatur von Schiffen.

Nowadays, the Blohm
+ Voss shipyard docks
opposite the landing
stages are used almost
exclusively for ship
repair and conversion
work.

pur, Kaohsiung (Taiwan), Rotterdam,
Pusan (Südkorea), Long Beach vor Los
Angeles, Antwerpen und Yokohama. Die
Hansestadt ist die wichtigste Drehscheibe im Im- und Export mit den skandina-
vischen Ländern und ihren 22 Millionen
Einwohnern. Seit der Öffnung des Eiser-
nen Vorhangs 1989 ist dem Handel auch
wieder das traditionelle Hinterland Ost-
europa zugewachsen. Ein kräftiger Schub
für den Hafen.

Was für die Vergangenheit und die
Gegenwart gilt, trifft auch auf die
Zukunft zu: Hamburgs ökonomisches
Schicksal hängt weitgehend von der flo-
rierenden Hafenwirtschaft ab. Die Handicaps sind größer als bei der Konkurrenz. Als Tidenhafen ist Hamburg

felt slippers for Finland and sewing-
machines for Nigeria to electric light
bulbs for Greenland, self-assembly furniture for South Africa and cuckoo clocks
for the USA and Canada.

In the worldwide competition between
container ports, Hamburg holds ninth
place after Hong Kong, Singapore,
Kaohsiung (Taiwan), Rotterdam, Pusan
(South Korea), Long Beach (California),
Antwerp and Yokohama. The Hanseatic
city is the leading turntable for import
and export trade with the Scandinavian
countries and their 22 million inhabitants. Since the opening of the Iron Cur-
tain in 1989 it has also gained trade with
its traditional hinterland in eastern
Europe. This gave the port a strong
boost.

As it was in the past and is in the present, so it will be in future. Hamburg's
economic fate depends to a large extent
on flourishing port activity. But it faces

abhängig von Ebbe und Flut. Mit der auflaufenden Flut die Elbe „raufzureiten" ist für die Schiffe ein leichtes. Um so schwieriger dann die Fahrt zurück zum Meer, wenn bei Ebbe rechts und links des Fahrwassers Sandbänke drohen. Das rund 100 Kilometer lange Flußstück zwischen Hafen und Elbmündung ist das Problemkind von Strom- und Hafenbau. Die gegen viel Widerstand beschlossene Vertiefung der Fahrrinne auf 16 Meter ist eine wirtschaftliche Notwendigkeit, die gegen ökologische Proteste durchge-

greater handicaps than its rivals. As a tidal port, Hamburg depends on high and low water. It is easy for ships to ride up the Elbe on a rising tide. All the more difficult is the journey back to the sea at low tide, with sandbanks threatening to right and left of the shipping lane. The hundred-kilometre-plus stretch of river between the port and the mouth of the Elbe is the problem child of river and port engineers. The decision, in the face of considerable opposition, to deepen the shipping lane to 16 metres is an economic necessity, carried against environmental protests, if even the largest container vessels are to be able to continue putting in to Hamburg.

Containerisation has rapidly altered the port's appearance in recent decades.

Ablaufendes Wasser am Strand von Blankenese. Die Schiffe müssen sich strikt an die Fahrrinne halten, damit sie nicht auf einer Sandbank stranden.

Ebb tide at Blankenese beach. Ships have to keep strictly to the shipping lane to avoid running aground on a sandbank.

setzt wurde, damit auch die großen Con-
tainerschiffe weiterhin den Hafen anlau-
fen können.

Die Containerisierung hat das Bild des
Hafens in den vergangenen Jahrzehnten
rasant verändert. Wie eine vielarmige
Riesenkrake sieht der Hafen von oben
aus. Wo sich der Fluß, von Osten kommend, in Norder- und Süderelbe teilt,
beginnen die Hafenbecken, die jedes für
sich ein Teil der Geschichte dieses nassen
Teils der Stadt sind. Holzhafen, Entenwerder Zollhafen, wo an der Billwerder
Bucht Liegeplätze für mehr als hundert
Binnenschiffe eingerichtet wurden, Reiherstieg, Kaiser-Wilhelm-Hafen, Oder-
und Travehafen, Kuhwerderhafen, Spree-
hafen, Kohlenschiffhafen. Ein Blick auf
den aktuellen Hafenplan macht schnell
deutlich, wieviel Raum die Container
heute für sich beanspruchen. Bei einem
avisierten Umschlag von vier Millionen
Stück im Jahr muß sowohl Platz für vor-
übergehende Lagerung als auch für das
Be- und Entladen der Schiffe rund um
die Uhr geschaffen werden.

Wie bunte Gebirge stapeln sich die
Behälter rechts und links der Autobahn
vor der südlichen Einfahrt in den neuen
Elbtunnel. Die 1975 eingeweihte sechs-
spurige Untertunnelung des Flusses ist
längst zu eng geworden für die vielen
Lkw, die die Container huckepack
weitertragen ins Binnenland. Im dritten
Jahrtausend werden dem Verkehr je vier
Fahrspuren zur Verfügung stehen.

Ein Hafenbahnnetz von 389 Kilometer
Länge sorgt ebenfalls für schnelle Zu-
und Abfahrt zu den Schiffen. Achtung
für Sightseeing-Lustige, die einem
Geheimtip folgen und das riesige Hafen-
gelände auf eigene Faust mit dem Fahrrad erkunden! Das Schienennetz, genau
wie das alte Kopfsteinpflaster der Straßen, die zu den Kaianlagen und Schup-
pen führen, ist schon manchem Radfahrer zur Falle geworden.

Seen from above, it looks like a many-
tentacled giant octopus. The docks, each
telling its own part of the story of this
city by the water, begin where the river,
flowing from the east, divides into two
arms – the Norder- and Süderelbe. The
timber dock, the Entenwerder customs
dock on Billwerder bay, where there are
berths for more than a hundred inland
vessels, Reiherstieg, the Kaiser Wilhelm
dock, the Oder and Trave docks, Kuh-
werder dock, Spree dock, the coal docks.
A glance at a map of the port soon
makes it clear how much space is now
occupied by containers. With a target
turnaround of four million each year,
there has to be room both for temporary
storage and for round-the-clock loading
and discharging of ships.

The containers tower like a colourful
mountain range to the right and left of
the autobahn just outside the southern
entrance to the new Elbe tunnel. The six
lanes of tunnel beneath the Elbe, opened
only in 1975, have long since ceased
being able to cope with the large number
of trucks that transport the containers to
other parts of Germany. Two further
lanes are due for completion in the new
millennium.

The speedy movement of goods to and
from the ships is further aided by a 389-
kilometre port railway network. A word
of warning to keen sightseers who follow
an insider tip to explore the enormous
docklands independently by bicycle. The
railways, combined with the old cobbled
surface of the roads leading to the quays
and sheds, have proved the downfall of
many bikes.

## Modernes Wahrzeichen: die Köhlbrandbrücke

Der spektakulärste Verkehrsweg des Hamburger Hafens ist die Köhlbrandbrücke – zugänglich nur für Autofahrer, nicht für Fußgänger und Radfahrer. Unter den 2453 Brücken von Hamburg ist sie die imposanteste und, wie viele meinen, auch die eleganteste. Mit einer Spannweite des Mittelteils von 520 Metern, aufgehängt an zwei 135 Meter hohen Pylonen, schlägt sie einen weithin sichtbaren Bogen über den Köhlbrand, wo Norder- und Süderelbe im Westen des Hafens wieder zusammenkommen.

Die Köhlbrandbrücke, eine Meisterleistung zeitgenössischer Ingenieurkunst, gilt heute als modernes Wahrzeichen des Hafens, dessen Logistik von Computern gesteuert wird, wo die Muskelkraft weitgehend von Maschinen übernommen ist. Ein Beispiel für diese Maschinenkraft

## A modern landmark: Köhlbrandbrücke

The most spectacular route in the docks is the Köhlbrandbrücke road bridge, accessible only to vehicles, not to pedestrians and cyclists. It is the most impressive, and many say the most elegant, of Hamburg's 2,453 bridges. The 520-metre-long central span is suspended on two 135-metre pylons, making it visible far and wide as it curves across the Köhlbrand, where the Norder- and Süderelbe meet up again to the west of the port.

Nowadays the Köhlbrandbrücke, a masterpiece of modern engineering, is regarded as the modern emblem of a port with computerised logistics, where muscle-power has largely given way to

Die Köhlbrandbrücke zweigt kurz vor dem neuen Elbtunnel im Süden von der A7 ab. Das 1974 für den Verkehr freigegebene Bauwerk löste zwei Trajektfähren ab, die vorher für die Überquerung der Süderelbe in den Hafen sorgten.

The Köhlbrand Bridge branches off from autobahn A7 close to the entrance of the new Elbe Tunnel. The bridge, opened to traffic in 1974, replaced two ferries that used to carry vehicles across the Süderelbe to the port.

Das einsamste Gottes-
haus Hamburgs. Die
Kirche von Altenwerder
mitten im Hafenerwei-
terungsgebiet. Wo einst
ein uraltes Fischerdorf
lag, entsteht der größte
Containerterminal in
Hamburg mit weitem
Umschlaggelände und
Verschiebebahnhof.

Hamburg's loneliest
church is at Altenwer-
der, in the midst of the
port expansion area.
The city's largest con-
tainer terminal, com-
plete with an extensive
transhipment area and
marshalling yard, is
under construction in
Altenwerder on the site
of an old fishing village.

sind die hochbeinigen VAN-Carrier, die
mit Leichtigkeit schwerste Container
zwischen ihre vier Beine nehmen und mit
Hilfe ihrer 300-PS-starken Motoren
dorthin transportieren, wo sie, laut Lage-
plan des Computers, hin sollen. Gesteuert wird der Carrier von einem von der
Straße aus winzig wirkenden Fahrer, der
in einer Glaskuppel auf dem Dach des
Transportgerätes sitzt. VAN-Carrier-Fah-
rer ist eins der neuen Berufsbilder, die die
rasante Modernisierung des Hafens mit
sich gebracht hat.

Der Hafen braucht Platz, um sich für
die Zukunft ausdehnen zu können.
Lange hatten sich die Bewohner des idyllischen Dorfes Altenwerder dagegen
gewehrt, Opfer einer Hafenerweiterung
zu werden. Doch heute zeugt nur noch
die kleine Backsteinkirche davon, daß
hier einmal Menschen gelebt haben.

Zu keiner Zeit hat der Hafen sein
Erscheinungsbild so schnell und gravie-
rend verändert wie in der zweiten Hälfte
des 20. Jahrhunderts. Wenn heute alljährlich über eine Million Menschen im
Mai zum Hafengeburtstag herbeiströmt,
wenn zwischen Fischmarkt und Kehrwiederspitze in vier Tagen 600 000
Würstchen, 100 000 Steaks und 50 000
Fischbrötchen verzehrt und mit 400 000
Litern Bier hinuntergespült werden,

machines. One example of this machine
power are the long-legged van carriers,
which lift the heaviest of containers
between their four legs with the greatest
of ease and, with the help of their 300-
horsepower engines, transport them to
where the computerised storage system
says they have to go. Each carrier is con-
trolled by what from road level looks
like a miniature driver sitting in a glass
dome on top of the machine. Van carrier
driver is one of the new professions the
rapid modernisation of the port has
brought in its wake.

The port needs space for future
growth. For many years the inhabitants
of the idyllic village of Altenwerder resis-
ted becoming victims of port expansion.
Nowadays, however, a small redbrick
church is the only sign that people once
lived there.

At no period in its history did the
port's appearance change so quickly and
drastically as in the second half of the
twentieth century. Nowadays, with more
than a million people swarming to the
annual Hafengeburtstag (port birthday)
celebrations in May, with 600,000
sausages, 100,000 steaks and 50,000
fish rolls being washed down with
400,000 litres of beer between Fischmarkt and Kehrwiederspitze in the space
of just four days, with tugs dancing a
ballet on the water in front of the jetties
and red fireboats gushing thick spouts of
water into the air to the delight of
onlookers, with blue police launches flit-
ting back and forth and green customs
boats almost disappearing in the hurly-
burly on the water, hardly anyone stops
to think about how it all began.

wenn die Schlepper vor den Landungsbrücken auf dem Wasser Ballett tanzen
und die roten Feuerwehrboote zum Vergnügen der Zuschauer dicke Fontänen in
die Luft spucken, wenn die blauen Poli-
zeiboote hin und her flitzen und die grünen Zollboote im Trubel auf dem Wasser
fast verschwinden, dann macht sich
kaum noch jemand ein Bild davon, wie
alles einmal anfing.

### Zollfreie Fahrt auf der Elbe

Der Hafengeburtstag geht zurück auf
einen Freibrief, den Kaiser Friedrich Barbarossa der Hamburger Neustadt am
7. Mai 1189 ausgestellt haben soll. Die
Urkunde, die das Ereignis verbürgt,
wurde allerdings später gefälscht. Der
Wortlaut jedenfalls sicherte Hamburg die
freie Schiffahrt auf der Elbe zu. Der
Handel prosperierte. Die Stadt wuchs
mit ihrem Hafen.

### Duty-free passage on the Elbe

The Hafengeburtstag dates back to a
royal charter said to have been issued to
Hamburg's Neustadt by Emperor Frederick Barbarossa on 7 May 1189. The document which vouches for this event was
actually forged at a later date. In any
case, the Emperor is said to have guaran-
teed Hamburg freedom to sail on the
Elbe. Trade flourished. The town grew
along with its port.

A no less crucial event was the establishment of the free port, which since
1888 has occupied sixteen of the port's
63-square-kilometre site. The year 1888
saw the coming into force of the customs
union which, under pressure from Reich

Die Schlepper bugsieren
mit ihren Hunderten
von Pferdestärken jeden
Schiffsriesen sicher in
den Hafen. Beim Ha-
fengeburtstag sind sie
einmal die Stars und
tanzen auf den Wellen
Ballett.

Tugs with hundreds of
horsepower manoeuvre
any gigantic vessel safe-
ly into port. At the port
anniversary festival it is
their turn to star, danc-
ing a ballet on the
waves.

Der Freihafen und die Speicherstadt kurz nach Fertigstellung der ersten Erweiterung aus der Vogelperspektive. Lithographie um 1890

A bird's-eye view of the free port and the Warehouse City shortly after completion of the first expansion project. This lithograph dates from around 1890.

Ein ebenso einschneidendes Ereignis war die Einrichtung des Freihafens, der seit 1888 sechzehn Quadratkilometer des insgesamt 63 Quadratkilometer großen Hafengeländes einnimmt. Im Jahr 1888 trat der Zollanschluß in Kraft, der Hamburg auf Druck von Reichskanzler Otto von Bismarck in das Zollinland des Deutschen Reiches eingliederte. Nur im Freihafen durften und dürfen bis heute die Waren unverzollt ein- und ausreisen. Der ungeheure Wirtschaftsboom bis zum Ersten Weltkrieg machte Hamburg trotz des Handicaps, das diese Einschränkung der Zollfreiheit bedeutete, dennoch in der Wilhelminischen Epoche zu einer Wirtschaftsmacht, der man den schmückenden Beinamen „Des Deutschen Reiches Tor zur Welt" gab.

Das Wilhelminische Zeitalter war auch für die großen Hamburger Reedereien eine Zeit des Aufschwungs. Die Namen der Männer, die diese Schifffahrtsunternehmen prägten, sind bis heute in der Hansestadt nicht vergessen. Albert Ballin (1857–1918) wurde 1899 Generaldirektor der HAPAG. Als Vertrauter von Kaiser Wilhelm II. genoß er großen Einfluß, konnte aber dessen englandfeindliche Politik nicht verhindern, die mit ein Auslöser des Ersten Welt-

Chancellor Otto von Bismarck, incorporated Hamburg into the customs area of the German Reich. Only in the free port were goods allowed to move in and out duty-free, a situation which continues to this day. Despite the handicap which this restriction on duty-free shipping signified, the tremendous economic boom which Hamburg experienced in the Wilhelminian period, especially in the years leading up to World War I, made it an economic power to be reckoned with, and earned it the flattering nickname "The German Reich's Gateway to the World."

The Wilhelminian era was a boom time for the large Hamburg shipping lines, too. The names of the men who shaped these shipping enterprises remain unforgotten in the city to this day. In 1899 Albert Ballin (1857–1918) became managing director of HAPAG. As a confidant of Kaiser Wilhelm II he enjoyed great influence, but was unable to prevent the Kaiser's anti-British policy, which was one of the causes of World War I, in which the whole HAPAG fleet was destroyed. The Hamburg-Amerikanische Packetfahrt Actien Gesellschaft and its ships with their yellow funnels with the black, white and red bands spelled destiny for many people. The shipping line transported thousands of emigrants on their journey to the New World, for which it relied on steamships. The first HAPAG steamship was launched in England in 1855. Its last sailing ship was taken out of service in 1868.

kriegs war, in dem die gesamte HAPAG-Flotte vernichtet wurde. Die Hamburg-Amerikanische Packetfahrt-Actien-Gesellschaft und ihre Schiffe mit den gelben Schornsteinen und den schwarz-weiß-roten Ringen wurden für viele Menschen zur Schicksalsstation. Die Reederei transportierte Tausende von Auswanderern auf ihrer Route in die Neue Welt. Dabei verließ man sich auf die Dampfschiffe. 1855 war das erste Dampfschiff für die HAPAG in England auf Kiel gelegt worden. 1868 wurde das letzte Segelboot ausgemustert.

### Fünfmaster zwischen Hamburg und Chile

Eine andere Hamburger Reederei, das 1824 von Ferdinand Laeisz gegründete Unternehmen, setzte dagegen ganz auf Tradition. Man ließ Segelschiffe bauen, die noch um 1900 den Dampfern davonfuhren. Die Fünfmaster von Laeisz' Flying-P-Line (alle Schiffsnamen begannen mit dem Buchstaben P) schrieben das letzte große Kapitel in der Geschichte der Segelschiffahrt. Pamir, Passat, Potosi, Preußen. Das sind nur einige der legendären Namen. Könige der Meere, mit denen die Reederei zu ihrer Zeit gute Kasse machte. Sie segelten schnell und zuverlässig, und wenn beispielsweise die 111 Meter lange Potosi mit 6500 Tonnen Salpeter an Bord aus Chile wieder in den Heimathafen einlief, war das nicht nur ein schön anzusehendes, sondern für den Reeder auch ein ökonomisches Ereignis.

Ein gebürtiger Bielefelder, Carl Woermann, der 1837 in Hamburg ein Handelshaus gegründet hatte, startete 1849 mit einem Segelschiff den Afrikahandel, der seine Reederei, später von seinem Sohn Adolph betrieben, groß machte.

Heute kann jeder an Bord eines dieser Schiffe gehen, die damals die sieben Weltmeere befuhren. Als Museumsschiff liegt an den Landungsbrücken die Rickmer Rickmers. Der Verein „Windjammer für Hamburg" hat den Segler vor der

Das Schmuckblatt zeigt Vater, Sohn und Enkel der Reederdynastie Laeisz.

This ornamental sheet shows father, son and grandson of the Laeisz shipping dynasty.

### Five-masters between Hamburg and Chile

In contrast, another Hamburg shipping line, founded in 1824 by Ferdinand Laeisz, relied totally on tradition. It commissioned sailing ships which even as late as 1900 were faster than steamers. The five-masters of Laeisz's Flying P Line (all the ships' names began with the letter P) wrote the last great chapter in the history of sailing vessels. Pamir, Passat, Potosi, Preussen are just four of the legendary names of these kings of the oceans, from which the shipping line earned a pretty penny in their day. They sailed fast and reliably and when, for example, the 111-metre-long Potosi returned to its home port carrying 6,500 tonnes of saltpetre from Chile, it was not just an attractive sight but a major economic event for the shipowner.

Das 1896 gebaute drei-
mastige Frachtschiff
RICKMER RICKMERS (r.)
liegt heute als
Museumsschiff an den
Landungsbrücken.
Die CAP SAN DIEGO (l.)
lief 1962 bei der Deut-
schen Werft vom
Stapel. Der Stückgut-
frachter kann an der
Überseebrücke besich-
tigt werden.

The three-masted
freighter RICKMER
RICKMERS (r.), built in
1896, is now a museum
ship berthed by the
Landungsbrücken.
The CAP SAN DIEGO (l.)
slid down the Deutsche
Werft slipway in 1962.
The general cargo
freighter is open to visitors at the Übersee-
brücke landing stage.

Verschrottung bewahrt. Das sattgrün
gestrichene Vollschiff von 1896 hat eine
Segelfläche von 3500 Quadratmetern.
Die erste Reise hatte die Rickmer Rickmers nach Hongkong gemacht, von wo
sie, mit Reis und Bambus beladen, in
ihren damaligen Heimathafen Bremerha-
ven zurückgekommen war. 1912 kaufte
sie eine Hamburger Reederei. Vier Jahre
später in portugiesischen Besitz gelangt,
kam der Segler erst 1983 auf Initiative
des Vereins wieder nach Hamburg.
    Kaum einen Steinwurf entfernt hat an
der Überseebrücke die Cap San Diego
ihren Liegeplatz, die als Museumsschiff
ebenfalls zu besichtigen ist. Gut ein hal-
bes Jahrhundert Schiffbaugeschichte
trennen die beiden Oldtimer voneinander. Die auf der Deutschen Werft Hamburg gebaute Cap San Diego war seit
1962 im Liniendienst der Reederei Ham-
burg-Süd nach Südamerika eingesetzt.
„Eins der schönsten Schiffe, die in Hamburg je gebaut wurden," schreibt der
Kunsthistoriker Hermann Hipp. Der Typ
wurde von dem Hamburger Architekten
Cäsar Pinnau entworfen. Es war die
Zeit, da das deutsche Wirtschaftswunder
die Erinnerung an die Zerstörungen des
Zweiten Weltkriegs schon wieder fast
vergessen gemacht hatte.

In 1849 Carl Woermann, who was
born in Bielefeld but founded a trading
company in Hamburg in 1837, started
trading with Africa, initially with just
one sailing ship. This was to prove the
making of his shipping line, which was
later run by his son Adolph.
    Nowadays one of the vessels which
travelled the seven seas in those days is
open for all to visit. The "Rickmer Rickmers," berthed at the Landungsbrücken
landing stages, is now a museum ship.
The Windjammers for Hamburg club
saved the sailing vessel from the scrap-
yard. Fully-rigged, the rich green-painted
vessel, built in 1896, has no fewer than
3,500 square metres of sail. Its maiden
voyage was to Hong Kong, from where
it returned to its home port of Bremer-
haven laden with rice and bamboo. In
1912 it was bought by a Hamburg shipping line, but passed into Portuguese
ownership just four years later. Not until
1983 did it return to Hamburg, thanks
to the club's initiative.
    Another museum ship, the Cap San
Diego, is berthed hardly a stone's throw

**Stapelläufe waren große Feste**

1945 hatten 2830 Schiffwracks den Hamburger Hafen nahezu unpassierbar gemacht. Sehr entschlossen steckte die Hansestadt sofort alle Energie in den Wiederaufbau des Hafens. Davon profitierten auch die Werften. Wer Anfang der siebziger Jahre nach Hamburg kam, konnte noch staunen über die Schiffbauplätze von Blohm + Voss oder HDW (Howaldtswerke Deutsche Werft AG), wo weithin sichtbar Tanker- und Containerneubauten in den Himmel wuchsen. Die Stapellauffeste waren nicht nur ein Ereignis für die feine Gesellschaft, sondern auch fürs Volk, das in Scharen am Nordufer der Elbe bei Teufelsbrück darauf wartete, wenn gegenüber auf Finkenwerder ein Neubau vom Stapel gelassen wurde. Die Spannung vorher, wenn das Schiff noch auf der schrägen Helling gehalten wurde. Der Moment, wenn es ins Rutschen geriet, ins Wasser glitt, freischwamm und von Schleppern gehalten wurde. Dann ging das Tuten der anderen Schiffe, das den Stapellauf begleitete, durch Mark und Bein. Aufatmen allerseits. Denn vorher hatten Geschichten über grausige Unglücke die Runde gemacht: wie ein Schiff beim Stapellauf auseinandergebrochen oder umgekippt war und daß früher Gefangene die letzten Stützbohlen wegschlagen durften, um dann vor dem in Bewegung kommenden Schiff davonzurennen in die Freiheit.

Ende der siebziger Jahre wanderte der Schiffneubau in Billiglohnländer ab. Hamburg hatte seine Werftenkrise, die das Bild des Hafens einmal mehr veränderte. Die Hellingen sind verschwunden.

away at Überseebrücke. A good half century of shipbuilding history separates the two veteran vessels. From 1962 the Cap San Diego, built at Hamburg's Deutsche Werft, sailed the South America route for the Hamburg Süd shipping line. "One of the finest ships ever built in Hamburg," wrote the art historian Hermann Hipp. The model was designed by the Hamburg architect Cäsar Pinnau. It was the period when the German economic miracle had almost banished the memory of World War II destruction.

**Launches were great occasions for celebration**

In 1945, around 2,830 shipwrecks had rendered the port of Hamburg almost impassable. Immediately, the city determinedly put all its energy into reconstructing the port, an endeavour from which the shipyards also profited. Anyone coming to Hamburg at the beginning of the 1970s could still be amazed at the number of ships being built by Blohm + Voss or HDW (Howaldtswerke Deutsche Werft AG), with new tankers and container vessels shooting skywards to be seen from far off. The launch of a ship was not only a high society event, but also one for the masses, crowds of whom stood waiting on the north bank of the Elbe by Teufelsbrück waiting for the new ship to be launched at Finkenwerder on the opposite bank. First, the tense anticipation while the vessel was still held fast on the sloping slipway. The moment when it started to budge, slipped into the water, floated and was held steady by tugs. Then the blast of hooters that went right through you from the other boats accompanying the launch. Sighs of relief all round. For stories of terrible accidents had been doing the rounds – how one ship had broken up or keeled over during the launch,

Der Hafen nach Bom-
benangriffen des
Zweiten Weltkriegs im
Jahr 1943

The port after World
War II air raids in 1943

Stapellauffeste gibt es nicht mehr. Ein
Ereignis ist aber immer noch das Ein-
docken großer Schiffe bei Blohm + Voss.
Die Ozeanriesen kommen zur Reparatur
oder nur zum „Rasieren und Haare-
schneiden", das ist die Pflege der Außen-
haut, Entfernung des Bewuchses von
Muscheln und Algen.

Die Lotsen und Schlepper leisten zenti-
metergenaue Präzisionsarbeit, wenn so
ein Schiffsriese ins Dock manövriert
wird. Das Dock, dieses schwarze Riesen-
becken zum Trockensetzen von Schiffen,
ist schon an sich ein Industriegigant von
eindrucksvoller Größe. Richtig atemberaubend sind aber die Nächte, wenn in
dieser dunklen Kiste ein hellerleuchteter
Schiffsriese liegt, wie ein umgestürztes
Hochhaus, und im Flutlicht Männlein zu
sehen sind, die die Reparaturarbeiten
ausführen. Was für die Sehleute ein tolles
nächtliches Spektakel ist, bedeutet für
die Beteiligten harte Arbeit. Zeit ist Geld
im Reparaturgeschäft. Das galt auch, als
das Kreuzfahrtschiff Hanseatic wie ein
schöner weißer Riese im Dock lag, bevor
es sich wieder auf die gefährliche Nord-
westpassage ins Polarmeer wagte. Die
Hanseatic gehört wie die Europa, die
Bremen und die Columbus zur Kreuz-
fahrerflotte von Hapag-Lloyd. Wenn

how prisoners had previously been
allowed to knock away the last chocks
before escaping from the path of the
moving vessel to liberty.

At the end of the 1970s, the building
of new ships shifted to countries where
labour was cheaper. Hamburg went
through a shipyard crisis which drastically altered the port's appearance yet
again. The slipways have disappeared.
Launch parties are a thing of the past.
Even so, it is still an event when a big
ship docks at Blohm + Voss. The ocean-
going giants come there for repairs or for
a "shave and haircut," that is, to have
their hulls cleaned and barnacles and
algae removed.

The pilots and tugs perform a high-
precision feat when a gigantic vessel like
this is manoeuvred into dock. The dock,
an enormous black basin where ships
can be lifted out of the water, is in itself
an industrial mammoth of impressive
size. But really and truly breathtaking
are the nights when a large brightly-lit
vessel lies in this dark box like an
upturned skyscraper, and in the flood-
light you can see little men carrying out
the repairs. What for onlookers is a fantastic nocturnal spectacle means hard
work for those involved. In the repairs
business, time is money. The same
applied when the cruise liner Hanseatic
lay in dock like a beautiful white giant
before venturing forth again to the Arctic to sail through the dangerous North-
West Passage. The Hanseatic, like the
Europa, the Bremen and the Columbus,
is part of the Hapag-Lloyd fleet of cruis-
ers. When these or other luxury liners tie
up in the port, there are often more people standing on the pier to watch and
catch a little of the breath of the big
wide world than there are passengers
disembarking to stretch their legs in
Hamburg for a few hours. Some passengers simply stay on board, leaning on the
railing, satisfied just to see the panorama
the city offers from that height, and to
dream of the voyage back downstream
to the sea, which is truly most attractive.

diese oder andere Luxusliner im Hafen festmachen, stehen auf der Pier oft mehr Menschen, die nur schauen, ein bißchen den Duft der großen weiten Welt schnuppern wollen, als Passagiere an Bord sind, die sich nun für ein paar kurze Stunden in Hamburg die Beine vertreten. Manche Passagiere bleiben gleich oben an der Reling, sind zufrieden mit dem Panorama, das die Stadt von so hoch oben aus bietet und träumen schon wieder von der Fahrt auf der Elbe seewärts, die in der Tat traumhaft schön ist.

Menschengedrängel gibt es heute nur noch auf der Hafenpromenade, die zugleich als Flutschutzmauer dient. Im Hafen selber werden immer weniger Arbeitskräfte gebraucht. Die Bilder, auf denen Hafenarbeiter zu den Barkassen strömen, sich nach der Arbeit in den zahllosen Hafenkneipen tummeln, die sind längst Geschichte. Doch der Alte Elbtunnel hat als Verbindungsweg für die im Hafen Beschäftigten immer noch nicht ausgedient. Als er 1911 eingeweiht wurde, galt er als ein technisches Wunderwerk. Die Doppelröhre war im Schildvortrieb durch den Elbgrund gebohrt worden. An jedem Ende sind Aufzüge für den vertikalen Transport eingebaut. Eine große Kuppel macht auf den Alten Elbtunnel aufmerksam, der im Westen die Anlage der St. Pauli-Landungsbrücken abschließt.

## St. Pauli-Landungsbrücken: für jeden etwas

Die St. Pauli-Landungsbrücken, die den Hafenrand heute repräsentativ begrenzen, liegen zwischen Fischmarkt und Hafenstraße im Westen und Baumwall im Osten, wo der Hamburgbesucher so richtig in der Hafenstadt anlandet. In

Nowadays, the only crowds are on the port promenade, which simultaneously serves as a protection against flooding. In the port itself, fewer and fewer workers are needed. The pictures of dock workers swarming to the launches or thronging the numerous dockside pubs after work are ancient history. That having been said, the old Elbe tunnel has still not served out its time as a link route for those who work in the port. When it was opened in 1911 it was regarded as a technical miracle. The twin tunnels had been bored through the Elbe bed by the shield driving method. Both ends of the tunnel are served by lifts for vertical transport. A large dome distinguishes the old Elbe tunnel, which rounds off the western end of the St Pauli-Landungsbrücken jetties.

## St Pauli-Landungsbrücken: something for everyone

The St Pauli jetties which now form a fitting boundary to the port perimeter run between Fischmarkt and Hafenstrasse to the west and Baumwall to the east, where visitors to Hamburg land in the port proper. In and around the grandiose 1910 buildings, which smack more of Wilhelminianism than of Hanseatic

Die Werft Blohm + Voss, dahinter die Stadtsilhouette. Im Dock wird das Kreuzfahrtschiff GALAXY auf Vordermann gebracht.

The Blohm + Voss shipyard against the backdrop of the city skyline. In the dock, the cruiser GALAXY is being licked into shape.

Die Röhren des Alten Elbtunnels verbinden seit 1911 St. Pauli und die Elbinsel Steinwerder.

The tunnels of the Old Elbe Tunnel have linked St Pauli with the Elbe island of Steinwerder since 1911.

Damals wie heute fasziniert die robuste Technik der offenen Autofahrstühle des Alten Elbtunnels.

The robust engineering of the Old Elbe Tunnel's open carlifts is as fascinating as ever.

den vom Wilhelminismus mehr als von hanseatischem Understatement geprägten pompösen Bauten aus der Zeit um 1910 und um sie herum gibt es alles, was das Touristenherz begehrt: Hafenrundfahrten, Krabbenbrötchen mit in Nordafrika gepultem Belag, Buscherumps, diese gestreiften Fischerhemden, Pudelmützen, Muschelkästchen. Nur Harry's Hafenbasar eine Etage höher in der

understatement, tourists can find everything their heart desires: boat tours of the port, rolls filled with shrimps peeled in North Africa, striped seamen's shirts known as Buscherumpen, bobble-hats, shell-covered trinket-boxes. Only Harry's Hafenbasar, for many years a favourite haunt of seamen and browsers, has moved from its basement to Bernhard-Nocht-Strasse, one storey higher. It was a basement where items from all over the world accumulated like colourful flotsam and jetsam – things which came not from serious port trade but reached Hamburg in the pockets of African, Indonesian, Chinese and Australian seamen. A bazaar that lived from the port. Now it has gone. The houses in Hafenstrasse with their wildly painted and graffitied facades have lost some of their attraction too, now that they are no longer the scene of riots

Bernhard-Nocht-Straße, den gibt es nicht mehr in dem Keller, der viele Jahre von See- und Sehleuten angesteuert wurde. Ein Keller, wo sich ein buntes Sammelsurium von Dingen aus aller Welt anhäufte, die im Hafen nicht ernsthaft gehandelt werden, sondern in den Taschen der afrikanischen, indonesischen, chinesischen, australischen Seeleute nach Hamburg kamen. Ein Basar, der vom Hafen lebte. Und auch die Hafenstraßenhäuser mit ihren wilden Fassadenmalereien haben an Attraktion verloren, seit es keine Randale mehr gibt. Wie der Hafen ändert sich auch sein Rand. Die Fähren nach England liegen nicht mehr direkt an den Landungsbrücken, sondern etwas abseits der Flaniermeile am Fährterminal, das selber aussieht wie ein Schiff aus Glas und Stahl. Wer die Vergangenheit sucht, muß noch etwas weiter elbabwärts wandern zum Museumshafen, wo die Oldtimer im Wasser

between squatters and police. Like the port itself, its perimeter has also changed. The ferries to England no longer berth directly at Landungsbrücken but a short distance away from the promenade at a ferry terminal which itself looks like a ship of glass and steel. Those in search of the past must walk a little further downstream to the museum harbour in Övelgönne, where veteran boats bob up and down on the water, stimulating the imagination to conjure up images of the port and the Elbe in days gone by.

Der auslaufende Dampfer CAP ARCONA wurde bei Blohm + Voss 1927 gebaut und passiert Anfang der 1930er Jahre St. Pauli-Landungsbrücken.

The departing steamer CAP ARCONA was built in the Blohm + Voss shipyard in 1927 and is seen passing the St Pauli landing stages in the early 1930s.

Der Terminal der Eng-landfähre in Altona-Altstadt ist nicht nur eine Attraktion für Passagiere, sondern auch für die Sehleute an Land.

The terminal for ferries to and from England in the old part of Altona is an attraction not only for passengers, but for onlookers on land.

schaukeln und die Phantasie anregen, sich Bilder von Hafen und Elbe aus vergangenen Zeiten auszumalen.

### Zukunftsmusik: die HafenCity

In die Zukunft kann man auch schon schauen. Die spektakulärste Auffrischung des ökonomischen Herzens der Hansestadt im dritten Jahrtausend trägt bereits konkrete Züge. Kurz vor Ende seiner Amtszeit 1997 brachte Bürgermeister Henning Voscherau die Pläne für

### A future dream: the Port City

One can look into the future, too. The most spectacular facelift of the economic heart of the city in the third millennium is already taking shape. Shortly before his term of office ended in 1997, Mayor Henning Voscherau tabled plans for Hamburg's new HafenCity, or Port City, a new district between the Speicherstadt and the Norderelbe bridges on the northern fringe of the port. It coincides with a development that Hamburgers have long dreamt of – to live, work and go out in the port, by the Elbe. With a prime inner-city location and one hundred hectares of land to build on, the Hafen-City provides plenty of scope for the realisation of attractive ideas. This once-in-a-lifetime project could turn out to be Hamburg's prime location. After all, the

Hamburgs neue HafenCity auf den
Tisch. Zwischen Speicherstadt und
Norderelbbrücken am nördlichen Hafen-
rand ist die Entwicklung eines neuen
Stadtteils angesiedelt, von dem die Hanseaten schon lange träumen. Wohnen,
Arbeiten und Ausgehen im Hafen, an der
Elbe. Die HafenCity mit bester Innen-
stadt-Lage am Wasser bietet auf einhundert Hektar Bauland viel Platz für die
Verwirklichung attraktiver Ideen. Ein
Jahrhundertprojekt, das zur besten
Adresse der Stadt werden könnte, die selber über anderthalb Millionen Einwoh-
ner zählt und ihre ohnehin große Anziehungskraft für die Millionen Menschen
im Hinterland mit der HafenCity noch
steigern wird.

city itself has more than one and a half
million inhabitants and the HafenCity
will increase its already considerable
powers of attraction for the millions
people in the hinterland.

Modellstudie zur
HafenCity. Es ist das
größte Stadterneue-
rungsprojekt Europas
zu Beginn des 21. Jahr-
hunderts.

A model of the Hafen-
City. This is Europe's
largest urban renewal
project at the start of
the twenty-first century.

# Die Speicherstadt
## Historisches Quartier mit Zukunft

## The Warehouse City
## Historic district with a future

Die Speicherstadt ist Teil des Freihafens. Ihr steht ein eigenes Kapitel durchaus zu, weil dieser zollfreie Basar mehr ist als nur Hamburgs herausragende Denkmallandschaft. Gebaut wurde die Speicherstadt aus rein merkantilen Gründen. Dieser 1888 eröffnete, bis heute größte Lagerhauskomplex der Erde hat seine praktische Bedeutung bis in die Gegenwart nicht verloren. Die dicken Backsteinwände der Speicher garantieren rund ums Jahr ideale natürlich klimatisierte Lagerräume für Tee, Kaffee, Gewürze, Tabak, Wein und viele andere Waren, die hier zollfrei gestaut werden.

### „Jedermann" zwischen Speicher und Fleet

Neben diesem praktischen Nutzen ist längst aber auch die eigentümliche Schönheit dieser Stadt in der Stadt entdeckt worden. Eine nordisch kühle Schönheit, die sich dem traditionellen Baumaterial der Hanseaten verdankt,

The Speicherstadt, or Warehouse City, is part of the free port. It thoroughly deserves a chapter to itself because this duty-free bazaar is more than just Hamburg's outstanding set of monuments. The Warehouse City was built for purely mercantile reasons. Opened in 1888 and still the largest warehouse complex on earth, it has retained its practical significance to this day. The warehouses' thick redbrick walls guarantee year-round, naturally air-conditioned, ideal storage for tea, coffee, spices, tobacco, wine and many other goods that are stored here duty-free.

### "Everyman" between warehouse and fleet

Apart from this practical use, the strange beauty of this city within a city was discovered long ago. A cool, Nordic beauty which it owes to the traditional Hanseatic building material, red brick. To anyone strolling along the promenade from Cremon island to the Deichtorhallen, the Warehouse City looks like a castle. The facades glow red in the sun, or at night loom like black cut-outs against the sky.

dem roten Backstein. Wie eine Burg, ein Schloß oder eine Festung präsentiert sich die Speicherstadt dem Spaziergänger auf der Promenade von der Cremoninsel zu den Deichtorhallen. Die Fassaden leuchten rot in der Sonne oder erscheinen nachts wie schwarze Scherenschnitte.

Wer die Stadt der zollfreien Waren südlich des Zollkanals über eine Brücke betritt, kann bei ruhigem Wetter die Verdoppelung der Speicher im Spiegel der Fleete erleben, die beim Bau des Lagerhauskomplexes neu angelegt wurden. Schwärmer begeistern sich auch für das Spiel der Schatten auf den Fassaden der Speicher. Die Ereigniskultur – immer auf der Suche nach neuen attraktiven Veranstaltungsorten – hat die Speicherstadt auch schon vereinnahmt. Ein überzeugender Vorreiter war hier die Theateraufführung des Hamburger „Jedermann", eine freie Adaption des Salzburger Mysterienspiels von Hugo von Hofmannsthal. Initiator des Spiels zwischen den Speichern am Fleet war Michael Batz.

Crossing one of the bridges into the city of duty-free goods south of the customs canal, in calm weather you can see a mirror image of the warehouses reflected in the canals that were rebuilt when the buildings were erected. Enthusiasts also rave about the play of shadows on the warehouse facades. Adventure culture – always in search of new, attractive event venues – has already taken over the Speicherstadt. A convincing forerunner was the performance here of the Hamburg "Everyman," a free adaptation of the Salzburg mystery play by Hugo von Hofmannsthal. The initiator of the play between the warehouses by the fleet was Michael Batz.

Anyone who has walked with open eyes across the uneven cobbles of streets such as Neuer and Alter Wandrahm, Dienerreihe, Holländischer Brook and St Annenufer will understand why the Speicherstadt has been used time and again as an enchanting film set.

In the nineteenth century, the land on Wandrahm and Kehrwieder islands where the Warehouse City now stands underwent an unprecedented change of use. The demolition of the historic buildings that had stood on the site after-

Die Speicherstadt um 1890. Im Ostteil der Brookinsel werden gerade weitere Speicherblöcke errichtet.

The Warehouse City in around 1890. Additional warehouse blocks are undergoing construction in the eastern part of Brookinsel.

Speicher am Alten Wandrahm, fotografiert um 1885 von Gustav Koppmann. An Land hieven Kräne die Waren, an den Speichern übernehmen Winden den Dienst.

This 1885 photograph by Gustav Koppmann shows a warehouse on Alter Wandrahm. Cranes hoist the goods onto land, while in the warehouses winches take over.

Daß die Speicherstadt auch immer wieder als hinreißende Filmkulisse dient, versteht jeder, der einmal mit offenen Augen über das holperige Pflaster der Straßen Neuer und Alter Wandrahm, Dienerreihe, Holländischer Brook und St. Annenufer gegangen ist.

Das Gelände der Speicherstadt auf der Wandrahm- und der Kehrwiederinsel erlebte im 19. Jahrhundert eine Umnutzung sondergleichen. Der Abriß der historischen Bebauung war für den Direktor der Hamburger Kunsthalle Alfred Lichtwark (1852–1914) ein Grund, Hamburg als „Freie und Abrißstadt" zu titulieren.

wards led Alfred Lichtwark (1852–1914), director of the Hamburg Kunsthalle, to describe Hamburg as the "Free and Demolition City."

In 1881, when Hamburg was forced to bow to the pressure of the German Reich and restrict the exemption from duty in the port as a whole, new storage facilities had to be created within the free port, and these had to be as close as possible to where the merchants had their offices. At that time, there were around 24,000 people living on Wandrahm and Kehrwieder islands, some in very grand houses of the Baroque era (Wandrahm had once been Hamburg's most exclusive residential area), and some in labourers' and craftsmen's quarters of a rather humbler type. All had to make way for the new port plans. There was no government-controlled resettlement plan for the poorer classes. People were just left to sort out somewhere to live for themselves. It is hard to imagine the dramas that took place during the demolition, which was on a massive scale for the time. Residents were not wanted in the new Warehouse City, no more than they are today.

The person responsible for this mammoth project was chief engineer Franz Andreas Meyer (1837–1901). He was a brilliant organiser with an eye above all to the use the new buildings were to be put to. Built on piles, the warehouses, each with up to 850 square metres of storage space, have frostproof walls. They are cool in summer and temperate in winter. Nowadays, the goods are mainly transported by truck, with only a few barges still using the Speicherstadt canals. The district often has a deserted air, for here, as everywhere, machines have taken over from muscle-power.

Als sich die Hansestadt 1881 dem
Druck des Deutschen Reiches beugen
mußte und die allgemeine Zollfreiheit
auf den Hafen eingeschränkt wurde,
mußten innerhalb dieses Freihafens neue
Lagermöglichkeiten geschaffen werden,
die möglichst nicht allzu weit entfernt
von den Kontoren der Kaufleute entstehen sollten. Auf der Wandrahm- und der
Kehrwiederinsel lebten damals etwa
24 000 Menschen. Teilweise in hoch-
herrschaftlichen Häusern aus der
Barockzeit (der Wandrahm galt einmal
als vornehmste Adresse Hamburgs), teilweise in Arbeiter- und Handwerkerquar-
tieren von eher ärmlichem Zuschnitt. Sie
alle mußten der Neuplanung für den
Hafen weichen. Ein staatlich gelenktes
Umsiedlungsprogramm für die ärmeren
Schichten gab es nicht. Jeder mußte zuse-
hen, wo er blieb. Welche Dramen sich
bei diesem für die damalige Zeit giganti-
schen Abriß abspielten, ist kaum auszu-
denken. Das Wohnen war in der neuen
Speicherstadt nicht erwünscht und ist es
bis heute nicht.

Verantwortlich für das Jahrhundertprojekt war der Oberingenieur Franz
Andreas Meyer (1837–1901). Ein genia-
ler Organisator, der vor allem den Nutzen der neuen Bebauung im Auge hatte.
Die auf Pfählen errichteten Gebäude mit
je bis zu 850 Quadratmeter Lagerfläche
haben frostsichere Wände. Sie sind im
Sommer kühl und im Winter gut tempe-
riert. Den Transport der Waren haben
heute überwiegend Lkw übernommen.
Nur noch wenige Schuten fahren auf den
Fleeten der Speicherstadt. Auch wirkt
das Quartier oft menschenleer. Maschinen haben die Muskelkraft hier wie
überall abgelöst.

## Museum mit „Kaffeeklappe"

Wie es früher in der Speicherstadt
zuging, ist in einem kleinen Museum zu
sehen, das als privat betriebene Außen-
stelle des Museums der Arbeit im Spei-

## Museum with "Coffee Hatch"

To see what it was like here in the old
days, you can visit a small privately-run
museum in the warehouse of the Eichholtz company at St Annenufer 2, which
is a branch of the Hamburg Museum of
Labour. The museum shows vividly how
as many as nine porters used to be
employed to transport mixed cargoes by
barge on the side facing the water. A
winchman, hatchman and stacker were
responsible for the separate work
processes. On the land side, bagged
goods were transported by horse and
cart.

Those are historic pictures. Time has
not stood still at the entrance to the
Warehouse City. The traditional ware-
housemen have become modern logistics
managers with computer systems that
are networked worldwide. But their task
has stayed the same. They take charge of
the transport of cargoes from ship to
store, check goods for damage, store
them and ensure that the packages are
labelled. Nowadays both the company

Schuten im Fleet an der
Holländischen Reihe
um 1881 von der
St. Annen-Brücke aus
gesehen. Die kiellosen
Transportboote konn-
ten wegen ihres gerin-
gen Tiefgangs die
Ladung auch in die
flachen Wasserstraßen
der Innenstadt bringen.

Barges on the Holländi-
sche Reihe fleet, or
canal, as seen from the
St-Annen-Brücke in
1881. Their shallow
draft allowed these
keel-less transport ves-
sels to bring goods even
into the shallow water-
ways of the inner city.

114

Traumschön, diese
Speicherstadt. Auf dem
Wasser ist es zuneh-
mend stiller geworden.
Nur noch wenige Wa-
ren werden heute mit
Schuten herangefahren,
fast alles kommt und
geht per Lkw.

Hamburg's Warehouse
City is simply gorgeous.
Less and less happens
on the water side of the
warehouses. Now-
adays, only a few goods
are brought in by
barge. Nearly every-
thing comes and goes
by truck.

Die Kannengießer-
brücke in der Speicher-
stadt. Der Name ver-
weist auf das ehemalige
Quartier der Kannen-
gießer, das aber schon
Ende des 17. Jahrhun-
derts bei einer Feuers-
brunst zerstört wurde.

Kannengiesserbrücke in
the Warehouse City.
The bridge's name
refers to a former dis-
trict of that name
which was destroyed by
fire back in the late
seventeenth century.

Im Speicherstadtmuseum wird über die Geschichte des Quartiers informiert.

Visitors to the Warehouse City museum are informed about the district's history.

Firmenschilder der Quartiersleute, die sich zusammenschlossen und nach dem bedeutendsten Teilhaber benannten. Die weiteren firmierten als Consorten (Cons.).

The company nameplates in the Warehouse City of the quartermen, dockers who joined forces and took the name of the leading partner. The other partners were known as Consorten (Cons. for short).

cher der Firma Eichholtz, St. Annenufer 2, eingerichtet wurde. Hier wird anschaulich vermittelt, daß für den wasserseitigen Umschlag von Stückgut über Schuten früher bis zu neun Träger eingesetzt wurden. Windenvize, Lukenvize und Stapelvize waren für die jeweiligen Arbeitsgänge verantwortlich. Auf der Landseite wurde Sackgut per Pferdegespann transportiert.

Das sind historische Bilder. Die Zeit hat vor der Speicherstadt nicht haltgemacht. Die traditionellen Quartiersleute haben sich zu modernen Logistik-Dienstleistern mit weltweit vernetzten Computersystemen entwickelt. Doch ihre Aufgabe ist die gleiche geblieben. Sie sorgen für den Transport der Waren vom Schiff zum Lager, prüfen Waren auf Beschädigung, speichern sie und sorgen für die Markierung der Verpackung. Heute werden sowohl die Firmeninhaber als auch

owners and their warehouse staff are described as "Quartiersleute" – a profession that exists only in the port of Hamburg, and referring to the fact that they have to find quarters for goods. The small museum also provides an opportunity to take part in tea tastings, doing for fun what a professional taster does to earn his daily bread. The small musem café is called the "Kaffeeklappe" (Coffee Hatch). The name originates from the dockworkers' bars, dozens of which once stood close to where they worked by and on the water. These typical Hamburg institutions have virtually disappeared, and with them the name "Kaffeeklappe."

Two more museums provide further excellent insights into this unusual warehouse complex. The old Customs House at Alter Wandrahm 15–16 has an exhibition on the history of the customs, ranging from the results of a successful hunt for smugglers to the customs vessel on which this hunt for minor and major criminals was carried out.

die Speicherarbeiter als Quartiersleute bezeichnet – ein Beruf, den es nur im Hamburger Hafen gibt. Das kleine Museum bietet auch die Möglichkeit, an Teeverkostungen teilzunehmen und das aus Spaß zu versuchen, was für den professionellen Teeverkoster das tägliche Brot ist. Die kleine Museumsgastronomie nennt sich „Kaffeeklappe". Das ist eine Bezeichnung für die Hafenarbeiterkneipen, von denen es früher Dutzende in der Nähe der Arbeitsstellen an und auf dem Wasser gab. Diese typisch hamburgischen Institutionen sind heute nahezu verschwunden und mit ihnen die Bezeichnung „Kaffeeklappe".

Zwei weitere Museen erschließen dem privaten Besucher dieses ungewöhnliche Lagerquartier auf das Schönste. Im alten Zollamt (Alter Wandrahm 15–16) wird die Geschichte des Zollwesens dargestellt. Was bei der erfolgreichen Jagd auf Schmuggler herauskommt, ist da genauso zu sehen wie das Zollboot, mit dem diese Jagd auf kleine und große Verbrecher vonstatten geht.

Das Gewürzmuseum „Hot Spice", Am Sandtor 32, hat sein Domizil ebenfalls in historischen Lagerräumen. Was man bei einem Spaziergang durch die Speicherstadt ohnehin schon mit der Nase wahrnimmt, ist hier noch mal auf kleinem Raum dokumentiert: Die Vielzahl von Gewürzen, die im Hafen lagern, wird in diesem Museum gezeigt, ihre Herkunft und Anwendung werden erklärt. In kleinen Portionen stehen sie auch zum Verkauf.

The Hot Spice spice museum at Sandtor 32 is also housed in a historic warehouse. In its small space you find documentary backing for what your nose has already told you on a walk through the Warehouse City: the large variety of spices stored in the port are shown in this museum and their origin and use explained. Small portions of them are also offered for sale.

Die Kornhausbrücke führt in die Speicherstadt. Auf der Stadtseite wurden Statuen der Entdecker Vasco da Gama und Christoph Kolumbus aufgestellt.

Kornhausbrücke leads into the Warehouse City. Statues of explorers Vasco da Gama and Christopher Columbus were erected.

Das Hafenfoto aus den
1920er Jahren zeigt den
Kaiserspeicher auf der
Kehrwiederspitze beim
Auslaufen des Schiffes
MONTE ROSA.

This 1920s photograph
of the port shows the
MONTE ROSA leaving
the Kaiser warehouse at
Kehrwiederspitze.

Die historisierende
Architektur der Spei-
cherstadt zeigt sich
aufs schönste beim
St. Annen-Fleet, am Sitz
der Hamburger Hafen-
und Lagerhaus-Aktien-
gesellschaft. Links der
Turm von St. Katha-
rinen

The Warehouse City's
neo-historical architec-
ture can be seen in all
its glory in the head-
quarters of the Ham-
burger Hafen- und La-
gerhaus-Aktiengesell-
schaft on St. Annen-Fleet.
On the left is the tower
of St Katharine's
Church

## Historisierende Architektur

Daß seine Speicherstadt einmal auch
museale Züge annehmen würde, hat ihr
Erbauer Franz Andreas Meyer sicher
nicht geahnt. Doch diese technisch
bestimmte Architektur vom Ende des 19.
Jahrhundert besitzt heute auch einen
hohen ästhetischen Reiz. Die historisierenden Fassaden sehen aus, als ob sie aus
der Zeit der Norddeutschen Backsteingo-
tik stammten. Keramische Ornamente,
Bänder mit Glasur- und Glassteinen und
vor allem in Gold ausgeformte Firmen-
namen lockern die Fassaden auf. Die
Grünspanhüte der Winden geben den
Dächern eine verspielte Silhouette. Kein
Wunder also, daß dieser kompakte
Architekturkomplex als Riesenschatztru-
he bezeichnet wurde.

Kurz nach 1900 erhielt die Speicherstadt das Gebäude, in dem auch heute

## Historicist architecture

Its builder Franz Andreas Meyer surely
never dreamt that his Speicherstadt
would one day take on some of the character of a museum. But this purpose-
built late nineteenth-century architecture
still possesses a large degree of aesthetic
appeal. The historicist facades look as if
they were built in the era of North German redbrick Gothic architecture.
Ceramic ornaments, strips of glazed and
glass bricks and above all the gold letter-
ing of company names relieve the
facades. The verdigris tips of the winches
give the roofs a playful silhouette. So it is
no wonder that this compact architectural complex is described as an enormous
treasure-chest.

Not long after 1900 the Warehouse
City was graced with the building which
remains its nerve centre to this day.
Richly adorned with turrets, arcades and
oriels, the headquarters of the Hamburger Hafen- und Lagerhaus-Aktiengesell-
schaft (HHLA) at Bei St Annen makes
such a grand impression you could take
it for the city hall. In fact it is the work
of three architects who had a hand in the
Hamburg Rathaus. Johannes Grotjahn,
Bernhard Hanssen and Emil Meerwein
designed the building in the Warehouse
City on the motto "What's good for the
port is good for Hamburg."

The new Speicherstadt's importance
for Hamburgers was illustrated among
other things by the richly ornate bridges
leading across to it. World War II
wrought much destruction. On the town
side, Kornhausbrücke is still flanked by
two statues erected in 1903, one of

noch alle Fäden zusammenlaufen. Reich
verziert mit Türmchen, Lauben und
Erkern macht das Verwaltungsgebäude
der Hamburger Hafen- und Lagerhaus-
Aktiengesellschaft (HHLA), Bei St.
Annen, einen so pompösen Eindruck, als
ob hier Rathaus gespielt würde. Tatsächlich ist es das Werk von drei Architekten,
die am Bau des Hamburger Rathauses
mitgewirkt hatten. Johannes Grotjahn
sowie Bernhard Hansen und Emil Meerwein bauten in der Speicherstadt nach
dem Motto: Was gut ist für den Hafen,
ist auch gut für Hamburg.

Wie wichtig den Hamburgern ihre
neue Speicherstadt war, zeigen auch die
reich dekorierten Brücken, die zu ihr
führen. Der Zweite Weltkrieg hat viel
zerstört. Die Kornhausbrücke wird zur
Stadt hin noch von den 1903 geschaffenen Statuen flankiert, die Christoph
Kolumbus auf der einen Seite und Vasco
da Gama auf der anderen Seite darstellen. Zwei Weltentdecker, deren Reisen
letztendlich auch dazu führten, daß sich
die Speicher der Hanseaten mit den Pro-
dukten aus aller Herren Länder füllen
konnten. Von Anis bis Zimt – A bis Z –
ist hier heute so ziemlich alles gut unter
Dach und Fach gebracht. Nach dem
Alphabet sind übrigens auch die einzelnen Speicher geordnet, beginnend mit
dem Block A im Westen, endend mit
dem Block X im Osten. Die Zerstörungen des Krieges machten nach 1945
einen Wiederaufbau nötig. Werner Kallmorgen (1902–1979) prägte diese Erneuerung mit einer klaren, modernen
Architektur. Die massive Bebauung der
Kehrwiederspitze in den neunziger Jahren war sehr umstritten. Wer diese
Architektur zu ideenlos findet, kann sich
mit einem Blick aus dem obersten Stock-
werk dieses Hauses trösten: da liegt
einem die Speicherstadt aufs faszinie-
rendste zu Füßen.

Christopher Columbus and the other of
Vasco da Gama. Two explorers whose
voyages ultimately enabled Hanseatic
merchants to fill their warehouses with
products from all over the world. Nowadays, pretty well everything from A to Z,
from Afghanistan to Zanzibar, is stored
safely under cover here. Incidentally, the
individual warehouses are also arranged
alphabetically, starting with block A to
the west and ending with block X to the
east.

The destruction of war made reconstruction essential in 1945. This renewal
was distinguished by the clear, modern
architecture of Werner Kallmorgen
(1902–79). The high-density building on
Kehrwiederspitze, the tip of Kehrwieder
island, in the 1990s was very controversial. Those who find the architecture
uninspired can console themselves with
the view from the top storey, with the
Speicherstadt spread out fascinatingly at
their feet.

Neubauten haben das
Gesicht des Geländes
westlich der histori-
schen Speicherstadt in
den neunziger Jahren
des 20. Jahrhunderts
stark verändert. Kehr-
wiederspitze von der
Niederbaumbrücke aus
gesehen

In the 1990s, new
buildings drastically
changed the appearance
of the area to the west
of the historic Ware-
house City. A view of
Kehrwiederspitze from
Niederbaum Bridge

# Die Elbe im Rhythmus der Gezeiten
## The Elbe in the rhythm of the tides

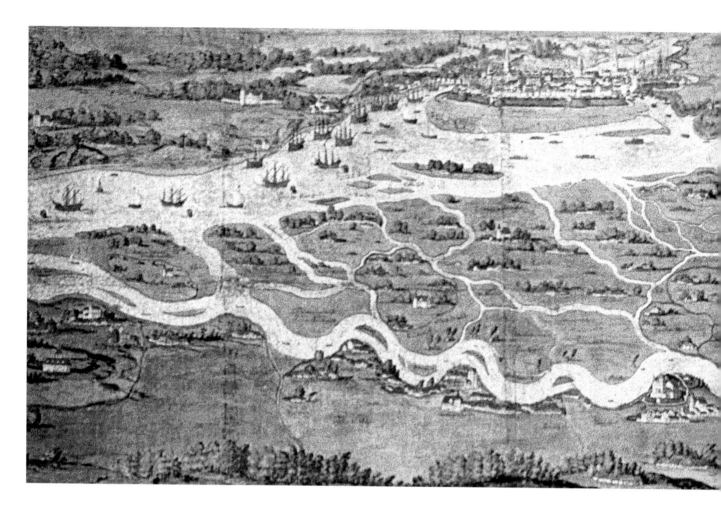

In keiner anderen Stadt gibt es so viele Segler wie in Hamburg. Sie machen zu Jahresbeginn in schöner Regelmäßigkeit ein kleines Büchlein zum Bestseller, das vor jedem Törn auf der Elbe zu Rate gezogen werden muß. Der Gezeitenkalender des Bundesamtes für Seeschiffahrt und Hydrographie gibt die Hoch- und Niedrigwasserzeiten an. Der alle sechs Stunden einsetzende Wechsel von Ebbe und Flut macht das Planspiel des Segelns auf dem großen Strom zusätzlich reizvoll und manchmal mühsam. Die Meeresgezeiten treiben das Nordseewasser zwar nur bis Glückstadt, aber noch im Hamburger Hafen wird ein Tidenhub von rund drei Metern gemessen. Flußaufwärts reichen Ebbe und Flut bis Geesthacht.

Wo die Alster in die Elbe mündet, ist Deutschlands verkehrsreichster Fluß nur 300 Meter breit. Doch auf ihrem rund 100 Kilometer weiten Weg zum Meer

In no other city are there as many yachtsmen as in Hamburg. Thanks to them, at the start of every year, with unfailing regularity, a little book becomes a bestseller, a book which has to be consulted before every trip on the Elbe. The calendar of tides published by the Federal Office of Marine Shipping and Hydrography gives the times of high and low water. The six-hourly pattern of high and low tides gives sailing on the Elbe a special thrill, but sometimes makes it hard going. Though the sea tides only wash the North Sea water as far as Glückstadt, even in the port of

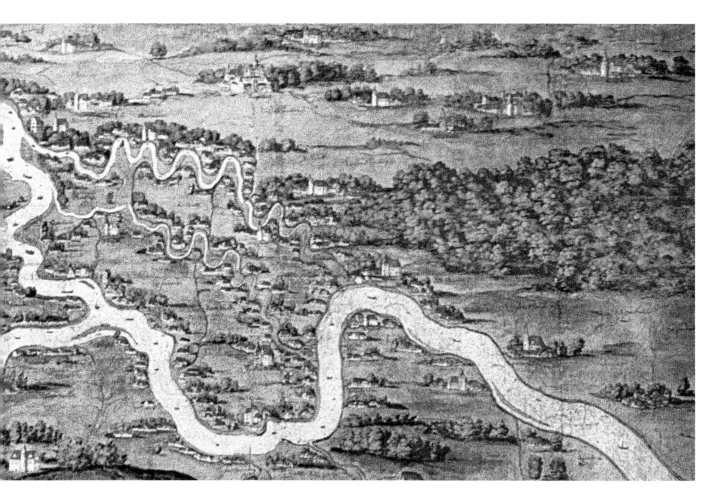

weitet sich die Unterelbe schon knapp
hinter dem Hamburger Hafen bei Blankenese auf zwei bis drei Kilometer. Bis
sie als graugelber Strom bei Cuxhaven in
die Nordsee einmündet, dehnt sie sich
auf 15 Kilometer Breite aus.

## „Autobahn" und schönes Ufer

Für die professionelle Schiffahrt gilt die
Unterelbe, deren Quellbäche 1165 Kilometer weiter südöstlich im Riesengebirge
entspringen, als tidenabhängige „Autobahn" zwischen Hafen und Meer. Früher
machten sich ständig verlagernde Sandbänke das Befahren nur bei Flut möglich.
Heute sorgen Schwimmbagger dafür, daß
Hafen und Fahrrinne von Schlick und
Sand nicht zugespült werden. Früher lie-
fen die flach gebauten Ewer bei Blanke-

Hamburg there is a change of around
three metres in the water level. Further
upstream, the river is tidal as far as
Geesthacht.

Where the Alster flows into the Elbe,
Germany's busiest river is just 300
metres wide. But on its hundred-kilometre-plus journey to the seat, the Lower
Elbe widens out, reaching between two
and three kilometres at Blankenese, not
far outside the port of Hamburg. By the
time the yellowish grey river flows into
the North Sea at Cuxhaven, it is a
sprawling fifteen kilometres wide.

Ausschnitt aus einer
Elbkarte, die der Maler
Melchior Lorichs 1567
im Auftrag des Rates
der Stadt malte. Und
zwar in einer Länge von
zwölf Metern und einer
Höhe von einem Meter.
Die Karte gehört heute
zu den schönsten Schät-
zen des Staatsarchivs
Hamburg.

Part of a map of the
Elbe commissioned by
the city council and
painted by Melchior
Lorichs in 1567. The
map, 12 metres long
and one metre high, is
now one of the finest
treasures in the Ham-
burg city archives.

Über die Jahrhunderte hat die Elbe immer wieder ihr Flußbild verändert und dabei eine Vielzahl von Inseln gebildet. Blick auf Schweine- und Pagensand bei Wittenbergen, westlich von Blankenese

Over the centuries the Elbe has regularly changed its course, creating a large number of islands in the process. A view of Schweine- and Pagensand near Wittenbergen, to the west of Blankenese

nese mit der Flut auf dem Strand auf, konnten bei Ebbe entladen werden und kamen mit der nächsten Flut wieder frei.

In Övelgönne können die Altonaer heute nur noch auf einem kleinen Streifen Sandstrand spielen und sonnenbaden. Erst hinter Blankenese, unterhalb des hohen Ufers von Wittenbergen, läßt der Strand schon ein wenig das nahe Meer ahnen. Vereinzelt sind mutige Schwimmer zu sichten. Vergiftungsgefahr besteht an der Unterelbe nicht mehr. Trotzdem, man sollte das Wasser nicht unbedingt schlucken. Gefährlich sind für Schwimmer aber nach wie vor die Strömungen und der von großen Seeschiffen ausgelöste Sog des Wassers.

## Motorway and pleasant banks

For professional shipping the Lower Elbe, which is fed by springs that rise 1,165 kilometres to the south-east in the Riesengebirge mountains, is a tide-dependent motorway between port and sea. In former times, constantly shifting sandbanks meant that the river was only negotiable at high tide. Nowadays, floating dredgers ensure that the port and the shipping lane are not clogged up by mud and sand. In former times the flat-bottomed coastal sailing-boats were washed onto Blankenese beach with the tide, could be unloaded at low tide and sailed out again on the next high tide.

Nowadays, the residents of Altona are left with only a narrow strip of land in Ovelgönne to play at sandy beaches and sunbathing. Only beyond Blankenese, beneath the steep bank at Wittenberge, does the beach give an inkling that the

Aber was ein richtiger Segler ist, der haßt das Schwimmen sowieso wie der Teufel das Weihwasser. Er werkelt auch im Hafen am liebsten an Bord und überläßt die Landgänge gerne seinen Mitseglern.

Die Unterelbe als grandioses Segelrevier zwischen Hamburg und Cuxhaven hat durch die Eindeichungen seit den siebziger Jahren viele reizvolle und verschwiegene Liegeplätze verloren. Durch die idyllische Schilflandschaft des Dwarslochs und das durch die Kuhweiden mäandernde Wasser direkt nach Haseldorf zu segeln, wo an Pfingsten traditionsgemäß ein Ochse am Spieß gebraten wird – das ist vorbei. Jetzt liegt der Haseldorfer Hafen außerhalb des Ortes.

sea is not far off. Occasionally, a courageous swimmer is sighted. There is no longer any danger of being poisoned in the Lower Elbe. Even so, swallowing the water is not recommended. What remains as dangerous for swimmers as ever are the currents and the undertow created by the large ocean-going ships.

But a true sailor hates swimming as much as the devil hates holy water. Even in port he prefers to potter about on board, leaving it to the others to go ashore.

The building of dykes since the 1970s has deprived the Lower Elbe of many delightful, secluded berths. Gone are the days when you could sail through the idyllic reed-overgrown landscape of the Dwarsloch and meander through cow-grazing pastures right into Haseldorf, where traditionally at Whitsun an ox is roast on a spit. Nowadays, Haseldorf marina is outside the village.

Vor Blankenese ist die Elbe drei Kilometer breit. Den einsamen Strandläufer können ozeanische Gefühle packen. Die kleine Personenfähre verbindet Blankenese und Cranz.

The Elbe off Blankenese is three kilometres wide. Walking alone on the beach, you can be overcome by oceanic feelings. The small passenger ferry connects Blankenese and Cranz.

Wer im Flugzeug die Elbe überquert, sieht den Hirschpark mit dem Mühlenberg und seinem Yachthafen unter sich liegen.

To anyone crossing the Elbe by plane, the Hirschpark with Mühlenberg and its marina appears like a small green patch of land below.

### Eigene Koje im City-Hafen

Trotzdem ist die Unterelbe heute immer noch eine so variationsreiche Wasserlandschaft, wie es nur wenige gibt. Daß dieses Freizeitrevier mit ozeanisch großartigem Atem direkt vor der Haustür der Millionenstadt beginnt, ist ein ebenfalls nicht zu unterschätzender Pluspunkt. Wer stadtnah in der eigenen Koje übernachten möchte, kann heute komfortabel mit seinem Schiff im City-Sporthafen festmachen. Kleine Yachthäfen für Freizeitkapitäne reihen sich dann elbaufwärts beiderseits des Stroms aneinander. Auf Hamburger Gebiet sind das die Häfen von Finkenwerder, Teufelsbrück, Mühlenberg und vom Blankeneser Segelclub.

### Your own berth in the city marina

Even so, the Lower Elbe is still an extraordinarily varied marine landscape. It is an advantage not to be underestimated for a major city like Hamburg to have this leisure ground with its magnificent breath of the ocean right outside its front door. Anyone wanting to spend the night in their own bunk close to the city can conveniently tie up in the city marina. Further downstream, small yacht harbours for amateur sailors are dotted along both sides of the river like a string of pearls. Hamburg alone has marinas at Finkenwerder, Teufelsbrück, Mühlenberg and the Blankenese Sailing Club.

The largest number of berths is at the Wedel yacht marina. Built in 1962, it is close to the Willkomm Höft, where passing ships from all over the world are welcomed and bidden farewell by the playing of their national anthem. There

Die meisten Liegeplätze bietet der
Wedeler Yachthafen. Diese 1962 eröffnete Anlage in der Nachbarschaft von Willkomm Höft, wo die großen Schiffe aus
aller Welt mit dem Abspielen der jeweiligen Nationalhymne begrüßt und verabschiedet werden, ist auch für Sehleute
immer wieder interessant. Luxusyachten,
Kutter, Jollen, Katamarane. Schwimmende Untersätze modernster und ältester
Bauart warten hier an den Stegen auf die
große und kleine Reise. Bei auflaufen-
dem Wasser entscheidet sich der Segler
für den Törn in Richtung Hamburg, bei
ablaufendem Wasser für die Fahrt in

is plenty to interest non-sailors, too.
Luxury yachts, cutters, dinghies, catama-
rans in every style from ancient to modern, wait here by the landing stages for
voyages both major and minor. When
the tide is coming in, the yachtsman
decides to sail towards Hamburg, when
it is running out, he heads in the opposite direction towards the North Sea.
Buoys and navigation lights mark out
the route to the sea. The Elbe Atlas helps
him to steer round the shallows. A
revised edition of the cartographic chart
of the river and its banks on a scale of
1:80,000 is published every two years.
But even with an atlas, those who ven-
ture outside the shipping lane into the
landscape of mud-flats and sandbanks
needs to know his way around and to
have a boat with as little draught as possible.

Blick auf den Blanke-
neser Kanonenberg mit
Leuchtfeuer, die Baum-
wipfel des Hirschparks,
den Mühlenberger
Segelhafen und die
Villen am Geesthang.
Die Vogelperspektive
macht die Schiffe auf
der Elbe kaum kleiner.

A view of Blankenese's
Kanonenberg and
beacon, the tree-tops of
Hirschpark, the Müh-
lenberg marina and the
villas that overlook it.
This bird's-eye view
hardly makes the ships
on the Elbe look any
smaller.

Der Museumshafen Övelgönne, der 1977 gegründet wurde, beherbergt u. a. Segler aus Fluß-, Küsten- und Hochseefahrt, ein altes Feuerlöschboot, das Feuerschiff Elbe 3 und einen Eisbrecher.

Övelgönne museum harbour, founded in 1977, is home to sailing ships that served in river and coastal shipping and on the high seas, to an old firefighting boat, to the lightship Elbe 3 and an icebreaker.

Richtung Nordsee. Tonnen und Leuchtfeuer markieren das Fahrwasser bis zum Meer. Der Elbe-Atlas hilft, Untiefen zu umschiffen. Das karthographierte Bild des Stroms und seiner Ufer im Maßstab 1 : 80 000 wird alle zwei Jahre in korrigierter Fassung neu aufgelegt. Aber auch mit Atlas gilt: Wer sich außerhalb des Fahrwassers in die Landschaft der Priele und Sandbänke wagt, braucht gute Ortskenntnis und ein Schiff mit möglichst wenig Tiefgang.

## Von Schweinesand bis Schwarztonnensand

Die ganz großen Sandbänke der Unterelbe liegen wie langgestreckte Inseln im Strom. Das beginnt bei Blankenese mit dem Schweinesand, der heute Naturschutzgebiet ist und mit Vorliebe von

## From Schweinesand to Schwarztonnensand

The largest sandbanks of the Lower Elbe lie like elongated islands in the river. They begin near Blankenese with the Schweinesand, now a nature reserve and a place where singing swans and storks stop over. Nesssand, Hahnöfersand (which is linked to the land), Hans-Kalb-Sand, Lühesand, Pagensand, Schwarztonnensand, Rhinplatte, Neufelder Sand, Vogelsand. Experienced Elbe sailors – whether or not they wear the eponymous "Elbsegler" cap – can reel off the names of the sandbanks in their sleep.

Singschwänen und Kranichen als Zwischenstation angeflogen wird. Neßsand, Hahnöfersand (er hat Landanschluß, und auf ihm sind Hamburger Strafvollzugseinrichtungen angesiedelt), Hans-Kalb-Sand, Lühesand, Pagensand, Schwarztonnensand, Rhinplatte, Neufelder Sand, Vogelsand. Erfahrene Elbsegler – mit dieser Mütze gleichen Namens oder auch ohne sie – können die Sände im Schlaf aufsagen.

Auch die Nebenflüsse und Kanäle zählen zum Reichtum dieser Landschaft mit großem Strom, die sich im Urstromtal der Elbe aus der Eiszeit breitgemacht hat. Este, Lühe, Schwinge, Oste am Südufer, Pinnau, Krückau, Stör am Nordufer. Die Schleifen dieser Elbnebenflüsse werden nicht nur von Lustschiffen, sondern immer auch noch von Lastkähnen befahren. Auch hier herrschen Ebbe und Flut.

Auf der einen Seite ist die Elbe bei Hamburg eine hochromantische Wasserstraße. Von den Sonnenuntergängen, die sich im Riesenwasserspiegel des Mühlenberger Lochs bei Blankenese verdoppeln, kann man noch lange träumen. Desgleichen vom Vollmond, wenn er ein silbernes Band auf die Wellen wirft. Die Heerscharen weißer Segel und bunter Spinnaker bei den Sommerregatten sind eine Augenlust, die vom Ufer oder von den Elbhöhen her gratis zu genießen ist. Treibeis im Winter und weiße Schollen, die sich am Ufer mannshoch auftürmen, ziehen ebenfalls zu ihrer Zeit Spaziergänger in Scharen an. Daß die Schiffe auch bei stärkstem Frost ungeschoren in Hamburg ankommen können, dafür sorgen Eisbrecher, die den Hafen und die Fahrrinne freihalten.

## Saubere Elbe – keine Utopie mehr

Doch die Unterelbe ist auch ein Arbeitsstrom, dem die Industrie arg mitgespielt hat. Die vier Atomkraftwerke Krümmel an der Oberelbe, Stade, Brokdorf und Brunsbüttel an der Unterelbe sind brisante Anrainer. Auch die Chemie-Indu-

Another of the riches of this broad river landscape which spread out in the Ice Age glacial valley of the Elbe are the tributaries and canals. The Este, Lühe, Schwinge, Oste on the south bank, and the Pinnau, Krückau and Stör on the north. These meandering tributaries are used not only by pleasure boats but still by barges carrying cargo. They, too, are tidal.

From one point of view, the Elbe near Hamburg is a highly romantic waterway. The sunsets reflected in the gigantic mirror of water at Mühlenberger Loch near Blankenese are something to dream about. The same goes for the sight of the full moon casting a silver ribbon across the waves. The armies of white sails and colourful spinnakers at the summer regattas are a feast for the eyes, which can be enjoyed to the full for free from a vantage point on the river bank or the hills overlooking the river. Ice drifts in winter and white lumps piled as high as a man along the bank draw hordes of walkers in their season. Icebreakers keep the port and shipping lane clear, ensuring that vessels can put into Hamburg unscathed even in the sharpest frosts.

## A clean Elbe – not longer a Utopian dream

However, the Lower Elbe is also a working river in which industry has played a leading role. The four nuclear power stations at Krümmel on the Upper Elbe, Stade, Brokdorf and Brunsbüttel on the Lower Elbe are controversial river-bank occupants. The chemical industry, too, has occupied large stretches of the bank below Hamburg. But in fact the Elbe,

strie hält die Ufer unterhalb von Hamburg stark besetzt. Doch Tatsache ist, daß die Elbe, der in den achtziger Jahren manchmal schier die Luft ausging, heute wieder besser durchatmen kann. Nach der Öffnung der Ostgrenzen wurde 1990 die „Internationale Kommission zum Schutz der Elbe" (IKSE) gegründet. Die von der deutschen und der tschechischen Regierung und der Europäischen Union getragene Institution hat ihren Sitz in Magdeburg und macht ihren Einfluß von der Quelle bis zur Mündung deutlich sichtbar. Neue Klärwerke, stillgelegte Fabriken und die allgemeine Verminderung der Einleitung von Schadstoffen haben die Wasserqualität deutlich verbessert. Ein Signal für diese Wende ist die Vielzahl der Fische, die jetzt wieder in der Elbe zu Hause ist. Experten haben 79 verschiedene Arten festgestellt. Das sind mehr als im Rhein heute überleben können. Aale, Barsche, Brassen, Plötze, Stinte, Störe und Zander. Sie gehen den Fischkuttern wieder in die Netze. Der Stint ist inzwischen zu einer Spezialität geworden, mit der die typischen Hamburger Fischlokale im Frühjahr auf ihren Speisekarten gerne renommieren.

## Hamburgs Vorposten im Wattenmeer

Am Ende der Segeltour von Hamburg die Elbe hinunter hat man so viele Eindrücke gesammelt, daß der Start in der Großstadt schon fast vergessen ist. Und doch taucht sie ganz zum Schluß wieder vor einem auf! Und zwar in Gestalt der Insel Neuwerk und ihrer unbewohnten Nachbarinnen Scharhörn und Nigehörn. Abgesehen von den Jahren 1937 bis 1969 gehört Neuwerk schon seit 1299 zu Hamburg. Der 1310 fertiggestellte Backsteinturm ist somit Hamburgs ältestes erhaltenes Bauwerk. Er hat seine

which in the 1980s was sometimes really running out of breath, can breathe more easily again now. After the opening of the borders with Eastern Europe, in 1990 the International Commission for Protection of the Elbe (IKSE) was founded. The commission, which is funded by the German and Czech governments and the European Union, has its headquarters in Magdeburg and has made its influence clearly felt from source to estuary. New waste-water treatment works, factory closures and a general reduction in pollutants discharged into the river has markedly improved the water quality. One sign of this change is the large number of fish that inhabit the Elbe once more. Experts have identified 79 different species, more than can now survive in the Rhine. Eel, perch, brace, roach, smelt, sturgeon and pike-perch are now caught in fishing-boat nets. In spring, smelts now feature as a speciality on the menus of traditional Hamburg fish restaurants.

## Hamburg's outpost in the mud-flats

By the end of a sailing trip down the Elbe from Hamburg, so many impressions have been gained that the start in the city is almost forgotten. But right at the end it is suddenly there again, in the shape of the island of Neuwerk and its uninhabited neighbours Scharhörn and Nigehörn. Neuwerk has belonged to Hamburg since 1299, with the exception of the period 1937 to 1969. And so its brick tower, built in 1310, is Hamburg's oldest surviving building. It long ago lost its role as Hamburg's advance observation post for Elbe shipping, but still has a lighthouse. Nowadays, Neuwerk has around 35 inhabitants. The ancient tower and the cemetery where unknown seamen found their last resting-place is a popular destination for mud-flat walkers. Those keen not to miss the unforgettable experience of walking through this muddily attractive landscape find them-

Funktion als Hamburgs vorgeschobener
Überwachungsposten der Elbschiffahrt
längst verloren, trägt aber noch ein
Leuchtfeuer. Neuwerk zählt heute etwa
35 Bewohner. Der alte Turm und der
„Friedhof der Namenlosen", auf dem
unbekannte Seeleute ihre letzte Ruhestät-
te fanden, sind ein beliebtes Ziel von
Wattwanderern. Wer sich dies unvergeß-
liche Erlebnis des matschig-schönen
Weges nicht entgehen läßt, durchquert
den Nationalpark Hamburgisches Wat-
tenmeer. Das 117 Quadratkilometer
große Gebiet wurde 1990 per Gesetz
festgelegt, wodurch zugleich die seit den
sechziger Jahren bestehenden Pläne zur
Anlage eines leistungsstarken Tiefwasser-
hafens endgültig aufgegeben wurden.

selves crossing the Hamburgisches Wat-
tenmeer national park. The 117-square-
kilometre area was designated in 1990,
thus putting a stop once and for all for
plans that had existed since the 1960s to
build a highly efficient deep-water port
in the area.

Eisgang bei Wittenber-
gen. Eisbrecher halten
die Fahrrinne frei,
damit die Schiffe auch
bei tiefsten Frosttempe-
raturen sicher im Hafen
einlaufen können.

Drift ice at Wittenber-
gen. Ice-breakers keep
the shipping-lanes clear
so that vessels can sail
safely into port even in
Arctic temperatures.

# Die Alster: Wassersport und Schöner Wohnen
## The Alster: water sports and elegant living

Eigentlich ist die Alster ja nur ein kleiner rechter Nebenfluß der Elbe. Aber die großen aufgestauten Wasserspiegel von Binnen- und Außenalster mitten in der Stadt sind vermutlich einer der Hauptgründe, daß Hamburg heute zu den schönsten Metropolen der Welt zählt. Die Alster ist viel besungen worden. Der Hamburger Dichter Friedrich von Hagedorn (1708–54), der als Angestellter des English Court (der Merchants Adventurers) ein so gutes Auskommen und viel freie Zeit hatte, daß er sich ausgiebig seiner Poesie widmen konnte, schenkte ihr besonders anmutige und spielerische Verse:

Beförderer vieler Lustbarkeiten,
Du angenehmer Alsterfluß!
Du mehrest Hamburgs Seltenheiten
Und ihren fröhlichen Genuß.
Dir schallen zur Ehre,
Du spielende Flut!
Die singenden Chöre,
Der jauchzende Mut.
Der Elbe Schiffahrt macht uns reicher,
Die Alster lehrt gesellig sein!
Durch jene füllen sich die Speicher;
Auf dieser schmeckt der fremde Wein.
In treibenden Nachen
Schifft Eintracht und Lust,
Und Freiheit und Lachen
Erleichtern die Brust.

     Wo die Alster in die Elbe fließt? Hauptsächlich durch das Alsterfleet, an dessen Ende die Schaartorschleuse liegt. Aber auch links und rechts davon, durch das Nikolai- und Herrengrabenfleet (Fleet bedeutet soviel wie Graben oder Kanal) fließt Alsterwasser in Richtung Elbe. Als die Alster noch nicht kanalisiert und durch Schleusen und Sperrwerke zur Elbe hin gesichert war, floß das Elbwasser bei Flut regelmäßig hoch bis in die Eppendorfer und Winterhuder Wiesen. Der Wasserspiegel hob und

Actually the Alster is just a small tributary to the right of the Elbe. But its damming to create the extensive expanses of water of the Inner and Outer Alster in the middle of the city is probably one of the main reasons why Hamburg is now one of the world's most attractive metropolises. The Alster's praises have often been sung. The Hamburg poet Friedrich von Hagedorn (1708–54), who as a Merchant Adventurer and employee of the English court had such a good living and so much free time that he could dedicate himself wholeheartedly to his poetry, dedicated some particularly charming and playful verses to it:

Sponsor of many festivities
Oh lovely Alster river
You increase Hamburg's rarities
And its merry enjoyment.
In your honour
Oh leisure-loving river
Sing choirs
Of jubilation.
Elbe shipping makes us richer
The Alster teaches conviviality
The former fills the warehouses
The latter is where we savour foreign wine.
In drifting barques
Float concord and joy,
And freedom and laughter
Lighten the heart.

     Where does the Alster flow into the Elbe? Mainly through the Alsterfleet, which ends in the Schaartor lock. But Alster water also flows toward the Elbe to the left and right of the Alsterfleet, through the Nikolaifleet and the Herrengrabenfleet ("Fleet" means "canal").

     In the days before the Alster was canalised to flow through locks and dams to the Elbe, at high tide the Elbe regularly flooded the meadows of Eppendorf and Winterhude. The water level rose and fell two metres between tides, at very high tides as much as seven metres. But that was long ago. The river was dammed in the Hamburg urban area at the end of the twelfth century, and water-driven grain mills supplied the

senkte sich durch die Gezeiten um zwei
Meter, bei Hochfluten um bis zu sieben
Meter. Doch das ist lange her. Schon
Ende des 12. Jahrhunderts wurde der
Fluß im Hamburger Stadtgebiet aufges-
taut. Die mit Wasserkraft betriebenen
Kornmühlen versorgten die Stadt mit
Mehl. 1842, beim Großen Brand von
Hamburg, fielen in der Innenstadt allein
acht Alstermühlen den Flammen zum
Opfer. Beim Wiederaufbau der Stadt
wurde der Fluß zum wichtigen Trans-
portweg für Ziegelsteine und Kalk. Der
Kalk kam aus den Steinbrüchen von Bad
Segeberg, wo heute Winnetou und Old
Shatterhand bei den Karl-May-Festspie-
len um die Wette reiten.

**Weiß gesprenkelt mit Segelbooten**

Die Lustschiffe haben die Lastschiffe
längst verdrängt. Bei schönem Wetter ist
die Außenalster heute weiß gesprenkelt
mit Segelbooten. Ruderer legen sich nach
Kommando in die Riemen. Paddler kurven zwischendurch. Tretbootfahrer
machen es sich gemütlich. Nur Schwimmer oder Badende sind nicht mehr zu
sehen. Die erste Alsterbadeanstalt – übrigens nur für Männer – an der Lombardsbrücke ist längst Geschichte. Das
berühmte Freibad am Schwanenwik, wo
sich noch um 1900 Männer und Frauen
getrennt tummelten, gibt es nur noch auf
alten Zeichnungen und Fotografien.
Schwimmen tun nur noch die Schwäne.
Für die Höckerschwäne ist im Haushalt
der Hansestadt extra ein Etat vorgese-
hen, damit sie in ihrem Winterquartier
genug zu fressen kriegen und sich im
Frühjahr wieder gestärkt ins Alstervergnügen stürzen können.

town with flour. In the Great Fire of
Hamburg in 1842, eight Alster mills
were consumed by the flames in the city
centre alone. When the city was rebuilt,
the river was an important transport
route for bricks and lime. The lime came
from the stone quarries of Bad Segeberg,
which are now used for performances of
the Wild West stories of Karl May, a
favourite German children's author.

**Sprinkled with white yacht sails**

Barges have long since given way to
pleasure boats. In fine weather the Outer
Alster is sprinkled with white yacht sails.
Oarsmen bend in rhythm over their
rowlocks. Paddle-boats twist in and out
between them. Pedal-boat drivers take it
easy. The only thing missing are swimmers and bathers. The first Alster swim-
ming-pool by Lombardsbrücke – which
was only for men – has long since been
history. The popular open-air pool at
Schwanenwik, where men and women
still frolicked separately in around 1900,
exists only in old drawings and photo-
graphs. Nowadays, the only swimming is
done by swans. They have their own
allocation in the city budget, so that the

Diese Mühle stand bis
zu ihrem Abriß 1865 an
der Lombardsbrücke.
Im Hintergrund zu se-
hen: die St. Petrikirche,
deren Turm noch fehlt.
Er wurde erst 1878
vollendet.

This mill by the Lom-
bardsbrücke was dem-
olished in 1865. In the
background you can see
St Peter's Church, still
without its tower. It
was not completed until
1878.

140                 Die Alster:
                      Wassersport und Schöner Wohnen          The Alster:
                                           water sports and elegant living

Damen und Herren planschten getrennt in der Außenalster, in der historischen Badeanstalt „Alsterlust" unweit der Lombardsbrücke.

Ladies and gentlemen splashed about separately in the Outer Alster, in the historic Alsterlust swimming pool not far from Lombardsbrücke.

Das sommerliche Alstervergnügen als organisierter Budenzauber rund um die Binnenalster ist auch den Menschen garantiert. Genauso wie das Feuerwerk zum japanischen Kirschblütenfest. Von der Laune des Wetters ist dagegen das größte Alstervergnügen auf dem Eis abhängig. Betreten der Eisfläche gestattet! Dieses offizielle Signal ist der Start zu einer Lustbarkeit ohnegleichen, zu einem Volksfest auf dem Eis mit Musik, Essen, Trinken und Polonäse Blankenese, mit Schlittschuhlaufen, Schliddern, Eishockeyspielen oder einfach nur Flanieren. Der Frost macht die Außenalster zu einer grandiosen Piazza, die nach Süden aufs schönste gesäumt wird von den Bögen der Kennedy- und Lombardsbrücke, dahinter wie filigrane Himmelszeichen die Türme der Hauptkirchen St. Jacobi, St. Petri, St. Katharinen, St. Nikolai und des Rathauses (von links nach rechts).

Wie bedeutsam die Alsterwasserflächen, die aus den mittelalterlichen Mühlenteichen entstanden, für das Bild der Stadt sind, ergibt sich schon aus ihrer Größe. Die Außenalster umfaßt 165 Hektar, die Binnenalster 18 Hektar und die kleine Alster am Rathaus 0,56 Hektar.

hump-billed swans have enough to eat in their winter quarters and are fortified to plunge back into the pleasures of the Alster in springtime.

The Alstervergnügen, or Alster fair, when colourful stands line the banks of the Inner Alster, is a regular annual event, as is the fireworks display that ends the Japanese Cherry Blossom Festival. The biggest Alster fair, however, depends on the whim of the weather, for it is held on the ice. The official go-ahead to step on the ice marks the start of an unparalleled junket, a true folk festival on ice, complete with music, food, drink and the Blankenese polonaise, with ice-skating, sliding, ice-hockey matches or simply strolls across the ice. The freezing weather turns the Outer Alster into a splendid piazza, beautifully lined to the south by the arches of the Kennedybrücke and Lombardsbrücke, with the towers of the churches of St James, St Peter, St Katharine, St Nicholas and the Rathaus (from left to right) rising behind like graceful signs from heaven.

The very size of the Alster lakes that emerged from the mediaeval mill-ponds reveals their importance to the city's appearance. The Outer Alster covers an area of almost 165 hectares, the Inner Alster 18 hectares and the Little Alster by the Rathaus another 0.56 hectares.

## The right and left banks

Those who see the Outer Alster as an urban piazza will also understand the separation between right and left banks that developed in the nineteenth century.

So schön kann die Außenalster im Winter sein. Kinder und Erwachsene haben in dieser Jahreszeit denselben Wunsch. Der Winter möge so viel Frost bringen, daß es wieder zum Alstervergnügen auf dem Eis reicht.

The picture shows how lovely the Outer Alster can look in winter. At this time of year, children and adults want the same thing: for winter to bring enough frost to hold the Alstervergnügen fair on the ice.

## Das rechte und das linke Ufer

Wer die Außenalster als städtische Piazza begreift, versteht auch die starke Trennung in rechtes und linkes Ufer, die sich im 19. Jahrhundert hier ausgebildet hat. Bezeichnend für die Bindung an das eine oder das andere Ufer ist das traditionelle Schachturnier der Schüler „Rechtes Alsterufer gegen linkes Alsterufer". Der Wettbewerb ist so stark besetzt, daß er sogar schon im Guinness-Buch der Rekorde steht.

Im Verlauf des 19. Jahrhunderts, als die Einheit von Wohnen und Arbeiten allmählich zerfiel, zogen die Menschen mehr und mehr aus der innerstädtischen Enge vor die Tore. Zunächst waren es nur die reichen Kaufleute, die dem Lärm und der Hektik nach Kontorschluß und an den Wochenenden entflohen. Es entstanden viele Villen jenseits des Dammtors. Am rechten Ufer der Außenalster reihten sich bald die noblen Wohngebäude und in ihrem Schatten Handwerker- und Dienstbotenunterkünfte aneinander. In der reichen Gründerzeit um 1900 kamen viele großartige Häuser hinzu.

Symbolic of the attachment to one bank or the other is the traditional "right versus left bank" schools' chess tournament. So many schoolchildren take part in the competition that it even features in the Guinness Book of Records.

In the course of the nineteenth century, as the unity of living and working gradually declined, more and more people moved out of the crowded inner city to the outskirts. Initially it was only the rich businessmen who fled from the noise and hubbub after office hours and at weekends. Many villas were built beyond Dammtor. Soon row on row of up-market residential buildings were strung out on the right bank of the Outer Alster, with craftsmen's and tradesmen's dwellings following in their shadow. In the prosperous period of rapid industrial expansion around 1900 they were joined by a large number of magnificent houses.

An der Alster kann jeder nach seiner Fasson selig werden.
In der Isestraße (rechts) wohnt „man". Die Harvestehuder lieben ihre schicken Häuserfassaden.
Richard Meier baute dem Reeder Rickmers ein Haus, das als Hommage an die klassische Moderne die Architektur des rechten Alsterufers auffrischt.

By the Alster, there are resting-places enough for everyone.
Isestrasse (right) is where "one" lives. Harvestehude people love their smart house facades.
This house was designed by Richard Meier for shipowner Rickmers. It pays tribute to classical modernism, lending a refreshing touch to the architecture on the right bank of the Alster.

Nach 1945 hat sich am rechten Alsterufer mit den Stadtteilen Rotherbaum, Pöseldorf, Harvestehude und Eppendorf viel geändert. Die Villengärten sind seit der Internationalen Gartenbauausstellung 1953 zum öffentlichen Park umgewandelt. Eine traumhaft schöne Anlage, die an Wochenenden heute regelmäßig zu einem Terrain des Sehens und des Gesehenwerdens wird, wo Spaziergänger, Hunde und Jogger sich auf die Füße treten.

Gewandelt hat sich auch die Funktion mancher historischen Villa. Die Hochschule für Musik und Theater an der Ecke Harvestehuder Weg/Milchstraße, der Hoffmann und Campe Verlag etwas weiter nördlich haben heute ihr Domizil

After 1945, a great deal changed in the districts of Rotherbaum, Pöseldorf, Harvestehude and Eppendorf on the right bank of the Alster. The villa gardens fronting the lake were turned into a public park for the 1953 International Garden Show, and have remained public ever since. At weekends, this highly attractive expanse of green becomes a place to see and be seen, with strollers, dogs and joggers all competing for space.

Some of the historic villas have been given a new function, too. The College of Music and Theatre on the corner of Harvestehuder Weg and Milchstrasse and Hoffmann und Campe publishers a little further north are housed in buildings dating back to the days of Hamburg's grand expansion. Many companies, too, have discovered the prestigious location on the right bank of the Outer Alster. Closest to the water is the Anglo-German Club in a villa by Krugkoppelbrücke.

For many years the right bank with its Hanseatic patrician houses, its spacious apartment buildings on both sides of

in Gebäuden aus der Zeit, als Hamburg sich hier auf das nobelste erweiterte. Und auch viele Wirtschaftsunternehmen haben die repräsentative Lage am rechten Ufer der Außenalster für sich entdeckt. Der Anglo-German-Club in der Villa vor der Krugkoppelbrücke ist dem Wasser am nächsten.

Das rechte Ufer mit seinen hanseatischen Patrizierhäusern, den großzügigen Etagenwohnungen rechts und links der Rothenbaumchaussee, rund um den Eppendorfer Baum, am Isekanal und im Universitätsviertel sowie den schicken Geschäften und den kulturellen Institutionen – diese Quartiere von schöner wohnen und teuer kaufen waren viele Jahre das Nonplusultra an der Alster. Doch das linke Ufer – früher als „falsches" Ufer diskriminiert – hat längst aufgeholt. An den Straßen Bellevue und Schöne Aussicht sind die Quadratmeterpreise heute mindestens so hoch wie auf dem „richtigen" Ufer westlich der Alster. Die Stadtteile Uhlenhorst und Winterhude haben auch in den von der Alster entfernteren Lagen an Attraktivität gewonnen. Nur schade, daß es keinen Personenfährverkehr mehr auf der Außenalster gibt, der rechtes und linkes Ufer verbindet. Noch um 1900 fuhr

Rothenbaumchaussee, around Eppendorfer Baum, along the Isekanal and in the university district, not to mention the smart shops and cultural institutions, this area of elegant living and expensive shopping was the non plus ultra on the Alster. But the left bank – formerly looked down on as the "wrong" bank – has long since caught up. Nowadays property prices on Bellevue and Schöne Aussicht are at least as high as on the "right" bank to the west of the Alster. The districts of Uhlenhorst and Winterhude, even those further away from the Alster, have increased their appeal. It is just a pity that there is no longer a passenger ferry linking the right and left banks of the Outer Alster. In around 1900 there was a ferry from Jungfern-

Ferienstimmung an der Alster (links).
Der Rondeelteich (oben) ist eine der idyllischen Ausbuchtungen der Außenalster.
Am Feenteich ist der Himmel weit. Die Villenstraße, die den Feenteich von der Außenalster trennt, heißt zu Recht Schöne Aussicht.

Vacation mood on the Alster (left).
The Rondeelteich (above) is an idyllic inlet of the Outer Alster.
A wide open sky over the Feenteich, or Fairy Pond. The mansion-lined road separating the Feenteich from the Outer Alster is appropriately named Schöne Aussicht, or Beautiful View.

Die Alster am Leinpfad lieben Wassersportler und Spaziergänger gleichermaßen. Im Hintergrund die Anlage des Damenstifts Kloster St. Johannis

Water sports enthusiasts and walkers find the Alster by Leinpfad, or Towpath, equally attractive. In the background is the St. Johannis nunnery complex.

regelmäßig alle 15 Minuten, nachts alle halbe Stunde, eine Fähre vom Jungfernstieg nach Eppendorf und Winterhude. Heute dient die Alsterflotte, deren Schiffe am Jungfernstieg starten, nur noch dem Sightseeing. Die weißen Schiffe der Flotte sind nach den Beken (niederdeutsch Bek gleich Bach), den kleinen Nebenflüssen der Alster, benannt. 27 Nebenflüsse, Bäche und Kanäle speisen die insgesamt 56 Kilometer lange Alster von der Quelle nahe dem schleswig-holsteinischen Ort Henstedt bis zur Mündung in die Elbe: Ammersbek, Bredenbek, Eilbek (eigentlich der Unterlauf der Wandse), Goldbek, Isebek, Osterbek, Rodenbek, Saselbek, Tarpenbek ...

stieg to Eppendorf and Winterhude every 15 minutes, and every half hour at night. Nowadays the Alster fleet of vessels departing from Jungfernstieg is purely for sightseeing purposes. The white boats in the fleet are named after the Beken (Bek is Low German for Bach, meaning stream), the small Alster tributaries. Twenty-seven tributaries, streams and canals feed the Alster as it flows along its 56-kilometre course from the source near Henstedt in Schleswig-Holstein to where it flows into the Elbe: Ammersbek, Bredenbek, Eilbek (actually the lower reaches of the Wandse), Isebek, Osterbek, Rodenbek, Saselbek, Tarpenbek ...

**In the labyrinth of canals**

Along with the extended and short tours of the port, a trip on a boat of the Alster fleet is one of the great attractions in

Der Hayns Park zwischen Eppendorfer Landstraße und Alsterlauf war ehemals Teil des Landsitzes von Max Theodor Hayn (1809–88), einem aus Breslau stammenden Kaufmann.

Hayns Park between Eppendorfer Landstrasse and Alsterlauf formed part of the estate of Max Theodor Hayn (1809–88), a merchant from Breslau, now in Poland.

## Im Labyrinth der Kanäle

Die Fahrten mit der Alsterflotte zählen nebst der großen und der kleinen Hafenrundfahrt zu den Attraktionen der Stadt am Wasser. Auch wo die Wasserwege der Alster nördlich der Krugkoppelbrücke für den Fremden unübersichtlich werden, wo sich der Kanufahrer oder Ruderer ohne Plan im Labyrinth der Kanäle verirrt, ist die Alster doch immer noch der klare Trennungsstrich zwischen den Stadtteilen. Wie der Fluß Eppendorf und Winterhude trennt, so markiert er auch die Grenzen zwischen Fuhlsbüttel und Groß Borstel einerseits sowie Ohlsdorf und Alsterdorf andererseits.

Daß das 587 Quadratkilometer große Entwässerungsgebiet der Alster lange Urwald und nur dünn besiedelt war,

Hamburg, the city on the water. North of Krugkoppelbrücke, where the Alster waterways become confusing for strangers, where canoeists and oarsmen without a map easily get lost in the labyrinth of canals, the Alster remains a clear dividing line. In the same way as the river separates Eppendorf and Winterhude, it also marks the boundary

Die Alster fließt bei Wellingsbüttel als ein verschwiegener Wasserlauf.

The Alster at Wellingsbüttel is a secluded stream.

sagen auch die Namen. Hude heißt Lagerplatz, Büttel bedeutet Siedlung. Die frühen Alsteranrainer trieben mit der Hansestadt regen Handel und bewegten sich mit ihren Waren längs der Treidel- und Leinpfade. Nur die zum Kloster Harvestehude zählenden Ansiedlungen gerieten nach der Reformation unter die Hoheitsmacht Hamburg.

Der Alsterwanderweg erschließt heute das Flußgebiet bis zur Quelle. Die Alster fängt klein an. Noch 26 Kilometer von der Hamburger Grenze entfernt, ist sie in Schleswig-Holstein zunächst nur ein wenig Aufsehen erregender Bach. Es braucht viel Regen, wenn Paddler sich auf die Tour von der Quelle bis zur Mündung machen wollen. Geest und Marsch, Heide und Moor sind am Oberlauf der Alster wahre Paradiese für Vögel und Frösche oder erholungsuchende Wanderer. Mehr als 100 Vogelarten haben die Ornithologen im Quellgebiet der Alster gezählt. Rohrweide, Schleiereule und Wachtelkönig sind hier zu Hause. Wo dann die Gartenhaussiedlungen und Schrebergartenanlagen beginnen, wird die Natur domestiziert. Kein Terrain mehr für Landschaftsmaler, die vor allem um 1900, als die Plein-air-Malerei ihre große Zeit hatte, die Alster immer wieder in Öl und Aquarell festhielten. Der Fluß hat vielen Orten seinen Namen gegeben: Alsterallee, Alsterarkaden, Alsterberg, Alsterblick, Alsterchaussee, Alsterfurt, Alsterglacis, Alsterkehre, Alsterkrugchaussee, Alsterterrasse, Alstertor, Alstertwiete, Alsterwiesen. Wer im Lokal ein Glas „Alsterwasser" verlangt, wird an Alster, Elbe, aber auch am Rhein anstandslos bedient. „Alsterwasser" – das ist Bier mit Zitronenbrause. Nur an der bayerischen Isar nennt man das Alsterwasser „Radlermoaß". Gemeint ist dasselbe.

between Fuhlsbüttel and Grossborstel on one side and Ohlsdorf and Alsterdorf on the other.

One of the indications that the 587-square-kilometre area drained by the Alster was once sparsely-populated primaeval forest are the names. Hude means camp, and Büttel means settlement. The people who lived beside the Alster in the early days traded with the Hanseatic town and transported their goods along the towpaths. Only the settlements belonging to Harvestehude convent became part of Hamburg after the Reformation.

Nowadays, you can walk right to the source of the river along the Alster Footpath. The Alster starts small. In Schleswig-Holstein, 26 kilometres from the Hamburg border, it is just an unprepossessing stream. Only if there is plenty of rain can canoeists paddle all the way from source to mouth. Along the upper reaches, heath, marsh and moorland are a true paradise for birds, frogs or hikers in search of relaxation. Ornithologists have counted over 100 species of bird in the region where the Alster rises. It is home to reed warblers, barn owls and corncrake. Where the summer-houses and allotments begin, nature becomes domesticated. It is no longer a place for landscape painters, who in the years around 1900, when open-air painting was in its heyday, captured the Alster in oil and water-colours time and again.

The river has bestowed its name on many places: Alsterallee, Alsterfurt, Alsterglacis, Alsterkehre, Alsterkrugchaussee, Alsterterrasse, Alstertor, Alstertwiete, Alsterwiesen. Ask for a glass of "Alsterwasser" (Alster water) in a pub, and you will have no trouble being served, whether on the Elbe, the Alster or the Rhine. An Alsterwasser is a beer with lemonade, in other words, what the British call a shandy. Only in Bavaria do they have another name for it – "Radlermoass." But they mean the same thing.

Ein unbekannter Künstler malte dies hübsche Aquarell von der Alsterschleife bei Mellingstedt im 19. Jahrhundert. Die Brücke mit dem Wehr stand an der heutigen Mellingburger Schleuse.

An unknown artist painted this attractive water colour of the horseshoe bend in the Alster at Mellingstedt in the nineteenth century. The bridge and weir were on the site of the present-day Mellingburg Lock.

# Die Hauptkirchen und andere Himmelsstürmer
## The main churches and other tall towers

In der Schönheitskonkurrenz der Städte liegt Hamburg mit zwei Pluspunkten ganz weit vorne. Nicht nur, daß zwei Flüsse das Bild der Stadt prägen. Wo die Alster in die Elbe fließt, hat sich zudem ein historisches Panorama erhalten, von dem andere Städte nur noch träumen können. Wie große Ausrufezeichen zeichnen die Türme der fünf Hauptkirchen Hamburgs Silhouette an den Himmel. Eine Silhouette, die schon im Mittelalter das Bild der Stadt prägte. Die älteste Kirche ist St. Petri an der Mönckebergstraße, die 1195 zum erstenmal als Marktkirche erwähnt wurde. Es folgten St. Nikolai am Hopfenmarkt, St. Katharinen gegenüber der heutigen Speicherstadt und St. Jacobi an der Steinstraße – drei Gotteshäuser, die im 13. Jahrhundert gegründet wurden. Die jüngste in der Reihe der fünf Hauptkirchen ist St. Michaelis an der Englischen Planke/ Krayenkamp, deren Grundstein Mitte des 17. Jahrhunderts gelegt wurde.

In the beauty contest between cities, Hamburg has two advantages that put it far ahead of the competition. Not only is its appearance graced by two rivers, but where the Alster flows into the Elbe a historic panorama has been preserved which other cities can only dream of. The towers of the five principal churches stand out on the skyline like big exclamation marks. A silhouette that shaped the town's appearance way back in the Middle Ages. The oldest church is St Peter's (Petrikirche) on Mönckebergstrasse, the first written record of which as a market church goes back to 1195. It was followed by St Nicholas's (Nikolaikirche) on Hopfenmarkt, St Katharine's (Katharinenkirche) opposite what is now the Warehouse City and St James's (Jacobikirche) on Steinstrasse – three churches established in the thirteenth century. The youngest of the five principal churches is St Michael's on Englische Planke and Krayenkamp, the foundation stone of which was laid in the mid-seventeenth century. At the end of the nineteenth century this historic skyline of towers was joined by the Rathaus tower, and in 1968 by the Heinrich Hertz Tower on the exhibition grounds, generally known in Hamburg

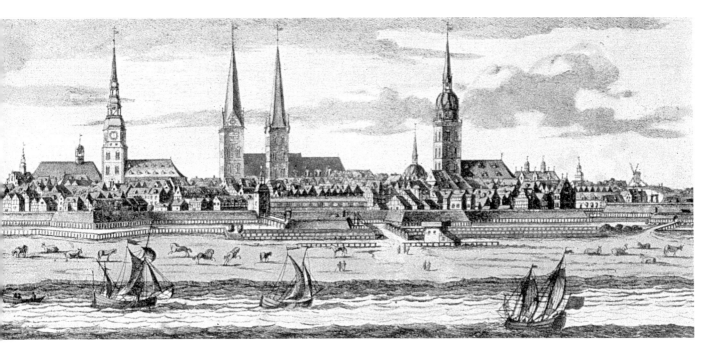

Zu dieser historischen Turmsilhouette gesellten sich Ende des 19. Jahrhunderts der Rathausturm und im Januar 1968 der Heinrich-Hertz-Turm am Messegelände, der in Hamburg kurz Fernsehturm oder „Tele-Michel" genannt wird. Sieben unübersehbare Himmelstürme, denen in der Silhouette der Stadt kein Hochhaus ernsthaft Konkurrenz macht.

### Hamburg von oben

„Der Michel" ist Hamburgs berühmtestes Wahrzeichen. Der markante Turm der St. Michaeliskirche ist aus allen vier Himmelsrichtungen von weither zu sehen. Von der Pförtnerloge bis zur Kirchturmspitze mißt „der Michel" 132 Meter. Von der Turmplattform aus – zu Fuß oder mit dem Fahrstuhl zu erreichen – geht der Blick weit bis zu den Harburger Bergen im Süden, über die Außenalster im Norden und bis Blankenese im Westen. Zu Füßen liegt dem Besucher die

as the Fernsehturm (TV tower) or the "Tele-Michel" (an allusion to the nickname for St Michael's church, which is commonly called the "Michel"). Seven towers that cannot be overlooked, and for which no skyscraper is serious competition in the town skyline.

### Hamburg from above

"Der Michel" is Hamburg's best-known landmark. The distinctive tower of St Michael's church is visible from afar in all four directions. From the porter's lodge to the tip of its tower, the Michel is 132 metres high. From the tower platform – which can be reached by lift or on foot – there is a panoramic view as far as the hills of Harburg to the south, across the Outer Alster to the north and to Blankenese to the west. At the visitor's feet lies the Neustadt, which acquired its magnificent triple-naved hall church when St Michael's was consecrated in 1661.

As chance would have it, in the very year when St Michael's was consecrated,

Hamburgs Stadtsilhouette um 1690. Von links nach rechts die Kirchtürme von St. Michaelis, St. Nikolai, St. Katharinen, St. Petri, St. Marien und St. Jacobi.

Hamburg's skyline in around 1690. From left to right are the church towers of St Michael's, St Nicholas', St Katharine's, St Peter's, St Mary's and St James'.

Zu Füßen der Micha-
eliskirche auf dem
Schaarmarkt herrschte
buntes Markttreiben.
Die 1857 von Wilhelm
Heuer gefertigte Litho-
graphie ist im Besitz des
Museums für Hambur-
gische Geschichte.

Schaarmarkt at the foot
of St Michael's Church
was the scene of bustl-
ing market activity.
This 1857 lithograph
by Wilhelm Heuer is
held by the Museum for
Hamburg History.

Baumeister der
St. Michaeliskirche
Ernst Georg Sonnin
(1713–94)

Architect of
St Michael's church
Ernst Georg Sonnin
(1713–94)

Neustadt, die mit der Einweihung der
dreischiffigen Hallenkirche St. Michaelis
im Jahr 1661 ihr großartiges Gotteshaus
erhielt.

Der Zufall wollte es, daß im Jahr der
Einweihung von St. Michaelis die abge-
dankte Königin Christine von Schweden
zum wiederholten Male in der Nachbarschaft der neuen Kirche ihren Einzug
hielt. Und zwar im Haus ihres zur jüdischen Gemeinde Hamburgs gehörenden
Finanzberaters Diego Teixeira. Die Königin gab an der Elbe Feste, von denen die
Stadt sprach. Daß die Tochter von
Gustav II. Adolf, der ein starker Streiter
für den Protestantismus war, je einen
Gottesdienst besuchte, ist eher unwahr-
scheinlich. Denn sie war längst zum
katholischen Glauben übergetreten.

Knapp neunzig Jahre nach der Einweihung wurde St. Michaelis vom Blitz
getroffen und sank in Schutt und Asche.
Die Kirche, wie wir sie heute kennen, ist
das Werk von Leonhard Prey und Ernst
Georg Sonnin. Das 1762 geweihte
Gebäude wurde noch zweimal ein Raub
der Flammen: 1906, als bei Reparaturarbeiten ein Brand ausgelöst wurde, und

who should turn up in the neighbourhood on one of many visits but Christine, queen of Sweden until she abdicat-
ed? She was on a visit to her financial
adviser Diego Teixeira, a member of
Hamburg's Jewish community. The ex-
queen held parties that were the talk of
the town. It seems unlikely that the
daughter of Gustaf Adolf II, who had
been a strong champion of Protes-
tantism, ever took part in a church service. For she had long since converted to
Catholicism.

Less than 90 years after its consecra-
tion, St Michael's was struck by light-
ning and was burnt to cinders. The
church we know today is the work of
Johann Leonhard Prey and Ernst Georg
Sonnin. The building consecrated in
1762 fell victim to fire twice more: in
1906, when a fire broke out during
repair works, and in World War II. Each
time, it was reconstructed on the histori-

im Zweiten Weltkrieg. Die Rekonstruktionen orientierten sich jedoch jeweils am historischen Vorbild. Der barocke, festliche Innenraum imponiert bis heute vor allem durch die geschwungene Empore. Lieblingsfigur vieler Besucher ist der auf Zehenspitzen auf einer Kugel schwebende Engel über der Kanzel.

## Musik in der Kirche

In der Gruft von St. Michaelis ruht nicht nur der Baumeister Sonnin, sondern auch der zweite Sohn von Johann Sebastian Bach. Carl Philipp Emanuel Bach (1714–88) war zu seinen Zeiten berühmter als sein Vater. Als Nachfolger seines Paten Georg Philipp Telemann wurde er 1768 Städtischer Musikdirektor und Kantor am Gymnasium Johanneum. Somit oblag ihm die Oberaufsicht über die gesamte kirchliche Musik in der Stadt. Die bis in die Gegenwart reichende große Tradition der Kirchenmusik in Hamburg hat ihre Wurzeln in dem Wirken Telemanns und Bachs.

Das Quartier rund um den Michel ist bunt und vielfältig. Eine breite Treppenanlage führt zum Verlagsgebäude von Gruner + Jahr. Der personalstarke Mediengigant am Hafenrand hat in den vergangenen Jahren in den Seitenstraßen neue Läden, Restaurants und Kneipen entstehen lassen. Die größte Anziehungskraft für Touristen hat aber eine kleine Gasse am Krayenkamp, deren älteste Häuser schon zu Beginn des 17. Jahrhunderts errichtet wurden. Die Krameramtswohnungen, ursprünglich errichtet für die Witwen der Händlerzunft, geben nach ihrer Restaurierung (1971–74) heute eine idyllische Vorstellung vom Wohnen im Hamburg vergangener Jahrhunderte.

Noch einmal rund 400 Jahre älter als die Krameramtswohnungen ist Hamburgs erste Pfarrkirche St. Petri. Der massige Backsteinbau an der Mönckebergstraße hat viele Vorläufer. Das erste schriftliche Zeugnis dieser Marktkirche

Hamburgs berühmtes Wahrzeichen steht in Flammen. Am 3. Juli 1906 fing der Turm der St. Michaeliskirche bei Sanierungsarbeiten Feuer, wurde aber innerhalb kurzer Zeit wieder rekonstruiert.

Hamburg's famous landmark in flames. St Michael's Church tower caught fire during renovation works on 3 July 1906, but was rebuilt soon afterwards.

cal model. To this day, the Baroque, formal interior impresses above all with its curving gallery. A favourite with many visitors is the angel poised on tip-toe on a ball above the pulpit.

## Music in the church

St Michael's crypt is the burial place not just of its architect Sonnin but also of the second son of Johann Sebastian Bach. In his day, Carl Philipp Emanuel Bach (1714–88) was more famous than his father. In 1768 he succeeded his godfather Georg Philipp Telemann as municipal director of music and cantor at the Johanneum high school. He was thus responsible for all church music in the city. Hamburg's great tradition of church music, a tradition that continues still today, has its roots in the work of Telemann and Bach.

Carl Philipp Emanuel Bach, zweiter Sohn von Johann Sebastian Bach, wurde 1768 Musikdirektor der fünf Hamburger Hauptkirchen.

Carl Philipp Emanuel Bach, the second son of Johann Sebastian Bach, became musical director of Hamburg's five main churches in 1768.

Der Innenraum der St. Michaeliskirche ist festlich schön. Ein herrlicher Rahmen auch für Konzerte

The formal beauty of St Michael's Church interior is also a wonderful backdrop for concerts.

stammt aus dem Jahr 1195. Im 14. und 15. Jahrhundert wurde neu gebaut und erweitert. Nachdem das Gotteshaus 1842 beim Großen Brand von Hamburg ein Opfer der Flammen wurde, schufen Alexis de Chateauneuf und Hermann Peter Fersenfeldt den heutigen Neubau, der sich an gotische Formen anlehnt, aber zugleich einen praktisch zu nutzenden Kirchenraum umgibt. Es ist noch nicht lange her, da zog in St. Petri sogar moderne Bühnentechnik ein, nämlich für das Musical „Jesus Christ Superstar".

The district around St Michael's is varied and interesting. A broad flight of steps leads down to the headquarters of publishers Gruner + Jahr. In recent years, this media giant on the edge of the port and its many staff have led to the opening of new shops, restaurants and bars in the surrounding side-streets. However, the greatest attraction for tourists is a narrow alley on Krayenkamp, the oldest buildings of which were erected at the beginning of the seventeenth century. Known as the Krameramtswohnungen, they were originally almshouses built for the widows of tradesmen. They were completely restored in 1971–74, and now provide an idyllic idea of what it was like living in Hamburg in centuries past.

Around 400 years older even than the Krameramtswohnungen is St Peter's, Hamburg's oldest parish church. The massive redbrick building on Mönckebergstrasse had many predecessors. The first written record of this market church dates back to 1195. In the fourteenth and fifteenth centuries it was rebuilt and extended. After it fell victim to the Great Fire of Hamburg in 1842, the present-day building was designed by Alexis de Chateauneuf and Hermann Peter Fersenfeldt. It is inspired by Gothic form while at the same time providing an interior space that can be put to practical use. It is not so long ago that modern stage engineering moved into St Peter's, for the musical "Jesus Christ Superstar."

**Meister Bertram's altar**

The most famous work of art from St Peter's interior can now be viewed in the Hamburger Kunsthalle. The high altar, completed by Meister Bertram in 1383,

## Meister Bertrams Altar

Das berühmteste Kunstwerk der Innenausstattung von St. Petri ist heute in der
Hamburger Kunsthalle zu sehen. Der
1383 von Meister Bertram vollendete
Hochaltar gilt als eins der bedeutendsten
historischen Kunstwerke der Hansestadt.

St. Petri steht wie eine heilige Trutz-
burg mitten im Einkaufstrubel der
Mönckebergstraße zwischen Rathaus
und Hauptbahnhof. Weniger Menschen,
dafür aber mehr Autos passieren die
benachbarte Hauptkirche St. Jacobi an
der Steinstraße. Der Name der Straße
weist zurück ins Mittelalter. Die Steinstraße wurde als erster innerstädtischer
Weg mit Steinen gepflastert.

St. Jacobi, wenig später als St. Petri
gegründet und urkundlich 1255 erstmals
erwähnt, wirkt von außen ebenso nord-
deutsch streng und verschlossen wie das
benachbarte Gotteshaus. Die Kirche liegt
heute im Kontorhausviertel. Chilehaus,
Sprinkenhof, Meßberg- und Mohlenhof
dominieren dieses Quartier der tausend
Bürofenster. Da ist es gut zu wissen, daß
gegenüber von St. Jacobi an der Steinstraße im 14. Jahrhundert Äpfel wuchsen
– in einem Pomarium, einem Apfelgar-
ten, den der Graf von Holstein-Stormarn
den Blauen Schwestern, den Beginen,
geschenkt hatte.

Die im Zweiten Weltkrieg ausgebrann-
te und in protestantischer Strenge
wiederhergestellte Kirche besitzt die
größte erhaltene Barockorgel Norddeutschlands. Sie ist ein Meisterwerk
Arp Schnitgers (1648–1719), der nicht
nur in Norddeutschland Orgeln baute,
sondern auch in den Niederlanden, in
Skandinavien, England, Rußland, Spanien und Portugal. Die Arp-Schnitger-
Orgel von St. Jacobi ist heute restauriert.
Ein Wunderwerk für Augen und Ohren.
Wie die Stadtsilhouette mit ihren berühmten Kirchtürmen im Jahr 1681 aussah – damals noch inklusive Domturm –
ist auf einem Gemälde en détail zu sehen,
das im Langhaus von St. Jacobi hängt.
Sehenswert ist auch der Lukas-Altar. Ein

is regarded as one of Hamburg's most
important historical works of art.

St Peter's stands like a sacred fortress
amidst the hustle and bustle of shoppers
on Mönckebergstrasse, between the
Rathaus and the main station. Fewer
people, but more cars, pass by the neighbouring principal church of St James on
Steinstrasse. The name of the street
(which means "stone street") goes back

Das Aquarell von Ru-
dolf Loewendei zeigt
die St. Jacobikirche von
Südosten um 1880.
Davor eine Anschlag-
säule

This water colour by
Rudolf Loewendei
shows St James's
Church from the south-
east in around 1880. In
front of it is an
advertising column.

Der Innenraum der St. Jacobikirche ist geschmückt mit einem der hervorragendsten Hamburger Kunstwerke, der aufwendig restaurierten Arp-Schnitger-Orgel aus dem späten 17. Jahrhundert.

The interior of St James' Church is adorned by one of Hamburg's most outstanding works of art, the lavishly restored late 17th-century organ by Arp Schnitger.

Kunstwerk, das eine Leihgabe der Hamburger Malerinnung ist. Lukas ist der Schutzheilige der Maler, und der Altar zeigt ihn, wie er Maria mit dem Jesuskind malt und sich von einem Gehilfen die Farben vorbereiten läßt.

Eine noch größere und schönere Orgel als für St. Jacobi baute Arp Schnitger für die Pfarrkirche St. Nikolai am Hopfenmarkt. Sie wurde zerstört, als das

to the Middle Ages, when it was the first road in the inner city to be cobbed with stones.

From the outside, St James's founded a little later than St Peter's and first mentioned in records in 1255, looks as North German, austere and reserved as the neighbouring church. St James's is now in a business district. This district of a thousand office windows is dominated by the Chilehaus, Sprinkenhof, Messberghof and Mohlenhof. So it is good to know that in the fourteenth century there were applies growing opposite the church in Steinstrasse – in a pomarium, or apple garden, which the Count of Holstein-Stormarn had given to the "blue nuns," the Beguines.

The church, which was burnt out in the World War II and restored in austere Protestant style, has North Germany's largest remaining Baroque organ. It is a masterpiece by Arp Schnitger (1648–1719), who built organs not only in northern Germany, but also in the Netherlands, Scandinavia, England, Russia, Spain and Portugal. St James's Arp Schnitger organ has been beautifully restored and is a treat for both eyes and ears. In the nave of St James's hangs a painting that shows in detail what the town skyline with its famous church towers – which at that time included the cathedral tower – looked like in 1681. Also worth seeing is the Lukasaltar (St Luke Altar), a work of art lent by the Hamburg Painters' Guild. St Luke is the patron saint of painters, and the altar shows the saint painting the Virgin Mary with the Christ child, while an assistant mixes his colours.

Arp Schnitger built an even bigger and better organ for the parish church of St Nicholas on Hopfenmarkt. It was destroyed when the building was burnt down in the Great Fire of 1842. The church was subsequently rebuilt in Gothic style. But as the city centre was increasingly transformed into a business and shopping area, the congregation in what had been a densely-populated

Gebäude 1842 beim Großen Brand den Flammen zum Opfer fiel und anschließend in gotischen Formen wieder aufgebaut wurde. Doch die Gemeinde in dem ehemals dicht bewohnten Kirchspiel schrumpfte, je mehr die Innenstadt sich zu einer „City", zu einer Büro- und Einkaufsstadt wandelte. Als das Gebäude im Zweiten Weltkrieg erneut in Schutt und Asche fiel, wurde beschlossen, die neue Kirche am Klosterstern anzusiedeln. Die Ruine der alten Kirche von St. Nikolai ist heute Gedenkstätte für die Opfer von Krieg und Gewaltherrschaft des Nationalsozialismus. Eindrucksvoll ragt der 1874 geweihte Turm in den Himmel. Mit 145 Metern ist er der höchste Kirchturm Hamburgs und nach dem Ulmer Münster und dem Kölner Dom der drittgrößte Steinkirchturm Deutschlands.

## Turmspitze mit goldener Krone

Von St. Nikolai nach St. Katharinen. Das ist nur ein Katzensprung über die Ost-West-Straße und das Nikolaifleet. Die goldene Krone auf der Turmspitze leuchtet von weitem. Doch die Kirche selber strebt nicht gotisch gen Himmel. Das Gebäude sitzt eher behaglich breit auf der Erde, beschützt von einem mächtigen Dach. St. Katharinen ist die „wohnlichste" der fünf Hauptkirchen, nicht so festlich wie St. Michaelis, nicht so streng wie St. Petri und St. Jacobi. Auch St. Katharinen wurde im Zweiten Weltkrieg erheblich zerstört. Den Bomben fiel die reiche Dekoration im Inneren zum Opfer. Die betont schlichte und moderne Innenausstattung, zu der man sich in den fünfziger Jahren entschloß, macht die Kirche geeignet für vielerlei Ereignisse. In den neunziger Jahren überstand sie unbe-

parish dwindled. When the building was reduced to ruins again in World War II, it was decided to move the new church to Klosterstern. The ruins of the old St Nicholas' are now a memorial to the victims of war and National Socialist tyranny. The tower, consecrated in 1874, still stretches impressively skyward. At 145 metres it is Hamburg's tallest church tower, and the third tallest in Germany after Ulm Minster and Cologne Cathedral.

## Spire with a golden crown

From St Nicholas to St Katharine, just a stone's throw away across Ost-West-Strasse and the Nikolaifleet. The golden crown on its spire gleams from afar. But the church itself does not reach heavenward, Gothic-style. Rather, it rests comfortably on the ground, protected by a massive roof. St Katharine's is the „homeliest" of the five principle church-

Der Turm der St. Nikolaikirche ist mit 145 Metern der höchste der Hamburger Kirchtürme und – nach dem Ulmer Münster und dem Kölner Dom – der dritthöchste Kirchturm Deutschlands. Er bleibt als Mahnmal gegen den Krieg erhalten, und die Kirchenruine wurde als Gedenkstätte eingerichtet.

The 145-metre tower of St Nicholas' Church is the tallest church tower in Hamburg, and the third tallest in Germany after Ulm Minster and Cologne Cathedral. It has been retained as an anti-war monument and the church ruins have been turned into a memorial.

Der Turm von St. Katharinen beherrscht die Hafenmeile gegenüber der Speicherstadt.

St Katharine's Church tower dominates the port area opposite the Warehouse City.

es, less formal than St Michael's, less austere than St Peter's and St James's.

It, too, suffered considerable destruction in World War II. Its rich interior decor also fell victim to the bombs. The very plain, modern interior the architects decided to go for in the 1950s makes the church a suitable venue for all kinds of events. In the 1990s it even survived a techno party unscathed. Walking round the outside of the building, you come across the portals of two historic town houses set into the the facade, providing a little idea of the urban milieu in which St Katharine's once set the tone.

The tower of the Rathaus, Hamburg's city hall, opened in 1897, is markedly different from those of the principal churches. In the over-zealous Wilhelminian era people did not go for plain and simple style, but for a great deal of ornamentation pregnant with symbolic meaning. Imperial eagles, heralds and phoenixes jostle for place on the tower. Its position at the Rathaus' central axis is not accidental either. The tower stands in the centre of the political power of the House of Burgesses (to the left) and the Senate (to the right). Be that as it may, anyone entering the Rathaus through the tower portal is deeply impressed by the grand gesture of a building which represents more than any other the self-assurance of the Free and Hanseatic City.

### A welcome from "Tele-Michel"

But taller than all the rest is a plain purpose-built tower completed in 1968, the Deutsche Bundespost telecommunications tower on Rentzelstrasse. The Fernsehturm, as it is commonly known,

schadet selbst eine Techno-Party. Wer um das Gebäude herumwandert, wird die Portale von zwei historischen Bürgerhäusern an der Fassade entdecken, die eine kleine Vorstellung von dem städtischen Milieu geben, in dem die St. Katharinenkirche früher einmal den Ton angab.

Der Turm des 1897 eingeweihten Rathauses unterscheidet sich deutlich von den Türmen der Hamburger Hauptkirchen. Im Übereifer der Gründerzeit war nicht die schlichte Form Trumpf, sondern vielfacher Schmuck mit hoher symbolischer Bedeutung. Am Turm tummeln sich Reichsadler, Herolde und Phönix. Auch seine Position in der Mittelachse des Rathauses ist nicht von ungefähr. Der Turm steht im Zentrum der politischen Macht von Bürgerschaft (links) und Senat (rechts). Wer durch das Turmportal das Rathaus betritt, ist auf jeden Fall tief beeindruckt von der pompösen Geste eines Hauses, das wie kein anderes das Selbstbewußtsein der Freien und Hansestadt repräsentiert.

Der Heinrich-Hertz-Turm – die moderne Konkurrenz der Hamburger Kirchtürme – ging 1968 in Betrieb. Es dauerte nicht lange, da machten die Hamburger aus ihm den „Tele-Michel".

The Heinrich Hertz Tower, a modern rival to the Hamburg church towers, was taken into operation in 1968. Before long, Hamburgers had nicknamed it the Tele-Michel.

### Der „Tele-Michel" läßt grüßen

Doch höher als alle anderen ist ein schlicht zweckdienlicher Turm, der 1968 als Fernmeldeturm der Deutschen Bundespost an der Rentzelstraße vollendet wurde. Der Fernsehturm, ein schlanker weißer Spargel, der durch mehrere Scheiben unterteilt ist, mißt immerhin 204 und mit Antenne sogar 271,5 Meter. In seinem Drehrestaurant zu sitzen und die Vogelperspektive auf Hamburg zu genießen, ist herrlich. Wer sich der Stadt heute mit Adleraugen nähert, wird sogar vom Fernsehturm noch früher begrüßt als vom Turm der St. Michaeliskirche, der ja der eigentliche „Begrüßungsmichel" der Stadt ist. Nicht nur, daß der Fernsehturm höher ist. Die 1996 fertiggestellte neue Kupferhaube des „Michel" hat auch noch nicht wieder den leuchtenden Grünspan angesetzt, der ihn sonst so weithin kenntlich macht.

a slim white building divided up by several saucers, is all of 204 metres high, and 271.5 if you include the aerial. To sit in its revolving restaurant enjoying a bird's-eye view of Hamburg is great experience. Approaching the town with an eagle eye, you are welcomed by the Fernsehturm even before that of St Michael's Church, which is the city's real "welcoming Michel." Not only is the Fernsehturm higher. The real Michel's new copper dome, completed in 1996, has not yet acquired the gleaming green verdigris that otherwise makes it recognisable from so far away.

# Die Reeperbahn
## St. Pauli olé – St. Pauli oh weh!

### The Reeperbahn
### St Pauli olé – St Pauli oh dear!

Berühmt und berüchtigt. Die Reeperbahn ist in aller Welt als Hamburgs populärste Straße bekannt. Auf dem 600 Meter langen „Boulevard der Sünde" zwischen Millerntor und Nobistor flanieren, drängen, schieben an Wochenenden bis zu 150 000 Menschen an den Etablissements des schillernden Vergnügens vorbei. Den einen reichen die Schaulust und eine Tüte Pommes frites, andere suchen sexuelle Abenteuer, was exorbitant teuer zu stehen kommen kann. Manche steuern nach Mitternacht gezielt ihre Lieblingsdisco an. Yuppies verschwinden hinter den Türen von Szenelokalen. Nebenan lagern Obdachlose. Taschendiebe – auf St. Pauli entschieden die harmlosesten Verbrecher – kommen auf ihre Kosten. In der berühmten Davidwache, die jeder Krimifan kennt, hat man für diese kleinen Fische nur ein freundliches, müdes Lächeln. Gedealt wird in bestimmten Seitenstraßen, die für Fremde wesentlich gefährlicher sind als die Reeperbahn.

Diese berühmte Straße ist das Herz von St. Pauli. Wenn die Fußballer vom FC St. Pauli spielen, wird hinterher auf der Reeperbahn gefeiert oder getrauert. Dieser Boulevard war immer ein öffentlicher Platz für Emotionen und Demonstrationen. Als die Revolution von 1848 in St. Pauli mobil machte, zogen die Demonstranten zwischen Millerntor und Nobistor auf. Als am 9. November 1989 die Berliner Mauer fiel, kam wenige Stunden später der Verkehr auf der sündigen Meile im Ansturm der Trabis zum Erliegen.

**Demonstration in der Herbertstraße**

St. Pauli ist im wohlhabenden Hamburg einer der ärmsten Stadtteile. Von den über 30 000 Einwohnern ist jeder zweite Ausländer. Die Arbeitslosenquote übersteigt bei weitem den Durchschnitt in der Hansestadt. In keinem Stadtteil wurden

Famous and notorious, internationally the Reeperbahn is Hamburg's best-known boulevard. At weekends, up to 150,000 people stroll, throng and push their way along past the gaudy pleasure domes of the 600-metre "street of sin" between Millerntor and Nobistor. Some are content just to slake their curiosity and eat a bag of french fries. Others are in search of sexual adventure, which can turn out exorbitantly expensive. After midnight, some head for their favourite disco. Yuppies disappear behind the doors of trendy bars and restaurants. Nearby, homeless people bed down for the night. Pick-pockets – by far the most harmless of crooks in St Pauli – do very well. The officers in the Davidwache police station, known to detective story fans all over Germany, have only a pleasant, weary smile for these small fry. Drug dealing goes on in certain side streets that are far more dangerous than the Reeperbahn for strangers.

This famous street is the heart of St. Pauli. It is where FC St Pauli soccer fans come to celebrate or commiserate after the match. It has always been a place for the public display of emotions and demonstrations. When the 1848 revolution started to sweep over St Pauli, demonstrators marched from Millerntor to Nobistor. When the Berlin Wall came down on 9 November 1989, within a few hours the rush of East German Trabant cars had brought traffic on the boulevard of sin to a standstill.

**Demonstration in Herbertstrasse**

St Pauli is one of wealthy Hamburg's poorest districts. One in two of its 30,000 residents is a foreigner. The unemployment rate is far above the city's average. And yet in no other district were so many myths born as in this red-light area, known to Hamburgers as the Kiez. Leaving aside the Reeperbahn's legendary reputation, there is the Hafenkrankenhaus, the former district hospital which has been immortalised in

Die Ansicht der Reeperbahn um 1800 zeigt noch sorgfältig gestaltete Gartenanlagen. Im Hintergrund das Millerntor und über den Bäumen der Turm des Michels

This view of the Reeperbahn in around 1800 still shows carefully tended gardens. In the background are the Millerntor and, peeping above the trees, the tower of St Michael's Church

so viele Mythen geboren wie auf dem Kiez. Der legendäre Ruf der Reeperbahn ist eine Sache. Doch wer kennt nicht das Hafenkrankenhaus, das es zwar in seiner früheren Funktion als Stadtteilklinik gar nicht mehr gibt, das aber in ungezählten Filmen, Krimis und Romanen verewigt ist.

Als 1997 ruchbar wurde, daß das seit 1900 bestehende Hafenkrankenhaus eingespart werden sollte, bildete sich spontan eine heilige Protestallianz von Punks und Pastoren, Krankenschwestern und Bordellwirten, Künstlern und Kiezfürsten. Krankenhausbesetzer luden zum Frühstück ein. Der Turmbläser der St. Michaeliskirche gab an der Hospitalpforte ein kleines Konzert. Das stärkste Ereignis für Kiezkenner war der Demonstrationszug durch die Herbertstraße. Gegen Abend öffneten sich die Eisentore zu der 300 Meter langen Straße der Bordelle, die sonst für Jugendliche unter 18

numerous films, detective stories and novels. In 1997 when rumours started circulating that the hospital, opened in 1900, was to be closed, a spontaneous holy alliance of punks and pastors, nurses and brothel-owners, artistes and local bigshots sprang up in protest. Protesters occupied the hospital, held breakfasts there, the Michaeliskirche trumpeter gave a concert outside the front

Die Davidwache: Hamburgs berühmteste Polizeistation

Everyone finds the Davidwache, Hamburg's best-known police station

Die Reeperbahn am Millerntor. Schön ist der Auftakt zu der sündigsten Meile der Welt nicht, aber bunt.

The Reeperbahn at Millerntor. The start of the world's most sinful street is not beautiful, but colourful.

Das Schanzenviertel ist das nördlichste Quartier von St. Pauli. Am Schulterblatt trifft sich die Szene.

The Schanzenviertel district is the northern-most part of St Pauli, and an area where members of the scene like to meet.

Jahren und für Frauen gesperrt ist. Die Schaufenster der Prostituierten blieben leer. Die Huren, für die das Krankenhaus traditionell an Weihnachten der liebste Zufluchtsort war, schlossen sich der Demonstration an. Ein Stadtteil stand auf. Doch vergebens. Das Hafenkrankenhaus überlebte nur als Notfallambu-

entrance. But for Kiez connoisseurs, the highlight was the protest march through Herbertstrasse. Towards evening the iron gates to this 300-metre street of brothels – otherwise banned to under-18s and women – were opened. The prostitutes' show-windows were empty because the women, for whom the Hafenkranken-haus was traditionally a favourite place of refuge at Christmas, had joined the demonstration. A whole district rose in protest, but in vain. The Hafenkranken-haus survived only as an emergency out-patients' clinic. Also gone is Harrys Hafenbasar next to what is now the PrivArt Museum in Bernhard-Nocht-Strasse. Until the mid-1990s this stuffy basement bazaar was chock-a-block with the sort of arts and crafts that sailors from all five continents bring into a port.

A legend that still lives is Hafen-strasse. In the 1980s Hamburg's mayor, Klaus von Dohnanyi, decided that the riots and rows over some squatted hous-es in Hafenstrasse were a job for the boss to tackle. Before long the political murals and graffiti painted on the houses had become a tourist attraction. In a later court case experts declared them to

lanz. Verschwunden ist auch Harry's Hafenbasar neben dem heutigen PrivArt Museum in der Bernhard-Nocht-Straße. Der Kellerbasar war bis Mitte der neunziger Jahre die schönste und stickigste Schwemme für Kulturgüter aus aller Welt, die Seeleute aller fünf Kontinente in einer Hafenstadt an Land bringen.

Legende ist heute auch „die Hafenstraße". In den achtziger Jahren machte der damalige Bürgermeister von Hamburg, Klaus von Dohnanyi, die Krawalle um die besetzten Häuser in der Hafenstraße zur Chefsache. Die politischen Wandmalereien der Hafenstraßenhäuser wurden bald zur Touristenattraktion. In einem Prozeß erklärten Experten sie später zu Kunstwerken. Die Häuser wurden privatisiert. Heute herrscht Frieden an der Hafenstraße.

### Kein Sonntag ohne Fischmarkt

Einen genehmigten Volksauflauf gibt es allerdings jeden Sonntag in aller Herrgottsfrühe zu Füßen der Häuser. Tausende von Nachtschwärmern und Frühaufstehern kommen auf dem traditionellen Fischmarkt zusammen. Die Meile der Imbißbuden, Südfrüchte- und Blumenstände, der Fisch- und Vogelhändler, Trödler, Marktschreier und Gewürzverkäufer verbindet St. Pauli mit Altona. Im Zentrum des morgendlichen Auftriebs steht die 1896 eingeweihte Fischauktionshalle – eine herrliche Eisen-Glas-Konstruktion aus der Gründerzeit, die von 1982–84 renoviert wurde. Schräg gegenüber liegt die Haifischbar, in der gestandene Nachtschwärmer mit einem letzten Absacker ihren Fischmarktbummel beenden.

be works of art. The houses were privatised. Nowadays, peace prevails in the street that runs along by the river.

### Every Sunday is Fischmarkt time

However, every Sunday a permitted public uproar takes place at the crack of dawn just below the Hafenstrasse houses, as thousands of night owls and early birds assemble at the traditional Fischmarkt or fish market, a row of snack bars, fruit and flower stalls, fish and

Der Altonaer Fischmarkt in den 1950er Jahren. Jeden Sonntag von 5.30–9.30 Uhr werden hier außer Fisch auch Blumen, Südfrüchte und sogar lebendiges Federvieh gehandelt.

Altona's Fischmarkt in the 1950s, when from 5.30 to 9.30 a. m. every Sunday not just fish but flowers, tropical fruit and even live poultry was sold.

So sah es in der prächtigen Altonaer Fischauktionshalle aus, als dort noch Fisch den Besitzer wechselte. Das Gebäude stammt aus dem Jahr 1895.

This is what the Altona fish auction hall looked like in the days when fish still changed hands there. The building dates back to 1895.

Mit Beginn des Jahres 1861 fiel in Hamburg die Torsperre. Ein wichtiges Ereignis für die Vorstadt, die der Rat der Hansestadt 1833 von Hamburger Berg in St. Pauli umbenannt hatte. Namensgeber war der Apostel Paulus beziehungsweise die ihm im 17. Jahrhundert geweihte Kirche nahe dem Pinnasberg. Daß an der Reeperbahn die Reepschläger seit 1626 ihre Schiffstaue (Reep) aus Hanf fertigten, sagt noch heute der Name. Daß die Wurzeln des Vergnügungs- und Rotlichtviertels von St. Pauli fast ebensoweit zurückreichen, wissen wenige. Schon vor 1800 etablierten sich vor den Toren der Hafenstadt am Spielbudenplatz, der parallel zur südlichen Seite der Reeperbahn verlaufenden Straße, Jahrmarkt- und Spielbuden und bald

poultry dealers, bric-à-brac merchants, market vendors and spice sellers that joins St Pauli with Altona. At the centre of this early-morning hustle and bustle is the 1896 fish auction hall, a superb Wilhelminian building of iron and glass that was renovated between 1982 and 1984. Diagonally opposite is the Haifisch Bar, where fully-fledged night owls round off their stroll round the Fischmarkt with a final drink.

At the beginning of 1861 the city of Hamburg stopped closing its gates at 8 p. m. every evening, an important event for the suburb whose name the Hanseatic city's council had changed from Hamburger Berg to St Pauli in 1833. It is named after St Paul the Apostle, or rather the seventeenth-century church near the Pinnaberg which was dedicated to him. The name Reeperbahn is a reminder is that this was the area where

auch Bordellwirtschaften in den Seitenstraßen. Die eigentliche Straße namens
Reeperbahn wurde zwischen 1820 und
1830 angelegt und hieß zunächst eine
kurze Zeit lang „Altonaer Allee". Das
Vergnügen, das an der Reeperbahn angeboten wurde, war manchmal durchaus
hochkarätig. In „Carl-Schultze's Theater" wurden gegen Ende des 19. Jahrhunderts die sozialkritischen Dramen
von Gerhart Hauptmann, Henrik Ibsen
und Johan August Strindberg aufgeführt
– lange bevor die etablierten Theater sich
dieser Stücke annahmen. Die berühmte
Eleonora Duse trat hier als Kamelienda-

from 1626 ropemakers used to make
ropes of hemp for ships. Few people
know that the roots of St Pauli as an
amusement and red-light district go
back almost as far. Already by 1800 fairground stalls and sideshows had established themselves outside the city gates
on Spielbudenplatz, the road that runs
parallel with the southern side of the
Reeperbahn – followed soon afterwards
by brothels in the surrounding side
streets. The actual Reeperbahn was built
between 1820 and 1830 and was initially named Altonaer Allee. The entertainment offered on the Reeperbahn in those
days was sometimes of a very high order.
Towards the end of the nineteenth century Carl Schultze's theatre staged the
socially critical plays of Gerhart Hauptmann, Henrik Ibsen and Johan August
Strindberg long before the established

1984 wurde die Alto-
naer Fischauktionshalle
im letzten Augenblick
vor dem Abriß gerettet
und detailgetreu restau-
riert. Heute dient sie als
Markt- und Veranstal-
tungshalle.

In 1984 the Altona fish
auction hall gained a
last-minute reprieve
from demolition and
refurbished to the origi-
nal design. It is now
used as a market hall
and event venue.

Das Tivoli und das Schmidt sind beste Adressen für Kleinkunst, Kabarett und Tingeltangel jeder Art am Spielbudenplatz. Links Schmidt's Tivoli, rechts das Schmidt

The Tivoli and Schmidt are the best places for cabaret and all kinds of night-club entertainment on Spielbudenplatz. On the left is Schmidt's Tivoli, on the right Schmidt.

me auf, und sogar der Wiener Walzerkönig Johann Strauß dirigierte seine Operetten auf St. Pauli.

Daß nach dem Zweiten Weltkrieg mit Damenringkämpfen im Schlamm an der Reeperbahn viel Geld verdient wurde und das Eros-Center als Zentrale der Prostituierten diente, gehört eher zu den traurigen Kapiteln in der Geschichte von St. Pauli. Die Auftritte der Beatles und des größten Teils der damaligen Crème de la crème des Rock'n Roll im Star-Club wurden erst zur Legende, als die Pilzköpfe aus England die Stadt längst wieder verlassen hatten und allmählich berühmt wurden. René Durants Sextheater „Salambo" blieb und wurde in den siebziger Jahren als Bühne mit den besten Inszenierungen der Stadt gehandelt. Heute heißt es „Dollhouse" und bietet eine Striptease-Show.

An die Tradition der berühmten Varieté-Theater auf St. Pauli knüpfte ein Kapitel an, das genau am 8.8.1988 begann. Damals machte Corny Littmann sein Schmidt-Theater auf, dem wenig später das schöne Tivoli folgte. Schwulentheater, Tingeltangel, Comedy- und Blödelshows, Chanson, Operette, türkische

theatre tackled their works. The famous actress Eleonora Duse performed here as La Dame aux Camélias, and Johann Strauss, king of the Viennese waltz, directed his operettas in St Pauli.

The fact that after World War II a great deal of money was earned on the Reeperbahn with women's mud-wrestling and that the Eros-Center became the headquarters of prostitution is one of the sadder chapters in St Pauli's history. The appearances of the Beatles – and many of the top rock 'n roll artistes of the day – at the Star Club only became a legend long after they had left Hamburg and gradually become famous. René Durand's Salambo sex theatre stayed put and in the 1970s was said to stage the city's finest performances. Now named Dollhouse, it is a striptease club.

A new chapter in St Pauli's famous vaudeville tradition began on 8 August 1988 when Corny Littmann opened his Schmidt-Theater, followed soon afterwards by the fine Tivoli. Gay theatre, club acts, comedy shows and slapstick, chansons, operetta, Turkish club

Clubabende. In Corny Littmanns Etablissements ist alles zu Hause, was unter
das Dach professioneller Vergnügungs-
theater gehört. Das Operettenhaus, das
St. Pauli-Theater und weitere hochkarä-
tige Musikklubs an Reeperbahn und
Großer Freiheit heizen der Kultur auf
dem Kiez zusätzlich ein.

## Der Rotlichtbezirk hat seine Grenzen

Der Amüsierbetrieb kennt keine Grenzen. Doch zumindest dem Rotlichtbezirk
wurden von offizieller Seite Grenzen
gesetzt. David-, Herbert-, Friedrich-,
Gerhard- und Silbersackstraße sowie der
Hans-Albers-Platz sind für die Prostitution freigegeben. Das große Geschäft mit
der käuflichen Liebe wird hinter geschlossenen Türen gemacht. In den achtziger Jahren sorgten die Kämpfe der
Zuhälterbanden um die Machtpositionen
auf dem Kiez für Schlagzeilen.

Der Schöne Mischa, Karate-Thommy,
Dakota-Uwe. Die Boulevard-Zeitungen
feierten die Kiezhelden. Als der Schöne
Mischa am 17. Oktober 1982 freiwillig
aus dem Leben geschieden war, bereitete
ihm die Szene einen würdigen Abschied.
Ein Korso edler Rennschlitten raste bei
Rot über die Reeperbahn zum Ohlsdorfer Friedhof. Über dem Sarg des Verstor-
benen schwebten ein weißer Rolls Royce
und der hawaiische Abschiedsgruß
ALOHA – geformt aus 3000 weißen
Nelken. Die Ganoven ließen sich nicht
lumpen und zeigten auf ihre Art Stil.

Seitdem sind die Sitten härter geworden. Die Kiezkriege werden von internationalen Banden geführt. Der Drogen-
handel spielt eine verheerende Rolle.

evenings' everything that can be classed
as professional entertainment culture
finds a home in Corny Littmann's establishments. The Operettenhaus, the St
Pauli Theatre and further high-class
music clubs on the Reeperbahn and
Grosse Freiheit help to turn up the cultural heat on the Kiez.

## The red-light district has its bounds

The amusement business knows no
bounds, but to the red-light district at
least officialdom has set some bounds.
Prostitution is allowed in Davidstrasse,
Herbertstrasse, Friedrichstrasse, Ger-
hardstrasse and Silbersackstrasse and on
Hans-Albers-Platz. In this area the big
business in sex for sale takes place
behind closed doors. In the 1980s the
battles between gangs of pimps for posi-
tions of power on the Kiez made head-
lines. The popular press celebrated Kiez
heroes with names like Schöner Mischa
(Handsome Mischa), Karate Tommy and
Dakota Uwe. When Schöner Mischa
took his life on 17 October 1982 the
red-light world gave him a fitting
farewell. A cortège of high-speed limou-
sines raced through red traffic lights
along the Reeperbahn on its way to
Ohlsdorf cemetery. Over the dead man's
coffin floated a white Rolls Royce and
the Hawaiian farewell salutation
ALOHA – in 3,000 white carnations.
His fellow-crooks had spared no expense
in giving him a send-off in what they
thought of as style.

Im legendären Star-
Club an der Großen
Freiheit begann die
märchenhafte Karriere
der Beatles.

The legendary Star
Club on Grosse Freiheit
is where the Beatles
began their fairy-tale
career.

Dem Entertainer Corny Littmann ist es zu verdanken, daß der Spielbudenplatz im Herzen von St. Pauli wieder Bühne für Straßentheater geworden ist.

We have the entertainer Corny Littmann to thank for Spielbudenplatz in the heart of St Pauli regaining its status as a street theatre stage.

Aktenkundig wurde die internationale Drogenmafia in Hamburg zum erstenmal 1926. Im Hafen wurden damals 114 Kilo Heroin aufgebracht, die als „Grabsteine" von Budapest nach Schanghai verschifft werden sollten.

In der Schmuckstraße, zwischen Großer Freiheit und Talstraße, hatte sich in den zwanziger Jahren auf engstem Raum eine mehr als 200 Köpfe zählende chinesische Kolonie angesiedelt. Mit kleinen Wäschereien, Gemüseläden und Restaurants hielt man sich über Wasser. Ob Chinesen aus der Schmuckstraße 1926 an dem Heroinhandel beteiligt waren, ist unbekannt. Gewiß ist das schreckliche Ende der Kolonie. 1944 wurden die noch in der Schmuckstraße verbliebenen Chinesen verhaftet und in ein Arbeitslager gebracht. Einige starben. Die Überlebenden verließen nach Ende des Krieges die Stadt.

Heute gibt es wieder zahlreiche Chinalokale auf St. Pauli. Doch hier, wie überall in Hamburg, ißt man am liebsten italienisch. Das erste ausländische Restaurant wurde denn auch von einem Italiener aufgemacht. 1905 eröffneten Maria und Francesco Cuneo in der Davidstraße 11 ihr Restaurant, das heute noch am selben Ort existiert und als Szenetreff aus der Ausgehkultur der Stadt gar nicht mehr wegzudenken ist.

65 Jahre vor der Eröffnung des „Cuneo" hatte sich eine Institution auf St. Pauli etabliert, die sich sehr viel umfassender um das „leibliche Wohl" ihrer Gäste sorgte. Gemeint ist das Israelitische Krankenhaus, das der Bankier Salomon Heine (1767–1844) stiftete. Es entstand an der Ecke Hein-Hoyer-Straße/Simon-von-Utrecht-Straße. Der Onkel des Dichters Heinrich Heine schuf damit ein Hospital, dessen medizinischer Ruf

Manners have got rougher since those days. The Kiez wars are now waged by international gangs, with drug dealing playing a devastating role. The international drugs mafia's presence in Hamburg was first recorded in 1926 when 114 kilograms of heroin was discovered in the port, labelled as "gravestones" on their way from Budapest to Shanghai.

In the 1920s a colony of more than 200 Chinese had settled in cramped quarters in Schmuckstrasse between Grosse Freiheit and Talstrasse. They kept their heads above water by running small laundries, greengrocer's shops and restaurants. It is not known whether Chinese from Schmuckstrasse were involved in the shipment of heroin for Shanghai in 1926. What is known for sure is the dreadful end to which the colony came. In 1944 all the Chinese still living in Schmuckstrasse were arrested by the Gestapo and sent to a labour camp. Some died, and those who survived left Hamburg after the end of the war.

Nowadays there are once again a large number of Chinese restaurants in St Pauli, though here as everywhere else in Hamburg the favourite food is Italian. Indeed the first foreign restaurant was Italian, back in 1905 when Maria and Francesco Cuneo opened the restaurant at Davidstrasse 11 which stands there still today as an essential part of Hamburg's going-out culture.

Sixty-five years before Cuneo opened, another institution had opened its doors in St Pauli, one which took much more comprehensive care of the "bodily wellbeing" of its its guests. This is the Israelitisches Krankenhaus, a hospital endowed by the banker Salomon Heine (1767–1844), which stood on what is now the corner of Hein-Hoyer-Strasse and Simon-von-Utrecht-Strasse. The medical reputation of the hospital founded by the uncle of the writer Heinrich Heine soon went far beyond the bounds of Hamburg. As a result of the dictatorial policies of the National Socialists, in

bald über die Grenzen der Stadt hinausging. Aufgrund der diktatorischen Politik der Nationalsozialisten mußte das Krankenhaus 1939 an die Stadt verkauft werden. Heute steht das restaurierte Gebäude unter Denkmalschutz und versammelt unter seinem Dach verschiedene gemeinnützige und soziale Einrichtungen.

## Wohnen auf St. Pauli

St. Pauli ist auch – was durch den grellen Amüsierbetrieb oft in den Hintergrund gerät – wegen seiner früh geförderten Wohnbebauung ein sehenswerter Stadtteil. Den Straßenzügen aus der Gründerzeit mit ihrer Hinterhofbebauung stehen die Häuserzeilen gegenüber, die im Zeichen des in der zweiten Hälfte des 19. Jahrhunderts allmählich einsetzenden Wandels im Wohnungsbau für Arbeiter entstanden. Durch Denkmal- und Ensembleschutz konnte in den vergangenen Jahrzehnten viel von dieser historischen Bebauung bewahrt werden. Die Jägerpassage in der Wohlwillstraße nördlich der Reeperbahn ist eines der ältesten erhaltenen Beispiele aus der Frühzeit des deutschen Arbeiterwohnungsbaus (1866–69, angeregt von der Patriotischen Gesellschaft). Wer auf St. Pauli wohnt, gehört also keineswegs zwangsläufig zum Amüsierbetrieb rund um die Reeperbahn. Auch Studenten und Yuppies haben den Kiez längst als facettenreiche Wohngegend für sich entdeckt. Rund um den Hein-Köllisch-Platz, der nur einen Steinwurf vom Hans-Albers-Platz entfernt liegt, spielt sich das Leben ebenso gemütlich wie international ab. Und an der Kante des Kiez werden die Wohnungen mit Hafenblick zunehmend begehrter und teurer.

1939 the hospital had to be sold to the city. The building, which has been restored, is now a protected monument that houses a number of charitable and welfare organisations.

## Living in St Pauli

St Pauli is also interesting for its early examples of subsidised housing, a fact which the loud entertainment scene often forces into the background. Along with streets of Wilhelminian houses with rear courtyards there are rows of houses built in the second half of the nineteenth century that reflect the gradual transformation that was coming about in housing for working people. Many of these historic buildings have been preserved thanks to protection orders in the last few decades. Jägerpassage in Wohlwillstrasse to the north of the Reeperbahn is one of the oldest remaining example from the early period of German working-class housing (built 1866–69 at the instigation of the Patriotische Gesellschaft). So it is by no means the case that everyone living in St Pauli is connected with the amusement business centred on the Reeperbahn. Students and yuppies, too, have long since discovered the Kiez as an interesting, lively residential area. Round Hein-Köllisch-Platz, just a stone's throw away from Hans-Albers-Platz, life is both easy-going and cosmopolitan. And on the edge of the Kiez, apartments with a view of the docks are becoming increasingly sought-after and expensive.

Eine der beliebtesten Wohnpassagen St. Paulis. Die Beckstraße verbindet das Schlachthofareal mit dem Schanzenviertel.

Beckstrasse, which links the Schlachthofviertel and Schanzenviertel districts, is one of St Pauli's most popular residential alleys.

# Altona: Hamburgs schöne Schwester
## Altona: Hamburg's lovely sister

Das Altonaer Rathaus im Stil der Neorenaissance wurde 1898 eingeweiht. Seine Schauseite mit dem Kaiser-Wilhelm-Denkmal ist gen Norden gewandt.

Altona's neo-Renaissance Rathaus, or City Hall, was inaugurated in 1898. Its north-facing frontage is rounded off by an equestrian statue of Kaiser Wilhelm I.

Mancher alteingesessener Altonaer kann sich noch heute darüber aufregen, daß seine Stadt 1937 nach Hamburg eingemeindet wurde. Altona hat sich jedoch seine Eigenständigkeit bewahrt, die in einem unterschiedlichen historischen Werdegang und in einer seit dem 17. Jahrhundert bestehenden Konkurrenzsituation zu der Hansestadt wurzelt. „All to nah" fanden die Hamburger diesen Anrainer im Westen, der im 16. Jahrhundert noch eine kleine Fischer- und Handwerkersiedlung gewesen war, aber im 18. Jahrhundert unter dänischer Herrschaft eine wahre Blütezeit erlebte und mit der Hansestadt auf wirtschaftlichem und kulturellem Gebiet erfolgreich wetteifern konnte. Altona wurde zu Hamburgs schöner Schwester.

Some long-established residents of Altona can still get hot under the collar at the fact that in 1937 their town was incorporated into Hamburg. However, Altona still retains an independence rooted in a different history and in a rivalry with Hamburg dating back to the seventeenth century. Hamburgers found their neighbour to the west "all too near" (a pun on its German name). In the sixteenth century it had still been a small settlement of fishermen and craftsmen but in the eighteenth century under Danish rule it experienced a real heyday and could successfully compete with the Hanseatic city in both the economic and cultural field. Altona became Hamburg's lovely sister.

### A demonstratively splendid building: the white Rathaus

Altona's self-assurance is most clearly reflected in the Rathaus or City Hall whose formal opening was celebrated in 1898. The showy building in the quadrangle between Max-Brauer-Allee, Platz der Republik, Christianskirche and Klopstockstrasse cannot be overlooked.

So prächtig sah der Altonaer „Hauptbahnhof" mit dem 1899 errichteten Stuhlmann-Brunnen um 1900 aus. Rechts das Hotel Kaiserhof. Das neugotische Bahnhofsgebäude wurde 1977–79 einem Kaufhaus geopfert.

This was how magnificent Altona's Hauptbahnhof, or main railway station, looked in about 1900, with the 1899 Stuhlmann fountain in the foreground and the Kaiserhof Hotel to the right. The neo-Gothic station building was demolished in 1977–79 to make way for a department store.

## Ein demonstrativer Prachtbau: das weiße Rathaus

Das Altonaer Selbstbewußtsein spiegelt sich am deutlichsten im Rathaus, dessen Einweihung die Stadt 1898 feierte. Das repräsentative weiße Gebäude im Viereck zwischen Max-Brauer-Allee, Platz der Republik, Christianskirche und Klopstockstraße ist nicht zu übersehen. Der Neorenaissancebau hat eine ungewöhnliche Geschichte. Das Rathaus wurde genau auf dem Platz errichtet, auf dem 1844 Altonas erster Bahnhof eingeweiht worden war. Hier hatte die Eisenbahnstrecke Altona–Kiel angefangen. Der Südflügel des Bahnhofs wurde in das neue Rathaus integriert. Die historische Fassade bietet heute den Brautleuten den für Hochzeitsfotos angemessenen prunkvollen Hintergrund. Das Standesamt im Altonaer Rathaus ist für Trauungen äußerst gefragt.

The neo-Renaissance edifice has an unusual history. The Rathaus was built on the very spot where Altona's first railway station had been opened in 1844, marking the start of the line from Altona to Kiel. The station's south wing was integrated into the new Rathaus. Nowadays the historic facade provides brides and grooms with a suitably magnificent and historic backdrop for their wedding photos. The registry office in Altona Rathaus is very much in demand for weddings.

More magnificent still is the north side facing Platz der Republik. The columned portico is crowned by a gable for which the sculptor Karl Garbers – together with the young Ernst Barlach – devised an allegorical depiction of Altona. The statue of Kaiser Wilhelm I on horseback has stood in front of the Rathaus portal since 1897. The town, which belonged to Schleswig-Holstein, passed to Prussia after the German-Danish war of 1864 and once and for all after the German War of 1866. Altona became the location for many kinds of industry. One of the most impressive manifestations of

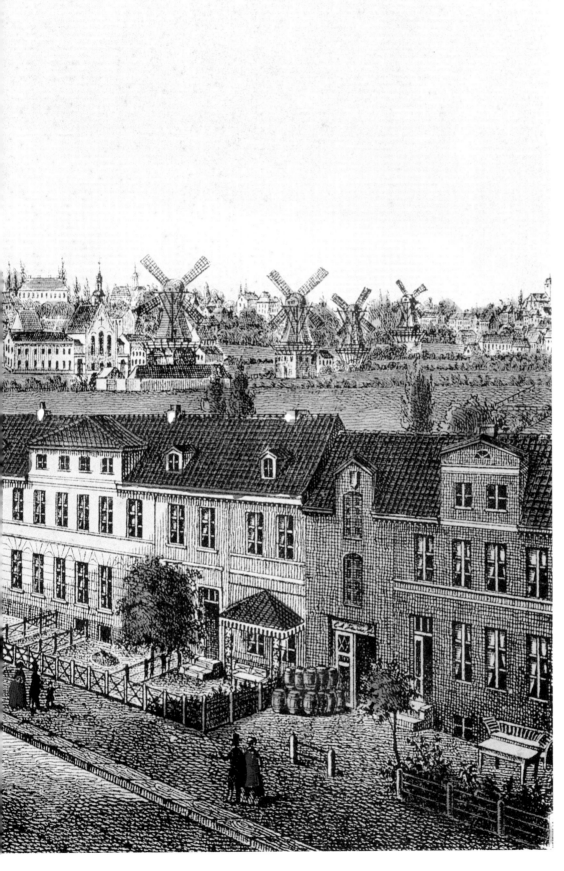

Die kolorierte Lithographie von Gustav Frank zeigt Altona um die Mitte des 19. Jahrhunderts. Im Hintergrund die Stadtsilhouette mit der Hauptkirche und fünf Windmühlen

This coloured lithograph by Gustav Frank features Altona as it looked in the mid-nineteenth century. In the background you can see the skyline, including the main church and five windmills.

Die klassizistischen Gebäude von Christian Frederik Hansen (1756-1845) wurden an der Palmaille weitgehend restauriert. Links das Wohnhaus des dänischen Baumeisters

These classicist buildings on Palmaille, designed by Christian Frederik Hansen, 1756-1845, have been largely restored. On the left is the house in which the Danish architect lived.

the prosperous Wilhelminian age was the new Altona main station to the north of the new Rathaus, which was opened in 1898. Until 1977 the neo-Gothic brick building with its five halls and the extensive network of tracks and points associated with a terminus remained one of Altona's main attractions. Then, despite fierce protests the monument was demolished and replaced by a faceless department store complex. A cultural loss that no financial advantage can justify.

## Palmaille – where high society lived in classical style

Die Palmaille wurde im 17. Jahrhundert als dreibahnige Spielstraße für das Ballspiel palle a maglio angelegt.

Palmaille was laid out in the seventeenth century as a three-lane alley for a ball game known as palle a maglio that found its way into English as Pall Mall.

Prächtiger noch geriet die Nordfassade am Platz der Republik. Der säulengetragene Vorbau (Portikus) wird von einem Giebel gekrönt, für den der Bildhauer Karl Garbers – unter Mitarbeit des jungen Ernst Barlach – eine allegorische Darstellung Altonas schuf. Das Reiterstandbild Kaiser Wilhelms I. hat seit 1897 seinen Platz vor dem Rathauspor-

Altona fared better to the west of the Rathaus where Palmaille runs parallel to the hilly slope above the Elbe bank towards the port. Now dominated once more by classical-style facades, the road was built in the seventeenth century as a generous track for the Italian ball-game palle a maglio. Palmaille acquired its well-known appearance in around 1800 when the Danish architect Christian Frederik Hansen (1756–1845) built a row of residences for wealthy merchants on Altona's showpiece street. During the

tal. Nach dem Deutsch-Dänischen Krieg von 1864 und endgültig nach dem Deutschen Krieg von 1866 war die zu Schleswig-Holstein gehörende Stadt an Preußen gekommen. Altona wurde Standort für viele Industriezweige. Zum eindrucksvollsten Dokument des prosperierenden Gründerzeitalters geriet der neue Altonaer Hauptbahnhof nördlich des neuen Rathauses, der 1898 eingeweiht wurde. Der neugotische Backsteinbau mit seinen fünf Hallen und dem weiten Gleis- und Weichennetz eines Kopfbahnhofs blieb bis 1977 eine der größten Attraktionen Altonas. Dann wurde das Monument trotz heftiger Proteste abgerissen und durch eine gesichtslose Kaufhausanlage ersetzt. Ein Verlust für die Kultur, der durch keinen finanziellen Vorteil gerechtfertigt werden kann.

## Palmaille – hier wohnte man klassizistisch vornehm

Besser erging es Altona östlich des Rathauses, wo die Palmaille parallel zum Geesthang am Elbufer Richtung Hafen führt. Die heute wieder von ganz überwiegend klassizistischen Fassaden geprägte Straße war im 17. Jahrhundert als großzügige Bahn für das italienische Ballspiel „palle a maglio" angelegt worden. Ihr berühmtes Gesicht erhielt die Palmaille um 1800. Damals errichtete der dänische Architekt Christian Frederik Hansen (1756–1845) für wohlhabende Kaufleute eine Reihe Wohnhäuser an Altonas Prachtstraße. Das einmalige klassizistische Ensemble wäre in der Nazizeit dem Abriß zum Opfer gefallen, wenn die Pläne des Hamburger Architek-

Nazi era the unique classicistic ensemble would have been demolished if plans by the Hamburg architect Konstanty Gutschow (plans which had taken shape a long time before) for Hamburg's development into a "Führer city" on the Elbe had come to fruition. Luckily his gigantomanic architectural ideas remained confined to paper. Palmaille was destroyed in another way. In 1943 two thirds of its buildings fell victim to bombing. After 1945 a few of Hansen's finest classical-style houses were restored at great expense. Nowadays Palmaille is

In diesem Hansen-Bau an der Palmaille ist heute eine Reederei zu Hause. Von der Parkanlage an der Südfront geht der Blick weit über den Hafen.

This building on Palmaille that Hansen designed now houses a shipping line. Its south-facing park enjoys an overview of the Port of Hamburg.

Das Porträt zeigt den dänischen Architekten Christian Frederik Hansen (1756–1845), der um 1800 als Landbaumeister in Altona wirkte.

A portrait of the Danish architect Christian Frederik Hansen, 1756–1845, who worked as state architect in Altona in about 1800.

ten Konstanty Gutschow für Hamburgs Ausbau zu einer „Führerstadt" an der Elbe verwirklicht worden wären. Die gigantomanischen Architekturvorstellungen blieben glücklicherweise Papier. Die Palmaille wurde auf andere Art zerstört. 1943 fielen zwei Drittel der Bebauung durch Bomben in Schutt. Mit viel Aufwand wurden einige der schönsten klassizistischen Hansen-Häuser nach 1945 restauriert. Die Palmaille ist heute keine Flanierstraße mehr. Aber mit ihrem unverwechselbaren Gesicht ist sie wieder ein städtebauliches Juwel, das an die glanzvollen dänischen Zeiten Altonas erinnert.

Anders als beim Hamburger Wappen stehen die Tore des Wappens von Altona weit offen. Tor zur Welt. Das war Hamburgs schöne Schwester durch die Jahrhunderte weit mehr als die Hansestadt, die sich gerne mit diesem Beiwort schmückt. Vor allem hielt das liberale Altona aber auch seine Tore offen, damit die Welt hereinkommen konnte. Die Straßennamen Große Freiheit und Kleine Freiheit sind eine Erinnerung an den Bezirk, in dem zuziehende Handwerker ab 1612 ihr Gewerbe ohne enge Reglementierungen ausüben durften, während anderswo noch die rigiden Gesetze der Zünfte herrschten. Vor allem galt hier aber auch uneingeschränkte Glaubensfreiheit. Nach der Reformation wurde Altona neue Heimat für Katholiken und niederländische Mennoniten. Portugiesische und deutsche Juden siedelten sich hier an. Von den rund 24 000 Einwohnern zählten um 1800, am Auslauf des „Goldenen Jahrhunderts" der Stadt, zehn Prozent zum jüdischen Glauben. Der älteste jüdische Friedhof Hamburgs an der Altonaer Königstraße zeugt von dieser Vergangenheit. Auf dem heute nicht mehr öffentlichen Areal, das 1613 eingerichtet wurde, befinden sich 2500 sefardische und 6000 aschkenasische

no longer a boulevard but its unmistakable appearance makes it once again a jewel of urban planning that recalls the glorious days when Altona was part of Denmark.

In contrast to the Hamburg coat-of-arms, the gates on the Altona coat-of-arms are wide open to the world. Through the centuries Hamburg's lovely sister was far more of a gateway to the world than the Hanseatic city that is so fond of adorning itself with this epithet. Above all, liberal Altona kept its gates open for the world to come in. The street names Grosse Freiheit and Kleine Freiheit (Great Freedom and Small Freedom) are a reminder of the district in which from 1612 on craftsmen from outside were able to practise their trade without strict regulation, while elsewhere the rigid guild laws still prevailed. First and foremost, however, there was unrestricted freedom of religion. After the Reformation Altona became a new home for Catholics and Dutch Mennonites. Portuguese and German Jews settled here. In 1800, at the end of the town's "golden century," of approximately 24,000 inhabitants ten per cent were Jews. The oldest Jewish cemetery on Altona's Königstrasse is testimony to this past. The cemetery, which was established in 1613 and is no longer open to the public, contains 2,500 Sephardi and 6,000 Ashkenazi graves. In 1989 a monument to the more recent past was erected on the north side of the Rathaus. A rectangular block of black stone designed by US artist Sol LeWitt recalls the persecution and extermination of Altona's Jewish community during the National Socialist period.

Gräber. 1989 wurde an der Nordseite des Rathauses ein Mahnmal errichtet. Ein von dem amerikanischen Künstler Sol LeWitt geschaffener schwarzer Steinquader erinnert an die Verfolgung und Vernichtung der jüdischen Gemeinde in Altona während der Zeit des Nationalsozialismus.

## Altona wächst durch Eingemeindungen

Zum Bezirk Altona mit seinen heute rund 240 000 Einwohnern gehörten um 1900 bereits die ehemalige Stadt Ottensen und die Dörfer Bahrenfeld, Othmarschen und Övelgönne. Weitere Eingemeindungen erfolgten 1927: Flottbek, Nienstedten, Blankenese, Sülldorf, Rissen, Osdorf, Lurup, Eidelstedt und Stellingen.

In der Zeit der Weimarer Republik wurde Altona wesentlich von zwei großen Persönlichkeiten geprägt. Der gelernte Glasbläser aus Ottensen, Max Brauer (1887–1973), wurde als jüngstes Stadtoberhaupt in Preußen 1924 zum Oberbürgermeister gewählt. Zusammen mit dem Architekten Gustav Oelsner (1879–1956), der im selben Jahr Bausenator wurde, trieb der Sozialdemokrat Brauer den Wohnungs- und Schulbau voran, schuf neue Parks und Sozialeinrichtungen. Brauer und Oelsner galten als die Schöpfer des sogenannten Neuen Altona. 1933 wurden beide von den Nationalsozialisten ihrer Ämter enthoben. Der Architekt deutsch-jüdischer Abstammung Oelsner, der Berufsverbot erhalten hatte, emigrierte 1939 in die Türkei, übernahm dann 1949 noch einmal für drei Jahre ein Amt in der Hamburger Baubehörde. Max Brauer flüchtete vor der Diktatur, die ihn 1934 ausbürgerte, und übersiedelte nach mehreren Exilstationen 1936 in die USA. Nach seiner Rückkehr verantwortete er als Erster Bürgermeister der Hansestadt von 1946 bis 1953 und von 1957 bis 1960 den Wiederaufbau Hamburgs nach den Zerstörungen des Zweiten Weltkriegs. Der

## Altona grows by incorporation

By 1900 the former town of Ottensen and the villages of Bahrenfeld, Othmarschen and Övelgönne were already part of the local government district of Altona with its population of 240,000. Further incorporations followed in 1927: Flottbek, Nienstedten, Blankenese, Sülldorf, Rissen, Osdorf, Lurup, Eidelstedt and Stellingen all became administratively part of Altona.

In the Weimar Republic period Altona was essentially shaped by two great men. In 1924, Social Democrat Max Brauer (1887–1973), a trained glass-blower from Ottensen, was elected mayor and became the youngest local government head in Prussia. In collaboration with the architect Gustav Oelsner (1879–1956), who became planning and building control senator in the same year, Brauer forged ahead with the building of apartments and schools and established new parks and welfare institutions. Brauer and Oelsner were regarded as the creators of the so-called New Altona. In 1933 the National Socialists removed both men from office. Oelsner, who was of German-Jewish origin, was forbidden to practise as an architect and in 1939 he emigrated to Turkey, to return in 1949 to work for three years in the Hamburg planning and building control authority. Max Brauer fled from the dictatorship, was expatriated in 1934 and after several stations of exile, in 1936 moved to the USA. After his return, as mayor of Hamburg from 1946 to 1953 and from 1957 to 1960 Brauer was responsible for the city's reconstruction after the destruction of World War II. Nowadays the politician from Ottensen is regarded as the most distinguished personality in the city's post-war history.

Max Brauer (1887–1973) wurde 1924 in Altona zum Oberbürgermeister gewählt und 1933 von den Nazis aus dem Amt entlassen. 1946–53 war er als Erster Bürgermeister von Hamburg der Motor des Wiederaufbaus der Stadt.

Max Brauer, 1887–1973, was elected mayor of Altona in 1924 and dismissed by the Nazis in 1933. From 1946 to 1953 he was mayor of Hamburg, playing a key role in the city's post-WWII reconstruction.

Am Ottenser Spritzen-
platz münden mehrere
Straßen, in deren Netz-
werk man sich gut ver-
laufen kann. Der Treff-
punkt verbindet Men-
schen aller Kulturen,
die diesen Stadtteil so
lebendig machen.

Several roads merge at
Spritzenplatz in Otten-
sen, and it is easy to
lose your way in the
network they make up.
Spritzenplatz is a meet-
ing-point for people of
all cultures, and they
are what makes this
district so full of life.

Ottensen – hier die sich
zum Alma-Wartenberg-
Platz öffnende Bahren-
felder Straße – ist ein
buntes Quartier.

Ottensen, here seen
where Bahrenfelder
Strasse opens out into
the square Alma-
Wartenberg-Platz, is a
colourful district.

aus Ottensen stammende Politiker gilt
heute als eine der markantesten Persönlichkeiten in der Nachkriegsgeschichte
der Stadt.

## Wohnen, arbeiten und ausgehen in Ottensen

Wer heute von Altona spricht, meint
häufig Ottensen. Das 1889 eingemeinde-
te Dorf hat sich seit den siebziger Jahren
zu einem bunten Kiez kleiner Läden,

## Living, working and relaxing in Ottensen

Nowadays when people talk about
Altona they often mean Ottensen. Since
the 1970s the village incorporated into
Altona in 1889 has developed into a
colourful district of small shops, bars
and restaurants and cultural establishments, a district in which foreigners set
the tone as much as yuppies, students
and ordinary workers and office clerks
with a German family history. Careful
renovation has preserved old buildings in
this district of tranquil rear courtyards
and a historic network of streets that can
soon become a labyrinth for strangers to
the area. In Ottensen living, working and
going out – work and leisure – are closely interwoven. In the second half of the
nineteenth century the Prussian village

Lokale und Kulturorte entwickelt, in dem Ausländer genauso den Ton angeben wie Yuppies, Studenten und einfache Arbeiter und Angestellte mit deutscher Familiengeschichte. Durch behutsame Sanierung wurde alte Bausubstanz erhalten. Es gibt stille Hinterhöfe und ein historisches Straßennetz, das für Fremde schnell zum Labyrinth wird. In Ottensen sind die Bereiche Wohnen, Arbeiten und Ausgehen – Arbeit und Freizeit – noch dicht ineinander verwoben. In der zweiten Hälfte des 19. Jahrhunderts war das preußische Dorf zum Standort für Tabak- und Fischindustrie, für Glashütten, Eisen- und Schiffbau mutiert. Viele Ottenser nennen ihr ehemaliges Dorf, das schließlich das größte in Preußen geworden war und 1871 zur Stadt erhoben wurde, noch heute Mottenburg. Ein ziemlich makaberer Beiname, denn er erinnert an die katastrophalen Arbeitsbedingungen der Glasbläser, Tabakdreher und Schweißer, die sich bei ihrem 16-Stunden-Tag nicht selten „die Motten" holten. Das hieß, sie wurden tuberkulosekrank.

Die Ummünzung Ottensens zum heutigen multikulturellen Stadtteil begann mit dem Zuzug ausländischer, vor allem türkischer Gastarbeiter in den sechziger Jahren und während der Krise der Industrie Anfang der Siebziger. Mit der Schließung zahlreicher mittelständischer Gewerbetriebe wurde Wohnraum frei und bezahlbar. Ein prägnantes Beispiel für den Strukturwandel von Ottensen ist die Entstehung der Medien-Fabrik Zeisehallen. 1868 hatte der Sproß einer Altonaer Großbürgerfamilie, Theodor Zeise, an der heutigen Friedensallee seine Eisengießerei gegründet. Ein Jahr zuvor war Ottensen in den deutschen Zollverein aufgenommen worden. Die Wirtschaft boomte. Das Handwerker- und Bauerndorf verwandelte sich zum Industriestandort. Genau 111 Jahre wurde auf dem Zeise-Gelände produziert. Die Schiffsschrauben, die bei Zeise gegossen

was transformed as tobacco and fish industries, glassworks, metalworks and ship-building established themselves there. Many local people still call their former village – which ended up being the biggest in Prussia and in 1871 was elevated to a town – Mottenburg, a rather macabre nickname recalling the dreadful working conditions of the glassblowers, tobacco rollers and welders who worked a 16-hour day and not infrequently fell victim to "Motten," a slang word for tuberculosis.

Ottensen's transformation into the present multicultural district began with the arrival of foreign, mainly Turkish, guest workers in the 1960s and during the industrial crisis in the early 1970s. The closure of many small and medium-sized commercial enterprises freed up affordable living space. One illustrative example of Ottensen's structural change is the birth of the Zeise media factory. Theodor Zeise, son of an upper-class Altona family opened his iron foundry on what is now Friedensallee in 1868, one year after Ottensen had been admit-

In Ottensen kann jeder nach seiner Fasson auftreten. Hier ein Feuerschlucker auf einer der Brachflächen, die im Bauboom des Stadtteils nach und nach verschwinden

In Ottensen, you do your own thing. Here, a fire-eater performs on one of the patches of waste land that are gradually disappearing as the construction boom fills them up.

So sah um 1918 Max Kuchel die Gießereihalle der Schiffsschraubenfabrik Theodor Zeise, die heute die Zeisehallen an der Friedensallee beherbergen.

This is how it looked in the foundry hall of Theodor Zeise's ship's propeller works in about 1918, which is now part of the Zeisehallen on Friedensallee.

wurden, hatten Weltruf. Daß die Firma 1979 in Konkurs ging, hing vor allem mit der deutschen Werftenkrise zusammen. Während in einem zur Straße gelegenen Verwaltungsgebäude mit dem Filmhaus und der Filmhauskneipe neues Leben einzog, verfielen die Produktionshallen zu Ruinen. 1993 wurde dann in den alten Mauern die Medien-Fabrik Zeisehallen eingeweiht. Eine bunte Mischung von Kulturunternehmen, mit Läden, Lokalen begann den öffentlichen Weg, der durch die Hallen führt, zu säumen.

ted to the German customs union. The economy was booming. The village of craftsmen and farmers was turning into an industrial location. Production continued at the Zeise works for exactly 111 years. The ships' screws manufactured by Zeise were known world-wide. The firm's bankruptcy in 1979 was mainly due to the crisis in the German shipyards. While the Filmhaus and Filmhaus bar breathed new life into the administrative building facing the street, the old factory fell into ruins. Finally, in 1993 within the old factory walls the Zeisehallen media factory was formally opened, a colourful mixture of cultural firms, shops and restaurants began to line the public footpath leading through the former factory halls.

## The Fabrik – Germany's first communications centre

However, it was not the Zeisehallen but the Fabrik (Factory) in Barnerstrasse that was the forerunner of structural change in Ottensen. In 1971 the programme of Germany's first communications centre, which became the model for the alternative cultural establishments shooting up at the time, began in this three-storeyed former engineering works, a wood-framed brick building dating back to 1830. In addition to a varied music programme it provided a venue for theatre, children's, youth and political workshops. More than a quarter of a century has passed since the Fabrik opened its doors, but the communication centre, still managed by its co-founder the painter and graphic artist Horst Dietrich,

## Die „Fabrik" – Deutschlands erstes Kommunikationszentrum

Vorreiter des Strukturwandels in Ottensen waren aber nicht die Zeisehallen, das war die „Fabrik" an der Barnerstraße. In der ehemaligen Maschinenfabrik von 1830, einer basilikagleichen Holzkonstruktion mit Backsteinaußenwänden über drei Etagen, begann 1971 das Programm des ersten bundesrepublikanischen Kommunikationszentrums, das zum Vorbild der damals aus dem Boden schießenden alternativen Kultureinrichtungen wurde. Neben einem bunten Musikprogramm gab es Workshops für Theater-, Kinder-, Jugend- und politische Gruppen. Seit der Gründung der „Fabrik" ist inzwischen mehr als ein Vierteljahrhundert vergangen. Doch das Kommunikationszentrum, das heute noch von seinem Mitbegründer, dem Maler und Graphiker Horst Dietrich, geleitet wird, besitzt nach wie vor ein Flair, das selbst hochberühmte Künstler immer wieder zu Auftritten auf der kleinen Bühne verlockt. Als Ort für Folklore-Musik und Jazz hat das Haus weltweit einen Ruf. Seit 1971 kommen viele Menschen nur deshalb nach Hamburg, nach Altona, ganz genau nach Ottensen, weil es dort die „Fabrik" gibt.

Die Ummünzung früherer Fabriken und Gewerbeanlagen hat Altona seit den siebziger Jahren sehr verändert. Borselhof oben links, Phönixhof oben rechts, unten die „Fabrik", die 1971 als Deutschlands erstes Kultur- und Kommunikationszentrum eröffnet wurde

Conversion of former factories and workshops has changed Altona greatly since the 1970s. Conversions include the Borselhof. above left, the Phönixhof, above right, and, below, the "Fabrik" (Factory), which opened in 1971 as Germany's first cultural and communication centre of its kind

still has the aura which attracts even famous artistes to perform time and again on its small stage. It enjoys a world-wide reputation as a folk music and jazz venue. Since 1971 many visitors have come to Hamburg, or rather Altona, or to be strictly accurate to Ottensen for one reason alone – because of the Fabrik.

# Die Elbchaussee am hohen Ufer des Stroms

Elbchaussee on the high bank of the river

Chaussee ist das französische Wort für Landstraße. Die Elbchaussee erhielt diesen schlichten Namen im Jahr 1830, als der etwa 8,5 Kilometer lange Sandweg zwischen Ottensen und Blankenese zur Schotterstraße ausgebaut wurde und der Verlauf am hohen Ufer des Stroms seine heutige Form bekam. Der Name ist schiere Untertreibung. Denn in Wirklichkeit ist die Elbchaussee eine der schönsten Straßen der Welt, Hamburgs feinste Adresse, der dem Flußverlauf harmonisch folgende Leitfaden durch die Noblesse gehobenen Wohnstils, eine Perlenkette weißer Landvillen und grüner Parks, eine Straße, an der Geschichte, Kulturgeschichte, Kommerz und Politik gemacht wurde und wird.

Über die Elbchaussee kann man aber durchaus auch fluchen. Denn Tatsache ist, daß sich jeden Morgen und jeden Abend zur Rushhour ein Strom von Autos von Ampel zu Ampel schiebt. Daß die Elbchaussee in den Zeiten, als man vom autogerechten Ausbau der Städte träumte, dank der Proteste der Anwohner nicht zu einer vierspurigen Schnellstraße ausgebaut wurde, ist dennoch ein Glücksfall.

### Sommervillen von gediegener Pracht

Trotz aller Veränderungen hat die Elbchaussee noch viel von der Prägung bewahrt, die sie um 1800 aufwies. Im 18. Jahrhundert zog es die Menschen, die es sich leisten konnten, mit Macht ins Grüne. Der Aufstieg des schön geschwungenen Sandpfades zur feinen Chaussee begann mit der Mode, daß sich reich gewordene Hamburger und Altonaer Kaufleute auf den Hügeln des Nordufers der Elbe Sommervillen von gediegener Pracht leisteten. Während die Väter im Stadtkontor ihren Geschäften nachgingen und nur sonntags in den Elbvororten erschienen, genossen die Familien sommermonatelang das Landleben.

Chaussee is the French word for a country high road. Elbchaussee was given this simple name in 1830 when the approximately 8.5 kilometre long dirt road between Ottensen and Blankenese was modernised as a grit road and its route along the high bank of the river took on its present shape. The name is pure understatement. For in reality Elbchaussee is one of the most attractive roads in the world, Hamburg's most exclusive address, a connecting thread harmoniously following the course of the river through the noblesse of an exalted lifestyle, a string of pearls of white country houses and green parks, a road along which history, cultural history, commerce and politics have been shaped and continue to be so.

It is perfectly possible to curse Elbchaussee too. For the fact is that every morning and evening rush hour a stream of cars push their way along it from one traffic light to the next. Nevertheless, it is fortunate that thanks to residents' protests Elbchaussee was not turned into a four-lane highway in the days when people dreamed of making cities fit for cars.

### Summer villas of tasteful grandeur

Despite many changes, Elbchaussee has retained much of the character it boasted in around 1800. During the eighteenth century, powerful people who could afford it were drawn to the countryside. The elevation of the attractively winding dirt track into a fine avenue began with the fashion for Hamburgers who had made a fortune and Altona merchants to buy themselves tastefully splendid sum-

Zu den vielfach im klassizistischen Stil errichteten Villen gehörten weitläufige Parks und Treibhäuser, deren Produkte bei den Gartenfesten stolz präsentiert wurden. Während die Parks nach englischem Vorbild gestaltet wurden, gab sich die feine Gesellschaft an der Elbchaussee um 1800 ansonsten auch gern französisch. Man parlierte in der Sprache jenseits des Rheins und las französische Autoren. Wohlhabende Revolutionsflüchtlinge aus Frankreich, die sich an der noblen Chaussee niederließen, brachten ihre Lebensgewohnheiten mit und lebten sie zur Nachahmung vor. Der schöne Atem dieser Vergangenheit kann heute von jedermann genossen werden. Die ehemaligen Privatparks der Wohlhabenden gehören der Stadt und sind frei zugänglich.

Die Elbchaussee ist dank ihres historischen Baumbestands und neuer Anpflanzungen zu allen vier Jahreszeiten eine

mer villas on the hills along the north bank of the Elbe. While fathers went about their business in the city offices, only turning up in the Elbe suburbs on Sundays, their families enjoyed the country life throughout the summer months.

The villas, many in classical style, had extensive parks and hothouses whose produce was proudly displayed at garden parties. While the parks were laid out in the English style, in other respects high society on the Elbchaussee in around 1800 was fond of French ways. They spoke and read French. Wealthy refugees from the French Revolution who came to settle on the high-class avenue brought their manners and customs with them and practised them for others to imitate. Nowadays the fine ambience of this past can be enjoyed by everyone.

Rainvilles Garten und Restaurant boten einen faszinierenden Blick über den Strom am Anfang der Elbchaussee. Das um 1815 gemalte Aquarell zeigt das damals so beliebte Ausflugsziel der Hamburger mit einer Vielzahl von liebevoll gestalteten Details.

Rainville's Garden and Restaurant enjoyed a fascinating view of the River Elbe at the beginning of Elbchaussee. This watercolour, painted in about 1815, shows what was in those days a favourite excursion destination for Hamburg people, complete with loving attention to detail.

Der Hirschpark mit
der 200 Jahre alten Lin-
denallee und der Rho-
dodendronwiese gehört
zu den Höhepunkten
der Elbchaussee – der
„schönsten Straße der
Erde".

Hirschpark with its
200-year-old avenue of
linden trees and its rho-
dodendron meadow is
one of the highlights of
Elbchaussee, the "finest
street on earth."

Attraktion. Blühende Mandelbäume, Japanische Kirschen, Magnolien, Kastanien im Frühjahr, Rotbuchen, Rosen im Sommer, flammender Ahorn, brennend rote Essigbäume im Herbst, schneebedeckte 200jährige Eichen und junge Birken im Winter. Die Fahrt auf der Elbchaussee ist, abgesehen von der Rushhour, zu allen Jahreszeiten eine Lustpartie. Wer die Chaussee per Fahrrad oder zu Fuß erwandert, Autolärm und Abgase irgendwann leid wird, kann aufs schönste flüchten. Nämlich direkt nach Süden ans Elbufer, wo zwischen den Gärten der ehemaligen Fischerdörfer Neumühlen und Övelgönne über Teufelsbrück, Nienstedten, Blankenese der Elbwanderweg parallel zur Chaussee verläuft.

**Reverenz an den Dichter**

Daß der Auftakt zur Elbchaussee heute den Namen Klopstockstraße trägt, ist eine Reverenz an den Dichter, dessen Grabstätte sich hier befindet. Im Schatten der 1783 geweihten Christianskirche ruht seit 1803 Friedrich Gottlieb Klopstock „bey seiner Meta und bey seinem Kinde", wie es auf dem Grabstein der schönen Anlage heißt.

Eine Straße wie die Elbchaussee ist immer auch Erinnerung an herausragende Persönlichkeiten. Nicht weit entfernt von Klopstocks Grab, Elbchaussee 31, wird in dem kleinen Gartenhaus Heinrich Heines (1797–1856) und Salomon Heines gedacht. Der Dichter und der Bankier, Neffe und Onkel, waren, jeder auf seine Art, wichtige Persönlichkeiten in der Geschichte der Hansestadt Hamburg. Der reiche Onkel hatte sich 1832 seine Landvilla an der Elbchaussee gebaut. Vom wortmächtigen Neffen wurde der Ort als „Affrontenburg" geschmäht. Denn sein Ersuchen um Geld endete häufig auch mit einem Affront,

The parks which once belonged to wealthy private owners now belong to the city and are open to all.

Thanks to its historic trees and newly planted flora, Elbchaussee is an attraction all year round. Blossoming almond trees, Japanese cherries, magnolias and chestnut trees in spring. Copper beeches and roses in summer, flaming maple and brilliant red stag's horn sumacs in autumn and snow-covered 200-year-old oaks and young birch trees in winter. Except in the rush hour, the journey along Elbchaussee is a joy in every season. Anyone exploring it on foot or by bicycle can make a wonderful escape if the traffic noise and exhaust fumes become too much – by striking off southwards straight down to the bank of the Elbe, where the Elbe footpath runs parallel with Elbchaussee between the gardens of the former fishing villages of Neumühlen and Ovelgönne, via Teufelsbrück, Nienstedten and Blankenese.

**Homage to the writer**

That the start of Elbchaussee is now called Klopstockstrasse is in honour of the writer whose gravestone can be seen there. Since 1803 Friedrich Gottlieb Klopstock has lain at rest "with his Meta and his child" as the inscription says, in the attractive churchyard of Christianskirche, which was consecrated in 1783.

A road like Elbchaussee always calls to mind outstanding individuals. Not far from Klopstock, at Elbchaussee 31, a small summer-house is a reminder of Heinrich Heine (1797–1856) and Salomon Heine. The writer and the banker, nephew and uncle, were each in their own way outstanding characters in the history of Hamburg. The rich uncle built his country house on Elbchaussee in 1832. His eloquent nephew often scornfully referred to the house as "Affrontenburg" on account of the fact that his pleading for money often ended in an affront, or at least that is how Heinrich Heine saw a rejection from his

einer Kränkung, wie die Ablehnung von dem Dichter verstanden wurde. Gartenhaus und Park sind die letzten Relikte des herrschaftlichen Anwesens aus dem 19. Jahrhundert.

Wer den Schleifen der Elbchaussee weiter nach Westen folgt, wird immer wieder von den Sehenswürdigkeiten dieser Prachtstraße gefangengenommen – u. a. fallen ins Auge: die Lichter und Brücken des Containerhafens von der „nassen" Chausseeseite aus gesehen, das verrückte „High-Tech-Barock-Haus" Nummer 96 auf der rechten, der „trockenen" Seite, die von Meinhard von Gerkan entworfene moderne Architektenburg Elbschlucht links, das weiße Säulenhaus rechts, das 1817 von Axel Bundsen für den Reeder Wilhelm Brandt errichtet wurde.

Uncle Salomon. The summer-house and park are all that remains of the grand nineteenth-century estate.

Travelling westward along the twists and turns of Elbchaussee you are constantly captivated by the sights of this magnificent boulevard. Some of things you notice are the lights and portainers in the container terminal on the left, the side nearest to the river, the crazy "high-tech" Baroque building at No. 96 on the right, Meinhard von Gerkan's modern architectural fortress Elbschlucht on the left and on the right a columned white mansion built by Axel Bundsen in 1817 for the shipowner Wilhelm Brandt. At Teufelsbrück, you reach what many people say is the most attractive section of Elbchaussee. On the right is Jenischpark, with a path leading up to the Jenischhaus, a fine mansion based on plans by Karl Friedrich Schinkel which the architect Franz Gustav Forsmann designed between 1832 and 1835 for the Hamburg Senator Martin Johann Jenisch. Nowadays the mansion is open to the public as a museum of nineteenth-century bourgeois lifestyle. To the east of the house, nestling behind 200-year-old oak trees is the Ernst Barlach Haus, a white atrium building designed by Werner Kallmorgen. Dedicated to the works of

Hier ruht bei seiner Meta der Dichter Friedrich Gottlieb Klopstock (1724–1803). Die Grabanlage vor der Christianskirche (links) war häufig Ziel des Dichters Heinrich Heine (1825–56), wenn er auf dem Landsitz seines Onkels Salomon weilte. Von dessen Besitz steht heute nur noch das kleine Gartenhaus (rechts).

Here lies alongside his wife Meta the poet Friedrich Gottlieb Klopstock, 1724–1803. His grave outside the Christianskirche (left) was frequently visited by the poet Heinrich Heine, 1797–1856, when he spent time at his uncle Salomon's country seat. All that now remains of the estate is the garden house (right).

Das „verrückte Haus" an der Elbchaussee, Ecke Fischers Allee, sorgt an allen Ecken und Enden für Aufsehen.

The "mad house" on Elbchaussee, at the corner of Fischers Allee, has created a widespread furore.

Bei Teufelsbrück gibt es eine Partie der Elbchaussee, die viele für die allerschönste halten: Durch den Jenischpark führt der Weg hoch zum Jenischhaus. Das von 1832 bis 1835 von dem Architekten Gustav Forsmann (mit verworfener Vorplanung von Karl Friedrich Schinkel) für den Hamburger Senator Johann Jenisch errichtete Herrenhaus ist heute als Museum für großbürgerliche Wohnkultur des 19. Jahrhunderts zugänglich. Östlich davon verbirgt sich im Jenischpark hinter 200 Jahre alten Eichen der weiße Atriumbau des Ernst Barlach Hauses (Architekt: Werner Kallmorgen). Das dem 1870 vor den Toren Hamburgs, im schleswig-holsteinischen Wedel geborenen Schriftsteller und bildenden Künstler gewidmete Haus ist eine Stiftung des Industriellen Hermann F. Reemtsma.

## Caspar Voght – der „grüne Baron"

Nur noch die Baron-Voght-Straße, die hinter dem Jenischpark rechts von der Elbchaussee abzweigt, erinnert mit ihrem Namen an den Schöpfer der grandiosen „ornamented farm", die hier in der ersten Hälfte des 19. Jahrhunderts entstanden war und von der der Jenischpark ein Teil ist. Caspar Voght (1752–1839), der „grüne Baron", war eine der herausragendsten Gestalten in der Vergangenheit der Hansestadt. Der Sohn aus reicher Hamburger Kaufmannsfamilie reiste als junger Mann mehrere Jahre durch Europa. Auf seinen Bildungsreisen durch Holland, England, Frankreich, Spanien und Italien knüpfte er Freundschaften mit Literaten, Philosophen und Politikern. Der sozial engagierte Aufklärer begründete in Hamburg eine Armenfürsorge, die Vorbild für gleiche Einrichtungen in vielen europäischen Städten wurde. Für die Reorganisation des Wiener Armenwesens verlieh ihm der deutsche Kaiser 1802 den Titel eines Freiherrn.

the writer and sculptor Ernst Barlach, who was born in 1870 in Wedel just outside Hamburg's western boundary, the gallery and museum was sponsored by the industrialist Hermann F. Reemtsma.

## Caspar Voght – the "green baron"

Nowadays only Baron-Voght-Strasse, the road that branches off from Elbchaussee after the Jenischpark, remains as a reminder of the man who created the grandiose "ornamented farm" that graced the area in the first half of the nineteenth century, a farm of which the Jenischpark formed part. Caspar Voght (1752–1839), the "green baron," was one of the outstanding figures in Hamburg's history. As a young man the son of rich Hamburg business people spent several years travelling round Europe. On his educational journeys through the Netherlands, Britain, France, Spain and Italy he made friends with writers, philosophers and politicians. In Hamburg, Voght, a socially committed man of the Enlightenment, founded a system of welfare for the poor which served as a model for similar facilities in many European towns. In 1802 the German Emperor awarded him the title of baron in recognition of his reorganisation of the system of welfare for the poor in Vienna.

The baron, who was a life-long admirer of beautiful women but never married, appreciated both the advantages of big-city life and the charms of the countryside. From 1785 onwards he began buying up farmland just outside Hamburg in Flottbek, which in those days was part of Holstein, ultimately becoming the owner of 260 hectares, four times the area of the present-day Jenischpark. On his English-style "ornamented farm" he planted potatoes and clover, reared orchids in hot-houses, established a tree nursery and laid out ponds and a waterfall, as well as setting up an "agricultural education institute" where around 30 pupils were taught how to grow crops,

Voght, der zeitlebens ein Liebhaber schöner, kluger Frauen war, aber nie heiratete, der die Vorzüge des Großstadtlebens genauso schätzte wie das Landleben, kaufte ab 1785 vor den Toren Hamburgs, im damals holsteinischen Flottbek, Bauernland auf, das mit 260 Hektar viermal soviel Fläche umfaßte wie der heutige Jenischpark. Auf seiner nach englischem Vorbild gestalteten „ornamented farm" baute er Kartoffeln und Klee an, züchtete Orchideen in Gewächshäusern, schuf Teiche, eine Baumschule und legte einen Wasserfall an. In einem „landwirtschaftlichen Erziehungsinstitut" wurden etwa dreißig

fruit and vegetables. He built homes for his staff and in 1794 had one built for himself, a rather modest country house north-west of what is now the Jenischpark, where he entertained guests from all over the world.

Since the mid-1990s there have been efforts to restore the historic shape of Voght's "ornamented farm" on the land to the west of the park. If you are wondering why it is call Jenischpark and not Voghtpark, the answer is simple. In 1828 Voght, once known as "the richest man

Abendgesellschaft bei Baron Caspar Voght auf seiner Ornamented Farm in Klein-Flottbek (oben links)
Porträt des vielgereisten, ideenreichen Weltmannes Caspar Voght (oben), dessen Wohnhaus an der heutigen Baron-Voght-Straße zu seiner Zeit ein lebendiger Hof der Musen war (unten)

A dinner party at the home of Baron Caspar Voght at his "ornamented farm" in Klein-Flottbek (above left)
A portrait of the much-travelled and imaginative man of the world Caspar Voght (above), whose home on today's Baron-Voght-Strasse was, in its day, a lively centre of the arts (below)

Das Jenischhaus ist heute Museum für die großbürgerliche Kultur des 18./19. Jahrhunderts, dessen Park zu den schönsten an der Elbchaussee zählt.

The Jenischhaus is now a museum of grand bourgeois culture of the eighteenth and nineteenth centuries, with a park and grounds that rank among the finest on Elbchaussee.

200

Die Blutbuche vor dem
Herrenhaus im Hirsch-
park wurde als im
Umfang stärkster Baum
von Hamburg vermes-
sen. In dem von Christi-
an Frederik Hansen
gebauten Landsitz für
die Familie Godeffroy
hat heute eine Tanz-
und Ballettschule ihr
Domizil.

The copper beech out-
side the Hirschpark
manor house was meas-
ured and found to be
the tree with the largest
circumference in Ham-
burg. A school of ballet
and dance is now hous-
ed in what was
designed by Christian
Frederik Hansen as a
country seat for the
Godeffroy family.

Mit Filzpuschen an den Füßen kann heute jedermann durch die großbürgerliche Wohnkultur im Jenischhaus wandern. Das schön geschwungene Tor zum Jenischpark, Ecke Elbchaussee/Holztwiete, lädt in das von Baron Voght geschaffene grüne Paradies ein.

Wearing felt slippers, anyone can now walk round the Jenischhaus and admire the grand bourgeois lifestyle it epitomised. The finely curved gateway to Jenischpark at the corner of Elbchaussee and Holztwiete invites you to visit Baron Voght's green paradise.

Schüler in Acker-, Obst- und Gemüseanbau unterrichtet. Er errichtete Wohnhäuser für seine Angestellten und ließ sich 1794 selber ein Landhaus bauen, in dem er Gäste aus aller Welt empfing. Es handelte sich dabei um ein eher bescheidenes ländliches Domizil nordwestlich des heutigen Jenischparks.

Seit Mitte der neunziger Jahre wird dem westlich des Parks liegenden Gelände von Voghts „ornamented farm" die

in the north," fell into financial difficulties and sold his estate to his friend Johann Martin Jenisch, retaining the right to occupy his country home for the rest of his life.

**Where wedding bells ring and celebrities are buried**

Continuing west from Jenischpark, you pass the palatial International Maritime Court building, where from time to time 21 highly specialised lawyers from all over the world meet to solve disputes

historische Form zurückgegeben. Daß
der Park heute nicht den Namen des
„grünen Barons" trägt, hat einen einfachen Grund. 1828 verkaufte der einst
„reichste Mann des Nordens", der in
finanzielle Schwierigkeiten geraten war,
seinen Besitz an den Freund Johann
Martin Jenisch, behielt aber ein lebens-
langes Wohnrecht in seinem Landhaus.

## Hochzeitskirche und Prominentenfried-hof

Vorbei am Justizpalast des Internationalen Seegerichtshofs, wo von Zeit zu Zeit
21 hochspezialisierte Juristen aus aller
Herren Länder Streitfälle klären sollen,
die außerhalb der Hoheitsgebiete und
Dreimeilenzonen auf den Meeren ihren
Ort haben, vorbei an dieser repräsentativen Institution, über der die meerblaue
UN-Fahne weht, führt der Weg über die

over international waters. From the
imposing building with the blue United
Nations flag fluttering over it the road
leads to the small country church of
Nienstedten, built in 1750 and now in
great demand for weddings – and to the
Nienstedten cemetery, with Caspar
Voght's rather grand gravestone by the
entrance. Engraved on it is a poem by his
friend Karl Sieveking.

Das Elbschlößchen an
der Christian-Frederik-
Hansen-Straße liegt
etwas im Verborgenen
(oben).
Das Barlachhaus im
Jenischpark ist dem
Bildhauer und Dra-
matiker Ernst Barlach
gewidmet und stellt
seine Werke aus
(unten).

The Elbschlösschen on
Christian-Frederik-
Hansen-Strasse, is
slightly hidden from
view (above).
The Barlachhaus in
Jenischpark is dedicated
to the sculptor and
playwright Ernst Bar-
lach and exhibits his
works (below).

Die Nienstedtener
Kirche wurde als Fach-
werkbau 1751 fertig-
gestellt und ist heute bei
Heiratswilligen sehr
beliebt (oben).
Der Internationale
Seegerichtshof (unten)
macht seit dem Jahr
2000 Staat an der Elb-
chaussee.

Nienstedten Church
was built as a half-tim-
bered building in 1751
and is now a highly
popular church in
which to wed (above).
The International Mari-
time Court (below) has
graced Elbchaussee
since 2000.

Elbchaussee zur 1750 errichteten Bau-
ernkirche von Nienstedten – heute als
Hochzeitskirche äußerst beliebt – und
zum Nienstedtener Friedhof, an dessen
Eingang sich der pompöse Grabstein für
Caspar Voght findet. Darin eingemeißelt:
selbstverfaßte Verse des Freundes Karl
Sieveking.

Another Hamburg celebrity buried in
the cemetery on Elbchaussee is the
writer, organ-maker and research scientist Hans Henny Jahnn (1894–1959), the
founder of the Hamburg Free Academy
of the Arts. Jahnn spent the last few
years of his life just a few bends further
along Elbchaussee in Hirschpark, in a
thatched cavalier's house that is now a
tea-room. Here on the river side of
Elbchaussee, in one of the loveliest parks
along Hamburg's loveliest road, Jahnn
lived in the shadow of the magnificent
mansion which the shipowner Johann
Cesar IV. Godeffroy had built between
1789 and 1792 by Christian Frederik
Hansen, the Danish master of classicism.
Nowadays the palatial columned mansion is let to a ballet school. Hansen's
building is another highlight from the
Elbchaussee's heyday in around 1800.
Finally, the illustrious road ends quite
unspectacularly in Blankenese in a rather

Auf diesem Prominentenfriedhof an
der Elbchaussee wurde auch der Schriftsteller, Orgelbauer und Forscher Hans
Henny Jahnn (1894–1959) zu Grabe
getragen. Seine letzten Lebensjahre hatte
der Gründer der Freien Akademie der
Künste in Hamburg wenige Elbchaussee-
kurven weiter im Hirschpark verbracht,
in dem reetgedeckten Kavaliershaus, das
heute eine Teestube und ein Restaurant
beherbergt. Hier, auf der Wasserseite der
Chaussee, in einem der schönsten Parks
an Hamburgs schönster Straße, hatte
Jahnn im Schatten des großartigen Her-
renhauses gelebt, das sich der Reeder
Johann Cesar IV. Godeffroy von 1789
bis 1792 von dem dänischen Meister des
Klassizismus, Christian Frederik Hansen,
errichten ließ. Heute ist eine Ballettschule Mieterin des Säulenpalastes.

Der Hansenbau ist noch einmal ein
Höhepunkt aus der Gründerzeit der Elbchaussee um 1800. Als eher schlichte
Wohn- und Ladenzeile endet die berühmte Straße in Blankenese dann ganz
unspektakulär. Nur noch gutbürgerliches
Milieu statt großbürgerlicher Prächtig-
keit, die der Chaussee ihren Ruf einge-
tragen hat.

Der Katharinenhof im
Baurs Park ist Domizil
städtischer Amtsstuben
(oben links).
Im ehemaligen Kava-
liershaus im Hirschpark
kann heute jeder im
„Witthüs" einkehren
(rechts oben).
Die Lindenallee im
Hirschpark ist als vier-
reihige Anlage eine Sel-
tenheit (unten rechts).

Katharinenhof in Baurs
Park houses municipal
offices (above left).
Witthüs, the former
gentlemen's quarters in
Hirschpark, is now
open to all (above
right).
The park's avenue of
linden trees, planted in
four rows (below right),
is distinctly unusual.

plain row of houses and shops – a solid
middle-class milieu rather than the grand
bourgeois pomp that earned Elbchaussee
its reputation.

# Blankenese: Dorf und Welt am Wasser

Blankenese: village and world by the water

Der vielbeschworene Zauber von Blankenese? Er liegt nicht in den stillen Wohnstraßen, in denen weiße Landhäuser und rote Backsteinvillen gehobenen hanseatischen Lebensstil demonstrieren. Auch nicht in dem Reichtum an gepflegten Gärten und Parks. Und nicht in der Vielzahl kleiner Geschäfte, in denen jeder nach seiner Fasson bedient wird. Das ist alles ganz vorzüglich und gehört auch zu Blankenese. Doch diese Vorzüge besitzen die anderen Elbvororte von Othmarschen bis Hochkamp auch.

Der besondere Zauber von Blankenese entfaltet sich da, wo die Wiege des heute so exklusiven Vorortes von Hamburg stand: am Strand und in dem sich darüber wie in einer Muschel an den Hang schmiegenden Treppenviertel. Die weite Wasserfläche der Elbe bestimmt den Blick, das Licht, die Luft und das Lebensgefühl. Auf drei Kilometern dehnt sich der Strom hier von einem Ufer zum anderen aus. Im Wechsel der Gezeiten steigt und fällt das Wasser. Bei Ebbe liegen südlich der Fahrrinne Sandbänke frei. Refugien für Segler und Tausende von Vögeln. Bei Sturmflut schlagen die Wellen manchmal bis an die Gartenmauern der Häuser am Strandweg. Wo spiegeln sich die Sonnenuntergänge so unglaublich schön wie hier, wo die Sonne im Winter oft wie ein riesiger feuerroter Ballon hinter dunklen Wolkenwänden im Westen im Strom versinkt und im Sommer den Turm des Süllbergs am Nordufer in letztes Licht taucht?

**Ozeanriesen und Optimisten**

In Blankenese am Wasser packen die romantische Seele ozeanische Gefühle. Die Phantasie kann mit den Ozeanriesen aufs Meer hinausziehen. Am Fuße vom Mühlenberg und von Baurs Park liegen in zwei kleinen Segelhäfen Kutter, Jollen, Yachten und Optimisten, die Segelkisten für Anfänger. Hier startete manche

The much-invoked magic of Blankenese does not lie in its quiet residential streets where white country houses and red-brick villas provide testimony to exclusive Hanseatic lifestyle. Nor in its wealth of well-kept gardens and parks. Nor yet in the large number of small shops where customers find personal service. All this is most excellent and an integral part of Blankenese, but the other Elbe suburbs from Othmarschen to Hochkamp boast the same advantages.

The special magic of Blankenese reveals itself in the cradle of this now so exclusive Hamburg suburb – down by the riverside and in the "staircase quarter" that nestles as if in a shell on the slope above it. Here the view is defined by the white surface of the Elbe, the light, the air and the feeling for life. Here the river stretches for three kilometres from one bank to the other. The water rises and falls with the tides. At low tide sandbanks are revealed to the south of the shipping lane, refuges for sailors and thousands of birds. At storm tide the waves sometimes beat against the garden walls of the houses down by the river. Where else are sunsets so beautifully reflected as here where in winters the sun often sinks like a gigantic, fiery red balloon behind dark banks of cloud on the south bank of the river and in winter the Süllberg tower on the north bank is bathed in the last rays of light?

**Oceangoing giants and Optimists**

Down by the water in Blankenese romantic souls are seized by sea-going emotions. The imagination can sail out on to the open sea with the giant oceangoing ships. In two small yacht marinas

Seglerkarriere. An Regattatagen stiehlt die Vielzahl der weißen Segel den Containerriesen und Tankern die Schau. Doch auf dem Wasser vor Blankenese, wo selbstredend strenge Vorfahrtsregeln befolgt werden müssen, kommen auch die Kleinen zu ihrem Recht. Bei Wind und Wetter sind die Paddler unterwegs, die ebenfalls am Strand ihre Stützpunkte haben.

„Bedenke immer, Du wohnst an einem großen Strom." So pflegte der Zeichner Horst Janssen einen traurigen Nachbarn zu trösten. Der 1995 verstorbene Künstler war nach Blankenese geraten und hat diesen Ort nie wieder verlassen. So, wie es vielen Zugereisten - und vor allem vielen Künstlern – hier ergeht. Janssen in seinem Gehäuse am Mühlenberger Weg, von dessen Altan aus er die Elbe durch die Bäume glitzern sehen konnte, wurde zur Legende. Die Geschichten, die sich

at the foot of Mühlenberg and Baurs Park you find cutters, sailing dinghies, yachts and Optimists – sailing tubs for beginners. Many a sailor's career began here. On regatta days the vast number of white sails on the water steals the show from the gigantic container vessels and tankers. But in the waters off Blankenese, where it goes without saying strict right-of-way rules must be observed, small boats too come into their own. Even in rough weather the canoeists who also have their base on the river bank here can be see moving through the water.

"Always remember you live by a great river," the artist Horst Janssen used to

Blankenese mit dem Süllberg und dem Fährhaus. Der Stich von Wilhelm Heuer zeigt den Elbhang um die Mitte des 19. Jahrhunderts.

A view of Blankenese, Süllberg and the Fährhaus (ferry house). Wilhelm Heuer's engraving shows the Elbe hillside in the mid-nineteenth century.

Der Zeichner Horst Janssen auf dem Altan seines Blankeneser Hauses

The artist Horst Janssen on the balcony of his Blankenese home

um seine genialische Person spinnen, sind längst in aller Munde. In seinem Haus zelebrierte er auf höchst unorthodoxe Weise eine Mischung aus Salon und Sozialstation. Und – was oft vergessen wird – er erarbeitete hier mit höchstem Fleiß ein fast uferlos erscheinendes Werk.

Anders als Horst Janssen, der einmal den Verzweifelungssatz über sich prägte: „Allein bin ich gut, zu zweit bin ich eine Katastrophe, ich kann nicht allein sein", leben die Berühmtheiten von Blankenese, die bildenden Künstler, Schriftsteller, Journalisten, Filmemacher, Musiker, eher zurückgezogen an dem Ort, an dem man es sehr schätzt, wenn man trotz Prominenz in Ruhe gelassen wird.

### „Treppenadel" gutbürgerlich

Es sind, anders als in Eppendorf oder Pöseldorf, auch nicht die Schönen und die Reichen, die am Strandweg, in der Einkaufsmeile, der Blankeneser Bahnhofstraße, und auf dem Wochenmarkt den Ton angeben und das Bild bestimmen. Da herrscht eher Gediegenheit als Eleganz, mehr Solidität als Schick. „Blankeneser Perlhühner", wie man die jungen Damen aus gutem Hause früher gerne nannte, die vorzugsweise in dunkelblauem Kostüm mit Perlenkette auftraten, sind Schmäh von gestern. Und der sogenannte „Blankeneser Treppenadel" ist durchaus nicht blaublütig, sondern gutbürgerlich und unauffällig.

say to cheer up a disconsolate neighbour. Janssen, who died in 1995, happened to come to Blankenese and never left the place again. The same thing happens to many other outsiders who come there – including a particularly large number of artists. Janssen and his house in Mühlenberger Weg, where he could stand on the balcony and see the Elbe glittering through the trees, became a legend. The stories woven around the brilliant draughtsman have long since been legendary. His home was a highly unorthodox mixture of salon and welfare centre. And – something that is often forgotten – it was here that he worked with enormous industry to produce what sometimes seems like a boundless number of artistic works.

Horst Janssen once described his desperate plight thus: "Alone I am fine, with another person I am a disaster, I can't be alone." Unlike him, the celebrities of Blankenese, the artists, writers, journalists, film-makers, musicians, live rather secluded lives in the place where people appreciate being left in peace despite their fame.

### The "staircase nobility" – solidly middle-class

Unlike in Eppendorf and Pöseldorf, it is not the rich and the beautiful who set the tone and define the image on the Elbe promenade, in Blankenese's main shopping street, Bahnhofstrasse, or at the weekly market. The aura is of quality rather than elegance, respectability rather than chic. "Blankenese guinea fowl," as people used mockingly to call well-bred young ladies with a predilection for navy-blue costumes and pearl necklaces, are a thing of the past. And the so-called "staircase nobility" is not blue-blooded at all, but solidly middle-class and inconspicuous.

With its hillside location overlooking the Elbe and its Italian charm, the staircase quarter may not be Blankenese's most up-market area, but it is the most

Die Hanglage mit Elbblick und italienischer Anmut ist nicht unbedingt das vornehmste Viertel von Blankenese, aber das schönste. Davon sind jedenfalls die Anwohner überzeugt. In der geschützten Südlage am Geesthang, im Labyrinth der Treppen, existiert eine geradezu unglaubliche architektonische Stilvielfalt. Im kunterbunten „Alles ist möglich" steht oft Wand an Wand, was woanders völlig unmöglich wäre. Fischerhäuschen mit Reetdach neben Gründerzeitvilla. Sechziger-Jahre-Bungalow neben spitzgiebeligem Fachwerkhaus. Groß neben Klein. Reich neben Arm. Häßlich neben Schön. Bauhausstrenge neben Barockremini-

attractive, at least the people who live there think so. To either side of the labyrinth of staircases on the south-facing riverside slope an incredible wealth of different architectural styles can be found, in a motley "free for all" where you come across combinations that would be completely impossible elsewhere: a fisherman's cottage with a thatched roof next door to a Wilhelminian villa, a 1960s bungalow side by side with a pointed-gabled half-timbered house, big next to small, rich next to poor, ugly next to beautiful, Bauhaus severity next to Baroque nostalgia. For those keen to trace the development of this apparently haphazard milieu the best place to start is on the beach.

Apart from a few small stretches, Blankenese's sandy beach is no more than a fond memory. Straightening,

Blick auf das Blankeneser Treppenviertel und den Süllberg vom Kiekeberg aus

A view of the Blankenese Treppenviertel (Staircase Quarter) and Süllberg from Kiekeberg

Die Annäherung an
Blankenese ist am
schönsten vom Wasser
aus. Der eng besiedelte
ehemalige Fischerort
wird wegen seines
Panoramas oft als
„Positano des Nor-
dens" bezeichnet.

Blankenese is best
approached from the
water. The densely
populated former
fishing village has
often been described,
on account of the
panoramic views of and
from it, as the Positano
of the North.

Die Terrassen und Balkons im Treppenviertel sind sommerliche Logenplätze zum großen Strom. Hier der Blick von der Terrasse des Restaurants „Sagebiels Fährhaus"

In summer, the Treppenviertel's terraces and balconies provide a privileged view of the river. This is the view to be enjoyed from the terrace outside Sagebiels Fährhaus restaurant.

szenz. Wer die Entwicklung dieses heute so zusammengewürfelt erscheinenden Milieus nachvollziehen will, fängt am besten am Strand an.

Der Blankeneser Sandstrand ist heute bis auf kleine Partien nur noch eine schöne Erinnerung. Begradigungen, Steinaufschüttungen und ein Betonstreifen haben das Ufer drastisch verändert. Der flache Sandstrand von Blankenese war die günstige Vorbedingung für eine Besiedelung an dieser Stelle. Bereits 1301 existierte hier eine Elbfähre. Schon 1060 hatte der Bremer Erzbischof auf dem Süllberg, der mit 74,7 Metern höchsten Erhebung über dem Strand, eine Burg anlegen lassen. Die Fähre transportierte seine Holsteiner Ochsen über die Elbe auf erzbischöflich-bremisches Gebiet. Um das ehemalige Fährhaus (heute Gaststätte

raised banks of stones and a strip of concrete have drastically altered the river bank. Blankenese's flat, sandy beach was the favourable precondition for settlement at this spot, where there was already a ferry across the Elbe in 1301. The archbishop of Bremen had had a castle built on the 74.7-metre-high Süllberg, the highest hill overlooking the river, way back in 1060. The ferry carried his Holstein oxen across the Elbe. Around the former ferry-house (now Sagebiels Fährhaus restaurant) fishermen, river pilots and seamen built their small houses on land owned by the arch-

„Sagebiels Fährhaus") bauten sich Fischer, Lotsen und Seeleute ihre kleinen Häuser. Man blieb unter sich, im Treppenviertel. Überliefert ist, daß von den 200 Einwohnern, die Blankenese im Jahr 1640 zählte, allein 80 Breckwoldt hießen. Die Familie spielte auch eine Hauptrolle, als nach dem Niedergang des Fischereiwesens in der napoleonischen Zeit zu Beginn des 19. Jahrhunderts in Blankenese eine Handelsflotte aufgebaut wurde, die zeitweise stärker war als die der Hamburger. Mit 243 seetüchtigen Schiffen übertrumpften die Blankeneser 1842 die Hamburger Konkurrenz um 31 Segler.

### Luftkurort mit Eisenbahnanschluß

Diesem wirtschaftlichen Wachstum war um 1800 schon eine Veränderung vorausgegangen, die vor allem den Nachbardörfern Dockenhuden und Mühlen-

diocese of Bremen. People in the staircase quarter kept themselves to themselves. Legend has it that of the 200 people living in Blankenese in 1640, 80 were called Breckwoldt. After the decline of the fishing industry, in the Napoleonic age at the start of the nineteenth century, the same family played a key role in establishing a merchant fleet that was sometimes stronger than Hamburg's. In 1842, for example, the Blankenese shipowners boasted 243 seaworthy sailing ships, 31 more that their Hamburg rivals.

Ein vielbewunderter Garten am Strandweg. Eine Augenlust für Anwohner und Ausflügler nicht weit vom Blankeneser Anleger

A much-admired garden on Strandweg in Blankenese and sight for sore eyes for residents and visitors alike, not far from the ferry landing pier

Das Interieur der alten Fischerhäuser (oben). Blankeneser Tracht (unten)

The interior of the old fishermen's houses (above). Traditional costume in Blankenese (below)

berg ein neues Gesicht gab. Reiche Kaufleute aus Altona und Hamburg bauten für sich und ihre Familien großzügige Herrenhäuser mit Parks als Sommersitze. 1867, als Blankenese mit ganz Schleswig-Holstein preußisch wurde, verkehrte die erste Eisenbahn zwischen Altona und Blankenese. Blankenese wurde Luftkurort mit kleinen Hotels und Tanzsälen.

Heute ist Blankenese nicht nur ein beliebter – der beliebteste? – Wohnvorort von Hamburg. Blankenese, was sich vom plattdeutschen „blanke Ness" (weiße, sandige Landzunge) herleitet, ist auch ein beliebtes Ausflugsziel. Man kann mit den HADAG-Fähren von den St. Pauli-Landungsbrücken anreisen, mit dem Schnellbus die Fahrt auf der Elbchaussee genießen oder die S-Bahn nehmen. Die meisten Besucher zieht es an den Strand. Im Treppenviertel verlaufen sich nur wenige.

## Health resort with railway connection

In around 1800 this economic growth had been preceded by a change that had given a new look above all to the neighbouring villages of Dockenhuden and Mühlenberg. Rich merchants from Altona and Hamburg established large mansions and parks there for themselves and their families. In 1867, when Blankenese and the whole of Schleswig-Holstein became part of Prussia, the first railway line was opened between Altona and Blankenese. Blankenese became a climatic health resort with small hotels and dance halls.

Nowadays, as well as being a popular, if not the most popular, residential suburb of Hamburg, Blankenese – which derives its name from the Low German "blanke Ness" (white, sandy strip of land) – is also a popular place for outings. It can be reached by HADAG ferry

Den weitesten Blick genießt man auf dem Süllberg. Wo früher einmal der Bremer Bischof residierte, befindet sich seit 1837 ein Restaurant. Seit Anfang der neunziger Jahre hatte es viel Streit um eine Neubebauung des lukrativen Plateaus gegeben. Einer Blankeneser Bürgerinitiative gelang es, drei Bebauungspläne zu kippen, doch nun ist die Neubebauung abgeschlossen. 1998 wurde das historische Restaurantensemble mit Rundturm unter Denkmalschutz gestellt.

from the St Pauli landing-stages, by express bus along Elbchaussee or by suburban train. Most visitors are drawn to the promenade, with just a few getting lost in the staircase district. The best view is from the top of Süllberg, where since 1837 there has been a restaurant where the archbishop of Bremen's residence once stood. From the early 1990s there was a great dispute over a planned redevelopment of the lucrative hilltop site. A local citizens' initiative succeeded in overthrowing three planned developments. Finally, in 1998, the historic restaurant complex complete with round tower was placed under a conservation order.

Osterfeuer in Blankenese. Vier Parteien wetteifern um das schönste Feuer, und manchmal kann es passieren, daß die kunstvoll aufgebauten Holzstapel bei Hochwasser „nasse Füße" kriegen.

Easter is bonfire time in Blankenese. Four groups vie with each other for the finest bonfire, and there are times when the decorative piles of wood get their "feet" wet at high tide.

# Die Stadt hat's Grün so gerne

## The city loves its greenery

Wo steht Hamburgs größter, schönster, ältester Baum? Die Frage brachte Anfang 1999 scharenweise Menschen auf die Beine, die die grünen Riesen der Hansestadt vermaßen. Siegerin bei den Laubbäumen wurde mit einem Stammumfang von 7,81 Metern die 220 Jahre alte Blutbuche auf der Rasenanlage vor dem Herrenhaus im Blankeneser Hirschpark. Im Alter übertroffen wird sie von einer 400 Jahre alten Eiche im Flottbeker Jenischpark, die jedoch hohl ist. Schön an Gestalt ist die Niendorfer Eiche am Garstedter Weg 9, die sich mit einem Efeumantel jedoch dicker gibt, als sie in Wirklichkeit ist. An Ebenmaß kaum zu übertreffen ist Norddeutschlands größte Atlaszeder, die an der Elbchaussee 352 steht. Doch dicke Riesen hin, dicke Riesen her! Am meisten liebt der Hamburger den Baum, der vor seinem Fenster wächst, und den Garten oder Park, der vor seiner Haustür liegt.

## Architektonisch geordnete Natur

Hamburg ist überaus reich an Grün. Parks und Gärten sind prägend für die harmonische Schönheit des Stadtbildes. Zahlreiche öffentliche Grünanlagen an Alster und Elbe gelten heute als kulturhistorisch bedeutsame Schöpfungen. Sie stehen unter Denkmalschutz. Die grünen Räume architektonisch geordneter Natur, wie wir sie heute in der Stadtlandschaft kennen, haben weit zurückreichende Vorläufer. In der Frühzeit gab es vor den Toren der Stadt Eichenwälder, Viehweiden und Getreidefelder. Apfelgärten (pomaria), Apotheker- und Klostergärten wurden im Mittelalter zur Wiege unserer heutigen Gartenkultur. Von den Barockgärten, die im Osten der Stadt die Festsäle großbürgerlicher Häuser ins Grüne erweiterten, sind kaum

Where is Hamburg's biggest, most beautiful, oldest tree? At the start of 1999 this question brought out crowds of people who set about measuring up the Hanseatic city's green giants. First place among the deciduous trees went to the 220-year-old copper beech on the lawn outside the manor house in Blankenese's Hirschpark: its trunk is 7.81 metres in circumference. It is beaten in seniority by a 400-year-old oak in Flottbek's Jenischpark. This, however, has a hollow trunk. Beautiful in form is the oak tree at Garstedter Weg 9, Niendorf, although the ivy growing over the trunk makes it look thicker than it really is. Almost unsurpassable in terms of its elegant proportions is northern Germany's tallest Atlas cedar at Elbchaussee 352. But large or small, what the Hamburger loves most is the tree growing in front of his window and the garden or park at his front door.

## Architecturally ordered nature

Hamburg possesses a wealth of greenery. Parks and gardens play a defining role in the harmonious beauty of the cityscape. Numerous public open spaces by the Alster and the Elbe are now seen as important features of cultural history and have been placed under conservation orders. The predecessors of the green areas of architecturally ordered nature which are a familiar sight in the city today go back a long way. In the early days there were oak woods, pastures and cornfields outside the gates of the city. In mediaeval times, apple orchards, apothecary's and monastery gardens were the cradle of our present-day garden culture. Hardly any traces remain of the Baroque gardens which were extensions to the banqueting halls of upper middle class houses in the east of the city. In contrast, the fashion for English-style landscaped gardens that was followed in around 1800 still makes its mark on the city in a most attractive way. The most important wave of greenery to bestow new parks

noch Spuren erhalten. Dagegen prägt die Mode der englischen Landschaftsgärten, die um 1800 gepflegt wurde, die Stadt bis heute aufs allerschönste. Die Idee des Volksparks wurde in der Bürgerstadt Hamburg früher in die Tat umgesetzt als in den meisten anderen deutschen Großstädten. Die bedeutendste Grünwelle, die Hamburg mit neuen Anlagen beglückte, war sozial motiviert. Hier sollten Körper und Seele gleichermaßen Erholung finden.

Der Stadtpark ist heute immer noch vorbildhaft als sozial bestimmte Grünanlage für die Millionenmetropole. Mit Luft- und Sonnenbad, Kurgarten, Festwiese, Stein-, Rosen- und Heidegarten,

and gardens on Hamburg was socially motivated. The idea of a people's park where both body and mind found equal recreation was put into practice in Hamburg earlier than in most other German cities.

The Stadtpark or municipal park is still an exemplary model of a socially-defined metropolitan open space. Every week more than 100,000 people go there to take the air, sunbathe, stroll through the Kurgarten, play or picnic on the festival meadow or enjoy the rock, rose and heather gardens, the open-air stage and the lake. The 180-hectare "open-air people's palace" to the north of the city centre was laid out and planted from 1911 onwards under the guidance of Hamburg's famous director of planning Fritz Schumacher. At that time the giant park signified a drastic change of style. The aim was no longer the idyllic nineteenth-century landscaped garden but a space clearly divided up on geometrical lines.

Dieses um 1770 geschaffene Ölgemälde zeigt den Blick von der Palmaille aus über den belebten Strom auf die Harburger Berge. Wo sich heute der Hafen ausgebreitet hat, war damals noch die großzügige Landschaft vor den Toren Hamburgs zu sehen.

This oil painting dating back to about 1770 shows the view from Palmaille across the busy river toward the Harburg Hills. Where now the Port of Hamburg extends, generously proportioned landscape outside Hamburg's city gates once was typical.

Der Stadtpark – hier die Mittelachse mit dem Planetarium im Hintergrund – wurde geschaffen als grüne Lunge und Freizeitraum für die vielen Bewohner der neuen Arbeitersiedlungen, die mit Beginn des 20. Jahrhunderts im Norden der Stadt gebaut wurden (links). Der Altonaer Volkspark hat viele verschwiegene Ecken und beherbergt den ältesten Dahliengarten Deutschlands (rechts).

The Stadtpark, of which you here see the central axis with the planetarium at the rear, was laid out as a green lung and recreational areas for the many residents of the new workers' housing estates that were built in the north of the city in the early years of the twentieth century (left). Altona's Volkspark boasts many secluded corners and features Germany's oldest dahlia garden (right).

Freilichtbühne und Parksee bietet er wöchentlich mehr als 100 000 Besuchern Erholung. Auf 180 Hektar nördlich der Innenstadt wurde das „Freiluft-Volkshaus" ab 1911 unter der Leitung von Hamburgs berühmtem Baudirektor Fritz Schumacher angelegt und bepflanzt. Der riesige Park bedeutete damals auch eine einschneidende Stilwende. Nicht mehr der idyllische Landschaftsgarten des 19. Jahrhunderts war das Ziel, sondern der geometrisch klar gegliederte Raum.

Sehen und gesehen werden. Das gilt, wenn auch vielleicht etwas weniger im Stadtpark, dafür um so mehr für die beliebteste grüne Flaniermeile der Metropole. Der Alsterpark ist die Krönung des Spaziergangs um Hamburgs schönsten Spiegel, die Außenalster. Bürgermeister Max Brauer setzte durch, daß die 14,5 Hektar des für die Internationale Gartenbauausstellung 1953 umgestalteten Alstervorlandes nicht wieder in die vorherigen Villengärten verwandelt wurden, sondern als öffentliche Grünanlage bestehen blieben.

Seeing and being seen is not so much of an issue in Stadtpark, unlike on the city's favourite green promenade, the Alsterpark, the crowning glory of a walk around Hamburg's loveliest stretch of water, the Outer Alster. The 14.5-hectare site by the Alster was newly laid out for the 1953 International Garden Show. Afterwards, Mayor Max Brauer insisted on its being retained as a public park instead of being reconverted into private waterside gardens belonging to the mansions behind.

### Moorweide close by the university

Whereas the Alsterpark was modelled on the nineteenth-century landscaped garden, the severe outlines of Moorweide on the edge of the university quarter west of the Outer Alster are distinguished by rows of magnificent chestnut trees. The description of Moorweide by Alfred Lichtwark (1852–1914), director of the Hamburg Kunsthalle and well-known in his day for the ideas he contributed to the design of parks and gar-

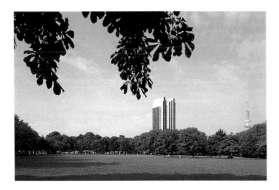

## Moorweide am Rande der Universität

Während der Alsterpark wieder an das Vorbild der Landschaftsgärten des 19. Jahrhunderts angelehnt wurde, besitzt die Moorweide am Rande des Universitätsviertels westlich der Außenalster eine strenge Form, die geprägt wird durch die Reihen herrlicher Kastanienbäume. Die Beschreibung der Moorweide von Alfred Lichtwark (1852–1914), der die Hamburger Kunsthalle leitete und für die Gestaltung von Parks und Gärten ein bekannter Ideengeber seiner Zeit war, kann als Eloge auf eine Grünanlage noch heute beeindrucken: „... eines der schönsten Raumgebilde in unseren Anlagen, fast noch die einzig ebene Grasfläche aus alter Zeit mit dem lotrechten Gegensatz der aufstrebenden Baumstämme und den hohen Laubmassen, oder malerisch genommen, der hellen Rasenfläche und des dunklen, waldartig dichten Baumbestandes rundum".

Hamburgs grüne Lunge aber sind die Wallringanlagen im Westen der City. Dieser zentrale Park der Stadt, ihre erste öffentliche Grünanlage, setzt sich aus vier sehr unterschiedlichen Teilen zusammen. Der alte Botanische Garten im

dens, remains an impressive eulogy to a green space: "... one of the most attractively designed of our open spaces, almost the sole remaining flat grassed area from olden days with the perpendicular contrast of tree trunks striving upward and the tall masses of foliage, or in terms of a painted scene, of the light area of lawn and the dark trees with their forest-like density all round."

However, Hamburg's green lung is the Wallringanlagen on the site of the former city walls to the west of the centre. The most central of the city parks and its first public open space, it now comprises four very different sections. The Old Botanical Garden to the north-east was opened in 1821 on the site of the fortifications which had been razed two years before. Planten un Blomen to the south of the Congress Center was formerly the site of a cemetery and a zoo and was given its present name – which is Low German for "plants and flowers" – on the occasion of the 1935 North German Horticultural Show. The park was completely redesigned for three International Garden Shows – in 1953, 1963 and 1973. To the south of Planten un Blomen a

Die Moorweide nördlich des Dammtorbahnhofs ist mit Kastanienbäumen dunkel umrandet und eine Grünanlage von strenger Schönheit (links). Die Wallanlagen verlocken zu Spaziergängen in der Büropause, weil sie „vor der Haustür" der Hamburger City liegen (rechts).

Moorweide, to the north of Dammtor railway station, is an oblong of austere greenery lined by mature, dark chestnut trees (left). The Wallanlagen, once the city's ramparts, are a handy park for city workers to head for during their lunch hour because they are right on the city's "doorstep" (right).

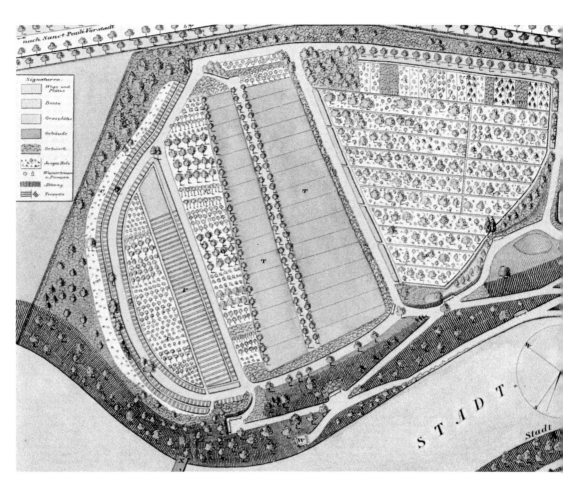

Nordosten wurde schon 1821 auf den
zwei Jahre zuvor geschleiften Festungs-
anlagen eröffnet. Planten un Blomen
südlich des Congress-Centrums, früher
Friedhofs- und Zoogelände, erhielt seinen Namen durch die Niederdeutsche
Gartenbauausstellung von 1935. Drei
internationale Gartenbauausstellungen
(1953, 1963, 1973) veränderten die
Anlage jeweils gründlich. Südlich von
Planten un Blomen geht es durch die
Kleinen und die Großen Wallanlagen
zum Hafen oder nach St. Pauli.

Wer die private Gartenlust der Hamburger erleben will, wandert am Elbufer
von Övelgönne nach Blankenese. Der
Spaziergänger muß über keinen Zaun

walk through the Kleine and the Grosse
Wallanlage takes you to the port or St
Pauli.

The best way to experience the Hamburgers' private love of gardens is to
take a walk along the Elbe bank from
Övelgönne to Blankenese. There is no
need to climb any fences, because the
attractive river bank is open to all, and
the view into private gardens is free.

Down by the river, small-scale garden-
ing art prevails, while up on the slope
the much-lauded ensemble of landscaped
areas, parks and architecture stretches
along Elbchaussee. The English-style
parks play the main role in this interplay.
The highspots of these products of the
former upper middle class love of gardens are Jenischpark in Flottbek, Hirschpark with its avenue of four rows of
200-year-old lime trees and Baurs Park,
both in Blankenese. They date from

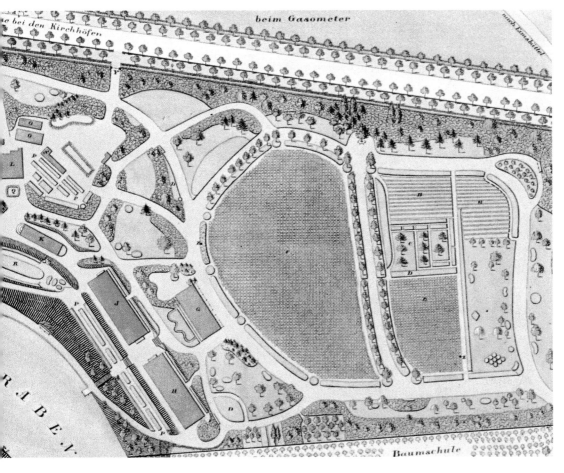

Der farbige Plan von 1855 zeigt die Anlage des Alten Botanischen Gartens in den Wallanlagen, die seitdem mehrfach umgestaltet wurde.

This coloured map dated 1855 features the Wallanlagen's old Botanical Garden, since redesigned on more than one occasion.

klettern. Denn das schöne Ufer ist jedermann zugänglich. Der Blick in die Privatgärten ist frei.

Während unten am Strand kleinteilige Gartenkunst vorherrscht, erstreckt sich oben am Hang längs der Elbchaussee das vielgerühmte Ensemble aus Landschaftsraum, Parks und Architektur. In diesem Zusammenspiel hatten die Parks im englischen Stil eine Hauptrolle inne. Höhepunkte dieser ehemals großbürgerlichen Gartenlust sind der Jenischpark in

around 1800, a time when painters were discovering the north German landscape as a motif. The landscape gallery in Altona Museum gives a historical overview of how green spaces are reflected in art.

### An educational garden and a pleasure-garden

Slightly away from Hamburg's best-known stretches of greenery are the University of Hamburg's New Botanical Garden in Klein-Flottbek and the Roman Garden on the western periphery of the slopes above the Elbe in Blankenese. An educational gardem and a pleasure-garden, in both of which a wonderful peace

Der Römische Garten
mit seinem kleinen
Freilichttheater in
Blankenese nimmt sich
stilistisch sehr unge-
wöhnlich im Grün der
Hansestadt aus (links).
Der Neue Botanische
Garten mit seiner faszi-
nierend gestalteten
Pflanzenwelt liegt nicht
weit vom Jenischpark
in Klein Flottbek.

Stylewise, Blankenese's
Roman Garden with its
pint-sized amphitheatre
is a far cry from the
city's usual greenery
(left).
The New Botanical
Garden with its fascina-
tingly laid-out world of
plants is not far from
Jenischpark in Klein
Flottbek.

Flottbek und der Hirschpark mit seiner
200 Jahre alten vierreihigen Lindenallee
sowie Baurs Park. Die beiden letztge-
nannten Anlagen gehören zu Blankenese.
Sie entstanden um 1800. In der Zeit ent-
deckten auch die Maler die norddeutsche
Landschaft als Motiv. Die Landschafts-
galerie im Altonaer Museum zeigt in
einem historischen Abriß, wie sich das
Grün in der Kunst wiederfindet.

### Ein Lehrgarten und ein Lustgarten

Etwas im Abseits der bekannten Hamburger Grünzüge liegen der Neue Botanische Garten der Universität Hamburg in
Klein-Flottbek und der Römische Garten
am Westrand der Blankeneser Elbhöhen.
Ein Lehrgarten und ein Lustgarten. In
beiden ist es meist wunderbar ruhig.
Genauso wie in den grünen Anlagen, die
dem Frieden der Toten gewidmet sind.
Mit dem Ohlsdorfer Friedhof besitzt
Hamburg eine Parklandschaft, die
zumindest in dieser Weitläufigkeit und
Qualität auf der Welt nicht ihresgleichen

and quiet usually prevails – as it does in
the green spaces where the dead rest in
peace. In Ohlsdorf cemetery Hamburg
has a stretch of parkland unparalleled in
the world. Walking through it you experience an inexhaustible symbiosis of garden and monumental art. The park,
begun in 1874, comprises several very
different sections. Wilhelm Cordes, who
as the cemetery's first director shaped its
romantic, picturesque part until 1914,
wrote that beauty should delight the eye
and plants should cover the grave. A
geometrical, functional section completed in 1920 was designed by landscape
gardener Otto Linne. The Hamburg
Memorial Cemetery north of the east-
west axis running through the cemetery
unites the city's luminaries from the
world of culture, business and politics in
one resting-place.

hat. Wer hier spazierengeht, erlebt eine unerschöpfliche Symbiose von Garten- und Grabmalkunst. Die 1874 begonnene Parkanlage setzt sich aus ganz unterschiedlichen Partien zusammen. Schönheit solle das Auge entzücken und die Pflanze das Grab verdecken, schrieb Wilhelm Cordes, der bis 1914 als erster Direktor den romantischen, malerischen Teil des Friedhofs prägte. Eine geometrisch zweckdienliche Anlage schuf bis 1920 der Gartenarchitekt Otto Linne. Auf dem „Hamburgischen Gedächtnisfriedhof" nördlich der Ost-West-Achse, die durch die Anlage führt, liegen die Honoratioren der Stadt aus Kultur, Wirtschaft und Politik in einem Quartier vereint.

Wie aus einem Guß erscheint dagegen ein heimlicher Lieblingsort für Spaziergänger, der Nienstedtener Friedhof an der Elbchaussee. Wer durch die grünen Gassen dieses rechtwinkeligen Labyrinths wandert, spürt das Alter dieser 1814 gegründeten Begräbnisstätte. Und er trifft meist keinen Menschen. Er ist mit der Natur allein, was in der Stadt, die's Grün so gern hat, sonst eher selten passiert.

In contrast, Nienstedten cemetery on Elbchaussee, a secret favourite with walkers, seems a unified whole. Strolling along the green pathways of this labyrinth of right-angles, you sense the age of the burial ground, which was established in 1814. Usually, you don't meet a soul. You are alone with nature, something rare in a city that is so fond of green spaces.

Der Ohlsdorfer Friedhof, der größte Park- und Landschaftsfriedhof der Erde, ist berühmt für seine Vielfalt (links u. rechts).

Ohlsdorf Cemetery, the world's largest landscaped, park-like cemetery, is renowned for its variety (left and right).

# Kultur kennt keine Grenzen
## Culture knows no bounds

Im schönen Saal des Literaturhauses ist die geistige Welt zu Hause. Man kann hier aber auch gut speisen.

Intellectuals feel at home in the attractive meeting hall of the Literaturhaus. You can dine well here too.

Hamburg ist traditionell eine Stadt des Theaters und der Musik. Seit der Eröffnung des Literaturhauses Ende der achtziger Jahre in einem unter Denkmalschutz stehenden Stadthaus am Ostufer der Außenalster, am Schwanenwik 38, ist auch die schreibende Kunst zunehmend ins Scheinwerferlicht gerückt. Die „gereizte Toleranz", die den Hanseaten früher in ihrem Verhältnis zur bildenden

Traditionally, Hamburg is a city of theatre and music. Since the late 1980s, when the Literaturhaus was opened at Schwanenwik 38 on the east bank of the Outer Alster in a building classified as a historic monument, writing has increasingly moved into the limelight. The "tetchy tolerance" with which Hamburgers were previously reputed to view painting and sculpture has also given way to a keener interest, aroused primarily through two new institutions. Since 1997 the Galerie der Gegenwart (Gallery of Contemporary Art) has occupied pride of place on the museum island between the main station and the Alster. Since then the white cuboid building designed by Cologne architect Oswald Mathias Ungers has established itself as an exciting location for contemporary art. The same goes for the Deichtorhallen, two steel and glass buildings erected between 1911 and 1914 by the former Klostertor that were originally wholesale market halls. Since 1989 they have provided spacious venues for changing exhibitions of contemporary art.

## A colourful, shimmering scene

The fact that Hamburg is now seen as an especially good place to live is due not least to its colourful, sometimes shimmering cultural scene. It has so many facets that there is something to satisfy everyone. A typical feature of Hamburg's metropolitan culture is that the sub-culture sometimes succeeds in rising to ranks of established culture and that small alternative events not infrequently get the opportunity to stand in the brightest of spotlights. This is partly thanks to an urbane media society which reacts flexibly and with curiosity to new cultural trends.

The distant, if not outright disapproving attitude towards art and culture of which Hamburgers are often accused, does exist, above all in political circles,

Kunst nachgesagt wurde, ist ebenfalls
einem wacheren Interesse gewichen, das
vor allem durch zwei neue Institutionen
geweckt wurde. Seit 1997 behauptet sich
auf der Museumsinsel zwischen Hauptbahnhof und Alster die Galerie der
Gegenwart. Der von dem Kölner Architekten Oswald Mathias Ungers entworfene weiße Würfel hat sich seitdem als
spannender Ort für die zeitgenössische
Kunst etabliert. Gleiches gilt für die
Deichtorhallen. Die 1911–14 errichteten
zwei Großmarkthallen aus Stahl und
Glas am ehemaligen Klostertor dienen
seit 1989 als großzügige Räume für
Wechselausstellungen und Gegenwartskunst.

**Eine bunte, schillernde Szene**

Daß Hamburg heute als Metropole gilt,
in der es sich besonders gut leben läßt,
ist nicht zuletzt einer bunten, manchmal
schillernden Kulturszene zu verdanken.
Sie ist so reich an Facetten, daß jeder
hier glücklich werden kann. Daß es der
Subkultur manchmal gelingt, in die
höheren Ränge der etablierten Kultur
aufzusteigen, daß kleine alternative
Ereignisse nicht selten die Chance haben,
plötzlich im hellsten Scheinwerferlicht zu
stehen – das ist typisch für Hamburgs
Großstadtkultur und verdankt sich auch
einer urbanen Mediengesellschaft, die
flexibel und neugierig auf neue Strömungen in der Kultur reagiert.

Die distanzierte bis ablehnende Hal-
tung gegenüber Kunst und Kultur, die
den Hanseaten oft nachgesagt wird, gibt
es aber auch. Vor allem in Politikerkrei-
sen. Nicht selten wird da Kultur mit Kul-
tiviertheit verwechselt. Es gibt Berüh-

where culture is often confused with
refinement. Afraid of contact, such people tend to view culture as a nice
appendage to life. No prince ever lav-
ished a crock of gold for the arts on the
city republic of Hamburg. For centuries,
the tradition has been for public spend-
ing on the arts to be either miserly or
economical, depending on your point of
view.

In contrast with this is a tradition of
citizens' initiatives in the field of culture
and the arts, the like of which very few
cities can boast. A glance back through
history shows that most theatrical, musical, literature and fine arts institutions
owe their existence to the private initiative of patrons and founders. When commerce was in good shape, art flourished.
With Meister Bertram (1340–1414 and
Meister Francke (c. 1385 to post–1436),
fourteenth-century Hamburg experienced a heyday of painting. Their altars
with their rich imagery are now on display in the Kunsthalle. 1479 saw the
founding of the Ratsbibliothek, the germ
cell of the present Staatsbibliothek and
university library named after the Ham-
burg-born Nobel laureate Carl von Ossi-

Das Universitätsgelände
mit dem Altbau der
Staatsbibliothek liegt
im Stadtteil Rother-
baum und damit in
direkter Nachbarschaft
zur City.

The university campus,
including the old build-
ing of the Staatsbiblio-
thek, is in Hamburg's
Rotherbaum district
and thus but a stone's
throw from the city
centre.

Die Oper wurde vor mehr als 300 Jahren als erstes von Bürgern getragenes Opernhaus gegründet. Die Lithographie von 1880 zeigt die Dammtorstraße mit dem Stadttheater auf der linken Seite.

Hamburg's opera house was founded over 300 years ago as the first of its kind to be supported entirely by citizens. This 1880 print shows Dammtorstrasse with the Stadttheater on the left.

rungsängste und die Vorstellung, daß Kultur ein netter Appendix des Lebens sei. Kein Fürst hat über der Stadtrepublik Hamburg jemals ein goldenes Füllhorn für die Kultur ausgeschüttet. Durch die Jahrhunderte hat es Tradition, daß den Künsten aus dem Staatssäckel nur, je nach Sichtweise, geizig oder sparsam Geld gegeben wird.

Dagegen steht eine Tradition kultureller Bürgerinitiativen, wie sie nur wenige Städte aufzuweisen haben. Ein Streifzug durch die Geschichte zeigt, daß die meisten Institutionen für Theater, Musik, Literatur und bildende Kunst sich der Privatinitiative von Mäzenen und Stiftungen verdanken. Wenn es dem Handel gut ging, blühte auch die Kunst. Mit Meister Bertram (um 1340–1414/15) und Meister Francke (um 1385–nach 1436) erlebte Hamburg im 14. Jahrhundert eine Blütezeit der Malerei. Ihre bilderreichen Altäre sind heute in der Kunsthalle ausgestellt. 1479 wurde die Ratsbibliothek gegründet, die Keimzelle der heute nach dem an der Elbe geborenen Friedensnobelpreisträger benannten

etzky. Both the Kunsthalle and the Staatsbibliothek were initiated by private sponsors. The founding in 1677/78 of the Hamburg Opera on Gänsemarkt was to be a trailblazing private initiative. As well as being the oldest German-language opera house, it was the first ever "standing" opera. In the second half of the twentieth century the opera house on Dammtorstrasse won world acclaim, above all for its premieres and new productions. This was largely due to the influence of its best-known director, the Swiss composer Rolf Liebermann (1910–1999), who led the opera from 1959 to 1973 and from 1985 to 1988.

In the early decades of the opera, Hamburg also became the centre of the North German organ school. The organbuilder Arp Schnitger (1648–1719) pro-

Mitte der 1950er Jahre wurde die Hamburgische Staatsoper nach einem Entwurf von G. Weber neu gebaut und erlangte bald Weltruf (links), den auch der Schweizer Komponist Rolf Liebermann (1910–1999) bewirkte. Er war von 1959 bis 73 und von 1985 bis 88 Intendant dieses Opernhauses.

In the mid-1950s the Hamburgische Staatsoper was rebuilt to a design by Gerhard Weber and soon gained world renown (left), toward which the Swiss composer Rolf Liebermann, 1910–1999, contributed. He was manager and artistic director of the Staatsoper from 1959 to 1973 and from 1985 to 1988.

Staats- und Universitätsbibliothek Carl von Ossietzky. Kunsthalle und Staatsbibliothek wurden durch private Förderer initiiert. Zu einer wegweisenden Bürgerinitiative wurde 1677/78 die Gründung der Hamburgischen Staatsoper am Gänsemarkt. Dieses älteste Opernhaus deutscher Sprache war die erste „stehende" Oper überhaupt. In der zweiten Hälfte des 20. Jahrhunderts gewann das Haus an der Dammtorstraße vor allem durch Ur- und Erstaufführungen Weltgeltung. Die prägende Intendantenpersönlichkeit wurde der Schweizer Komponist Rolf Liebermann (1910–99), der die Oper von 1959 bis 1973 und von 1985 bis 1988 leitete.

In den frühen Jahrzehnten der Oper wurde Hamburg auch zum Zentrum der Norddeutschen Orgelschule. Arp Schnitger (1648–1719) baute für St. Nikolai und St. Jacobi wahre Wunderwerke der Klangkultur. Die restaurierte Arp-Schnitger-Orgel in St. Jacobi lockt heute Kenner aus aller Welt an.

duced real music-making miracles for St Nikolai and St Jacobi churches. Nowadays connoisseurs from all over the world come to see the restored Arp Schnitger organ in St Jacobi.

## Telemann, Lessing and many more

The eighteenth century bestowed an unparalleled heyday on the Hanseatic city and its privately-financed public cultural institutions. Georg Philipp Telemann, Johann Mattheson and Carl Philipp Emanuel Bach, three composers still famous today, all worked in Hamburg. In 1767 Gotthold Ephraim Lessing came to Hamburg to spend some years as dramatic director of the Nationaltheater. Performances were held in the Commödienhaus building on Gänsemarkt, which had been established four years previously. Serious plays had a

Alfred Lichtwark (1852–1914) war von 1886 bis zu seinem Tod Direktor der Hamburger Kunsthalle (oben). Die 1997 eröffnete Galerie der Gegenwart ist das dritte Gebäude der Hamburger Kunsthalle (rechts). Der erste Erweiterungsbau mit prachtvoller Rotunde und Kuppel wurde 1919 eröffnet (unten).

Alfred Lichtwark, 1852–1914, was director of the Hamburg Kunsthalle from 1886 until his death (above). The Galerie der Gegenwart, opened in 1997, is the Kunsthalle's third building (above right). The first extension, with its magnificent rotunda and cupola, was opened in 1919 (below).

### Telemann, Lessing und viele andere

Das 18. Jahrhundert bescherte der Hansestadt und ihren privat finanzierten öffentlichen Kulturinstitutionen eine Blütezeit ohnegleichen. Mit Georg Philipp Telemann, Johann Mattheson und Carl Philipp Emanuel Bach wirkten drei bis heute berühmte Komponisten in der Stadt. 1767 kam Gotthold Ephraim Lessing für einige Jahre als Dramaturg ans „Nationaltheater". Spielstätte war das vier Jahre zuvor gegründete „Commödienhaus" am Gänsemarkt. Die

hard time of it competing with the frequently slapstick-type entertainment provided by travelling players. The Nationaltheater survived until 1769.

In 1803 the painter Philipp Otto Runge moved from Wolgast to Hamburg, and worked there until his death in 1810. In 1806 lovers of painting and sculpture founded a "Society for the Promotion of Good Taste," the forerunner of what eleven years later became the first art society in Germany to be funded by private individuals, the Kunstverein. The idea caught on, and still now the Kunstverein is dedicated to the cause of promoting contemporary art. The nineteenth century in Hamburg was the age of privately-founded museums and galleries. In 1868 the Kunsthalle art gallery, which emerged from a Kunstverein foundation, moved into its own building on Glockengiesserwall. In 1876 the Museum für Kunst und Gewerbe (Arts and Crafts Museum) established itself in the parkland behind Glockengiesserwall where the main railway station now stands. All trace of greenery is gone but the yellow museum building is unmistakable. Even now, the museum's collection

anspruchsvollen Sprechstücke hatten es schwer gegen die oft klamaukig-grelle Unterhaltung der gastierenden Schauspieltruppen. Das „Nationaltheater" bestand noch bis 1769.

1803 zog der Maler Philipp Otto Runge von Wolgast nach Hamburg, wo er bis zu seinem Tode 1810 tätig war. 1806 gründeten Liebhaber der Malerei und Bildhauerei einen „Verein zur Beförderung des guten Geschmacks", aus dem elf Jahre später der erste von Bürgern getragene Kunstverein Deutschlands hervorging. Ein Verein, der Schule machte, der sich bis heute die Förderung der Gegenwartskunst auf die Fahnen geschrieben hat. Das 19. Jahrhundert war in Hamburg auch die Zeit der von Bürgern initiierten Museumsgründungen. Die Kunsthalle, aus einer Stiftung des Kunstvereins hervorgegangen, zog 1868 in ein eigenes Gebäude am Glockengie-

is heavily influenced by its founding director Justus Brinckmann (1843–1915), a sponsor of Alfred Lichtwark (1852–1914), who was director of the Hamburg Kunsthalle from 1886. As well as shaping the Kunsthalle, Lichtwark did some pioneering work as a museum educationalist and in the art education movement. He invited many artists to Hamburg – Max Liebermann, Lovis Corinth, Wilhelm Trübner, Leopold Graf von Kalckreuth and the French painters Pierre Bonnard and Edouard Vuillard. Many of their works are now on show in the Kunsthalle.

Das Museum für Kunst und Gewerbe – oben erster Direktor Justus Brinckmann (1843–1915) – am Hauptbahnhof gehört zu den renommiertesten Institutionen seiner Art (oben links). Es konnte im Jahr 2000 die Eröffnung einer Erweiterung u. a. für eine Sammlung von Tasteninstrumenten feiern (unten).

The Museum für Kunst und Gewerbe, or Museum of Arts & Crafts – above first director Justus Brinckmann, 1843–1915 – is one of the world's prestigious museums of its kind (above left). In 2000 it opened an extension where among other exhibits, a collection of keyboard instruments can be seen (below).

Das Museum für Hamburgische Geschichte am Holstenwall zählt zu den schönsten Bauten von Hamburgs berühmtem Baudirektor Fritz Schumacher (links).
Das Hamburger Museum für Völkerkunde an der Rothenbaumchaussee beherbergt die Kulturen der Welt und besitzt einen wenig bekannten wunderbaren Hörsaal (rechts).

The Museum of Hamburg History on Holstenwall is one of the finest buildings designed by the city's famous director of public works Fritz Schumacher (left).
The Museum für Völkerkunde, or Museum of Ethnology, on Rothenbaumchaussee is home to the civilisations of the world and boasts a little-known but magnificent lecture theatre (right).

ßerwall. Das Museum für Kunst und Gewerbe etablierte sich 1877 in der Parklandschaft jenseits des Glockengießerwalls am heutigen Hauptbahnhof – in einem Grün, von dem keine Spur mehr zu sehen ist. Dafür ist das gelbe Museumsgebäude unübersehbar. Sein bis heute die Sammlung prägender Gründungsdirektor war Justus Brinckmann (1843–1915), ein Förderer Alfred Lichtwarks (1852–1914), der als Leiter der Hamburger Kunsthalle seit 1886 dem Haus sein Gesicht gab und als Museumspädagoge sowie in der Kunsterziehungsbewegung bahnbrechend wirkte. Lichtwark lud viele Künstler nach Hamburg ein: Max Liebermann, Lovis Corinth, Wilhelm Trübner, Leopold Graf von Kalckreuth sowie die Franzosen Pierre Bonnard und Edouard Vuillard. Viele Bilder von ihnen finden sich heute in der Kunsthalle.

## "Nana" in a new light

One of the gallery's most famous works, Edouard Manet's "Nana," came to the Kunsthalle from a private Hamburg collection, a fact which casts a light on the hitherto rather discreet chapter of private art collections in the Hanseatic city. The Commetersche Kunsthandlung, founded in 1821, was the first Hamburg gallery to arrange access to contemporary art. Only now is the enthusiasm with which private individuals collected gradually becoming clear. On of the leading patrons of young art (Edvard Munch, Emil Nolde and the Brücke painters) was the lawyer Gustav Schiefler (1857–1935). Together with his wife, he ensured that shortly after the founding of the Brücke group of Expressionist painters in Dresden, two thirds of their passive sponsors lived in Hamburg.

Werner Hofmann, director of the Kunsthalle from 1969 to 1990, dedicated a exhibition to "Nana" as part of a series entitled "Art in Around 1800" designed to cast a new light on the era.

## „Nana" im neuen Licht

Eins der berühmtesten Gemälde des Hauses, Edouard Manets „Nana", kam aus einer hamburgischen Privatsammlung in die Kunsthalle. Eine Tatsache, die ein Licht auf das bislang sehr verschwiegene Kapitel privater Kunstsammlungen in der Hansestadt wirft. Die 1821 gegründete Commetersche Kunsthandlung vermittelte als erste Hamburger Galerie den Zugang zur Gegenwartskunst. Wie engagiert die Bürger sammelten, kommt nach und nach erst heute ans Tageslicht. Einer der wichtigsten Förderer junger Kunst (Edvard Munch, Emil Nolde und die Brücke-Maler) war der Jurist Gustav Schiefler (1857–1935), der zusammen mit seiner Frau erreichte, daß kurz nach der Gründung der Dresdner Malervereinigung Brücke zwei Drittel der passiven Förderer in Hamburg ansässig waren.

Der „Nana" widmete Werner Hofmann, Direktor der Kunsthalle von 1969 bis 1990, eine wunderbare Ausstellung in der Reihe „Kunst um 1800", mit der er diese Zeit in neues Licht setzte.

Das Museum für Hamburgische Geschichte verdankt seine Entstehung dem 1839 gegründeten Verein für Hamburgische Geschichte und dessen „Sammlung hamburgischer Alterthümer". Das herrliche Backsteindomizil des Museums wurde von Hamburgs Baudirektor Fritz Schumacher entworfen und 1914-22 fertiggestellt.

Das Museum für Völkerkunde, begründet auf einer ethnologischen Privatsammlung, erhielt 1911 ein eigenes Haus an der Rothenbaumchaussee. Das nach seinem Stifter August Helms benannte Helms-Museum für die

The Museum für Hamburgische Geschichte (Museum of Hamburg History) owes its existence to the Society for Hamburg History, founded in 1839, and the society's collection of Hamburg antiquities. The splendid redbrick museum building was designed by Hamburg's director of planning Fritz Schumacher and built between 1914 and 1922.

The Museum für Völkerkunde (Museum of Ethnology), based on a private ethnological collection, moved into its own building on Rothenbaumchaussee in 1911. The Helms Museum, named after its founder August Helms, dates back to 1898. It is in Harburg, which is now part of Hamburg, and a few things have changed inside the museum, too. Its official name now is the Hamburger Museum für Archäologie und die Geschichte Harburgs – Helms-Museum. The Altona Museum, too, would be much poorer if it were not for the support of private sponsors. Only the most recent of the major Hamburg museums, the Museum der Arbeit (Museum of Labour), owes its existence since 1982 to the state. Since 1999 the Hamburg museums have been operating as independent public foundations, so a whole new era awaits them.

Der Jurist und Kunstkenner Gustav Schiefler (1857–1935)
Das Museum der Arbeit wurde 1990 als siebtes staatliches Museum auf einem ehemaligen Industriegelände in Barmbek eröffnet.

Lawyer and art connoisseur Gustav Schiefler, 1857–1935
The Museum der Arbeit, or Museum of Labour, was opened in 1990 as the city's seventh state-owned museum on a former industrial site in the Hamburg suburb of Barmbek.

Der Saal der Galions-
figuren ist eine der
größten Attraktionen
im Altonaer Museum.

The hall with the ship's
figureheads is one of
the main attractions at
the Altonaer Museum.

Die Musikhalle am Johannes-Brahms-Platz wurde kurz nach 1900 errichtet. Eine Stiftung des Reederehepaares Carl Heinrich und Sophie Laeisz (links). Das Thalia Theater am Alstertor konnte die Restaurierung seiner Fassade auch aus Spendengeldern finanzieren (rechts).

The Musikhalle on Johannes-Brahms-Platz was built shortly after 1900 by a foundation set up by shipowner Carl Heinrich Laeisz and his wife Sophie (left).
The Thalia Theater on Alstertor was similarly able to finance a restoration of its facade by raising donations (right).

Geschichte Hamburgs in Harburg geht in das Jahr 1898 zurück. Seit 1937 gehört Harburg zu Hamburg, und im Museum hat sich einiges geändert. Heute heißt es: Hamburger Museum für Archäologie und die Geschichte Harburgs – Helms-Museum. Auch das Altonaer Museum wäre ohne Unterstützung privater Förderer um vieles ärmer. Nur das jüngste Haus im Reigen der großen Hamburger Museen, das seit 1982 bestehende Museum der Arbeit, verdankt seine Existenz dem Staat. Im Zeichen der Verselbständigung der Hamburger Museen – seit 1999 werden sie als Stiftungen öffentlichen Rechts betrieben – kommen auf die Häuser ganz neue Zeiten zu.

Auch die neubarocke Musikhalle, die 1904–08 am Gorch-Fock-Wall unweit des Geburtshauses des Komponisten Johannes Brahms entstand, wurde als Konzerthalle mit über 1800 Plätzen gestiftet: von dem Reeder Carl Heinrich Laeisz und seiner Frau Sophie.

### Leuchtfeuer der Kultur und Orte der Wissenschaft

Die Flaggschiffe der Hamburger Theaterszene sind das Schauspielhaus an der Kirchenallee und das Thalia Theater am Gerhart-Hauptmann-Platz. Beide Häuser können auf eine große Tradition zurück-

The neo-Baroque Musikhalle, built between 1904 and 1908 on Gorch-Fock-Wall not far from the house where the composer Johannes Brahms was born, was another private foundation. The money to build the concert hall seating more than 1,800 people was donated by the ship-owner Carl Heinrich Laeisz and his wife Sophie.

### Beacons of the arts

The flagships of Hamburg's theatre scene are the Schauspielhaus on Kirchenallee and the Thalia Theater on Gerhart-Hauptmann-Platz. Both can look back on a great tradition. Both regularly earn themselves a place in the first rank of German-language theatre by staging sensational productions. Without the three great beacons of its cultural scene – the Opera, the Schauspielhaus and the Thalia Theater – Hamburg would be

blicken und spielen sich mit aufsehener-
regenden Inszenierungen immer wieder
in die erste Reihe der deutschsprachigen
Bühnen. Hamburg wäre arm ohne die
drei großen Leuchtfeuer seiner Kultur:
Oper, Schauspielhaus, Thalia Theater.
Und gar nicht hoch genug zu schätzen
sind auch die vielen privatwirtschaftlich
funktionierenden kleineren und größeren
Lichter, deren Schein die Stadt reich
macht an Kunst und Kultur – Galerien,
Musikclubs, kleine Theater. Eine schnell
fluktuierende alternative Szene und nicht
zuletzt eine vitale Kinoszene machen die
Stadt zur Metropole von tausend Künsten.

Die Wissenschaft etablierte sich in
Hamburg erst sehr spät in der deutschen
Universitätslandschaft. Die Universität
Hamburg wurde 1919 gegründet. Während bis dato Universitäten zumeist
durch Gründungsakte von Fürsten entstanden waren, erlebte die Hansestadt
die erste parlamentarisch-demokratische
Universitätsgründung in Deutschland.
Unter den zahlreichen wissenschaftlichen
Institutionen an Alster und Elbe gibt es
heute eine Einrichtung, auf die man
besonders stolz ist. Weltweit eines der
bedeutendsten Forschungszentren für
Elementarteilchenphysik hat seit 1959
seinen Sitz in Bahrenfeld. Das Deutsche
Elektronen-Synchroton (DESY) ist eine
wissenschaftliche Stiftung. Der größte
Teilchenbeschleuniger HERA (Hadron-
Elektron-Ring-Anlage) läuft in bis zu 20
Meter Tiefe als Tunnel von 6,3 Kilome-
ter Länge unterirdisch durch Hamburgs
Westen.

poor. However, one cannot speak highly
enough of the many private-sector establishments, both large and small, which
make the city rich in art and culture.
Galleries, music clubs, small theatres, a
rapidly changing alternative scene and
not least a lively cinema scene make
Hamburg a metropolis of a thousand
arts.

Hamburg did not enter the German
university scene until very late on. Hamburg University was founded in 1919.
Up till then, universities had usually been
founded by princely decree, and Hamburg's was the first university in Germany to be established by order of a
democratic parliament. Among the
numerous academic institutions on the
Alster and the Elbe there is one of which
the city is particularly proud: since 1959
one of the world's leading research cen-
tres for elementary particle physics has
been based in Bahrenfeld. The Deutsches
Elektronen-Synchroton (DESY) is a scientific foundation. Its largest particle
accelerator, HERA (Hadron-Elektron-
Ring-Anlage), is a 6.3-kilometre subter-
ranean tunnel running up to 20 metres
below the surface of west Hamburg.

Das gläserne Audito-
rium Maximum ist das
Zentrum auf dem Cam-
pus der Hamburger
Universität (links).
Das Deutsche Schau-
spielhaus am Haupt-
bahnhof zählt, wie das
Thalia Theater, zu den
renommiertesten
deutschsprachigen Büh-
nen (rechts).

The glass-clad Audito-
rium Maximum, or
main lecture theatre,
forms the centre of the
Hamburg University
campus (left).
The Deutsches Schau-
spielhaus opposite the
main railway station,
like the Thalia Theater,
is one of the most high-
ly-regarded theatres in
the German-speaking
world (right).

# Die Feste feiern, wie sie fallen
## High days and holidays

Hamburger Prominenz und internationale Ehrengäste treffen sich alljährlich seit 1356 im Februar im Großen Festsaal des Rathauses zum Matthiae-Mahl.

Leading Hamburg public figures and international guests of honour have met annually in February since 1356 in the Grosser Festsaal of the Rathaus, or City Hall, for the Matthiae-Mahl, or gala dinner held on the feast day of St. Matthew.

No tips for party-goers, whose terrain is in any case much too fast-moving and very much the same in any large city. The typical Hamburg calendar of events starts with the Matthiae-Mahlzeit in the Great Banqueting Hall of the Rathaus at the end of February each year. The world's oldest formal banquet, it was first held on St. Matthew's Day (24 February) 1356. On this evening the city-state rolls out its finest pomp and splendour for 400 guests from the worlds of politics, business, the arts and sport. The civic silver is brought out of the walk-in silver chamber onto the tables – precious centrepieces, chalices, cutlery, all gifts received by the Senate. However, politicking also goes on beneath the three large crystal chandeliers in the banqueting hall. The formal addresses by the guests of honour – usually leading politicians – are regarded as having programmatic status.

## An intimate repast for businessmen

The next exclusive event follows hot on the heels of the Matthiae-Mahlzeit. In March the Ostasiatischer Verein (East Asia Society) plays host to a far-eastern love banquet (Liebesmahl) in the Hotel Atlantic. This event, too, goes back a long way. The society, founded by Hamburg and Bremen merchants in 1900, held its first Liebesmahl in 1901. The event is attended by the leading East Asia experts. Ladies were admitted for the first time in 1964. The Liebesmahl, held in aid of business rather than love, derives its often misunderstood name from parties known as love banquets thrown for German businessmen in the

Keine Tips für Partytiger. Deren Terrain ist ohnehin viel zu schnellebig und in jeder Großstadt ein bißchen ähnlich. Der typisch hamburgische Festkalender beginnt mit der Matthiae-Mahlzeit im Großen Festsaal des Rathauses jeweils Ende Februar. Zu diesem ältesten Festbankett der Welt wurde zum erstenmal im Jahr 1356 eingeladen, und zwar am Tage des Heiligen Matthias (24. Februar). Für die 400 Gäste aus Politik, Wirtschaft, Kultur und Sport wird an diesem Abend im Rathaus der höchste Glanz entfaltet, den die Stadtrepublik in petto hat. Aus dem Safe der begehbaren Silberkammer wird das Ratssilber auf die Tische gebracht: kostbare Tafelaufsätze, Pokale, Bestecke – alles Geschenke an den Senat. Unter den drei großen Kristallüstern im Festsaal wird während des Essens aber auch Politik gemacht. Die Festreden der Ehrengäste – meist prominente Politiker – gelten als programmatisch.

## Liebesmahl für Kaufleute

Der Matthiae-Mahlzeit folgt die nächste exklusive Veranstaltung auf dem Fuß. Im März lädt der Ostasiatische Verein im Hotel Atlantic zum Ostasiatischen Liebesmahl ein. Auch dieses Fest hat Tradition. Der von Hamburger und Bremer Kaufleuten im Jahr 1900 gegründete Verein veranstaltete 1901 sein erstes Liebesmahl. Bei diesem Fest sind die tonangebenden Ostasienexperten versammelt. 1964 wurden zum erstenmal auch Damen zugelassen. Das Liebesmahl, das mehr der Wirtschaft als der Liebe dienen soll, führt seinen oft mißverstandenen Namen auf die Feste zurück, die unter der Bezeichnung Liebesmahl im Rahmen der bewaffneten Seefahrt an Bord des Ostasiengeschwaders der Offiziere der kaiserlichen Flotte für deutsche Kaufleute in Fernost gegeben wurden. Ihr Initiator war der Kommandeur der Flotte, Prinz Heinrich von Preußen, der bis 1914 auch Stammgast beim norddeutschen Liebesmahl war.

Anschließend an diese beiden Festveranstaltungen wird es im Hamburger Festkalender volkstümlich. Die Osterfeuer am Strand von Övelgönne bis Rissen und neuerdings auch im Hinterland führen am Ostersamstag jedesmal zu einem wahren Volksauflauf. Genauso wie der Hafengeburtstag, der jeweils Anfang Mai zwischen Baumwall und St. Pauli-Landungsbrücken mit einem gewaltigen Aufgebot an Buden und Veranstaltungen an und auf dem Wasser gefeiert wird. Am schönsten ist das Fest vom Wasser aus zu erleben. Höhepunkt der Geburtstagsereignisse ist für die meisten die Fahrt der großen und kleinen Segelschiffe, die sich zwischen Blankenese und Teufelsbrück zur Parade formieren. Im Jahr 1989 wurde der 800. „Geburtstag" des Hafens begangen. Man beruft sich dabei auf eine angeblich am 7. 5. 1189 von Kaiser Friedrich I. Barbarossa verfaßte Urkunde. Ein Dokument, das nie gefunden wurde. Was existiert, ist eine vom

Far East on board the ships of the East Asia command of the German imperial fleet. They were initiated by Prince Heinrich von Preussen, commodore of the fleet, who was a regular guest at the Hamburg Liebesmahl until 1914.

After these two formal occasions, the Hamburg events calender strikes a popular note. The Easter bonfires lit along the Elbe beach from Övelgönne to Rissen – and of late in the hinterland – on Easter Saturday each year draw hordes of people. The same goes for the Hafengeburtstag (Port Birthday), which is celebrated each year in early May with a vast array of stalls and events on and around the water between Baumwall and St Pauli-Landungsbrücken. The best way to experience this event is from the water. For most people, the highspot of the birthday celebrations is the parade of large and small sailing boats which form up between Blankenese and Teufelsbrück. The port's 800th "birthday" was celebrated in 1989. The date was fixed on the basis of a document allegedly written by Emperor Frederick Barbarossa on 7 May 1189. The document has never

Ein Volksfest mit alter Tradition sind die Osterfeuer am Elbstrand, zu denen jedes Jahr Tausende von Schaulustigen zusammenkommen.

Easter bonfires on the beach by the River Elbe are a longstanding tradition and are attended annually by people in their thousands.

Jedes Jahr Anfang Mai
wird zwischen Baum-
wall und St. Pauli-Lan-
dungsbrücken an Land
und zu Wasser gleicher-
maßen Hafengeburtstag
gefeiert.

The Port's birthday, or
anniversary of the Port
of Hamburg, is cele-
brated annually at the
beginning of May
between Baumwall and
the St Pauli landing
stages on land and on
the water.

Hamburger Rat um 1265 veranlaßte Fälschung, in der die Privilegien festgeschrieben sind, die Barbarossa 1189 möglicherweise bereits gewährte.

### Feuerwerk über der Alster

Nicht von der Historie, sondern von der Natur abhängig ist das Kirschblütenfest, das die japanische Kolonie in Hamburg alljährlich im Mai feiert und mit einem herrlichen Feuerwerk über der Außenalster zu der zauberhaftesten pyromanischen Veranstaltung macht, die die Hamburger kennen und lieben.

Die populärsten Volksfeste der Hansestadt finden auf dem Heiliggeistfeld statt. Wo sich im Mittelalter die Kornkammer des Hospitals zum Heiligen Geist befand, werden unter dem Markenzeichen Hamburger Dom heute der „Frühlingsmarkt", das „Hummelfest" im Sommer und der „Dommarkt" im Spätherbst durchgeführt. Die Riesenkirmes bietet ständig neue technische Attraktionen. Wer die „Spuckmaschinen" nicht liebt, kann sich mit Labskaus und Zuckerwatte den Magen verrenken.

### Woher der Name Dom kommt

Warum dieser größte Jahrmarkt Norddeutschlands Dom heißt, das ist eine weit zurückreichende Geschichte. Urkunden weisen erstmals für das Jahr 1329 ein marktartiges Treiben im und um den Hamburger Dom aus, der dort stand, wo heute neben dem Pressehaus am Speersort ein großer Parkplatz liegt. 1892 fand dieser Jahrmarkt, der sich inzwischen zu einer großen Volksbelustigung ausgewachsen hatte und 1804 auf den Gänsemarkt umgezogen war, zum erstenmal auf dem Heiliggeistfeld genug Platz.

been found. What does exist is a forgery ordered by the Hamburg Council in around 1265, setting out the rights and privileges which Barbarossa may have granted in 1189.

### Fireworks over the Alster

A festival dependent on nature rather than history is the Cherry Blossom Festival which Hamburg's Japanese community celebrates each year in May. It culminates in a magnificent fireworks display over the Alster, the most magical of the pyromaniac events which Hamburgers know and love.

The Hanseatic city's most popular folk festivals are held on Heiligengeistfeld, which in the Middle Ages was the site of the Holy Ghost Hospital granary. It is now the venue of the Hamburg Dom, a brand-name which covers the Spring Fair, the Hummelfest in summer and the Dommarkt in late autumn. This gigantic fairground constantly comes up with new technical attractions. Those who are not keen on the "sick-making machines" can torture their stomachs with corned-beef, fish and beetroot hash or candy-floss instead.

### How the Dom got its name

The story of how North Germany's largest fair came to be called the Dom goes back a long way. The first record of market-type happenings in and around the Hamburg Dom, or cathedral, go back to 1329. In those days the Dom stood on the site of what is now a large car-park next to the Pressehaus on Speersort. In 1892 this fair, which in the meantime had grown into a large popular amusement and had moved to Gänsemarkt in 1804, was held for the first time on the more spacious Heiligengeistfeld. Although the cathedral was demolished in 1807, the folk festival kept its name. Nowadays very few of the many thousands of visitors to the Dom know where the name comes from. Putting

Obwohl die Domkirche bereits 1807 abgerissen worden war, behielt das Volksfest seinen Namen bei. Woher der Name kommt, wissen heute nur die wenigsten der zigtausend Dombesucher. Das Riesenrad stimmt im Frühjahr, Sommer und Herbst auf den Dombummel ein. Ein festlich leuchtender Kreis, der sich in langsamer Drehung am Himmel bewegt und seinen Mitfahrenden im Zenit einen wunderbaren Blick über die Stadt bietet.

people in the right mood for a stroll round the Dom in spring, summer and autumn is the Giant Wheel, a brightly-lit circle that revolves slowly in the sky, offering passengers a wonderful view of the city from its highest point.

Der Hamburger Dom auf dem Heiligengeistfeld versammelt dreimal im Jahr die neuesten Kirmes- und Jahrmarktattraktionen zu einem der größten Volksfeste Norddeutschlands.

Hamburg's funfair, known as the Dom and held on Heiligengeistfeld three times a year, features the latest funfair attractions and is one of the largest funfairs in north Germany.

# Hamburgs Obst- und Gemüsegarten:
## Altes Land und Vierlande

Hamburg's fruit and vegetable gardens:
Altes Land and Vierlande

Eine Millionenstadt will versorgt sein. Unter anderem täglich mit tonnenweise Obst, Gemüse, Blumen, die in aller Herrgottsfrühe auf den Markt kommen. Aber auch mit ländlichen Ausflugszielen, die den urbanen Pflastertretern und Bürohockern am Wochenende Erholungsmöglichkeiten bieten. Für beides sind die Riesengärten vor den Toren der Hansestadt gut. Südlich der Elbe im Westen, auf etwa 25 Kilometer Länge zwischen Süderelbe und Schwinge, erstreckt sich das Alte Land, traditioneller Obstgarten für Hamburg und die ganze Region. Nördlich des Stroms liegen im Osten der Stadt die Vier- und Marschlande, eine fruchtbare Niederung, deren Bauern die Hansestadt seit Jahrhunderten mit Gemüse und Blumen versorgen.

## Grabenspringen unter Apfelbäumen

Das Alte Land rühmt sich, das größte zusammenhängende Obstanbaugebiet im Norden der Erdkugel zu sein. Geprägt wurde das Marschgebiet an den drei Nebenflüssen der Elbe – Este, Lühe, Schwinge – von holländischen Siedlern, die im 12. Jahrhundert von den damaligen Landesherren, den Erzbischöfen von Bremen, ins Land geholt wurden. Sie durchzogen das Alte Land mit einem rechtwinkeligen Netz von Entwässerungsgräben. Was sich heute hier und da noch als Kinderspiel findet, das Grabenspringen, gehörte für die Bewohner des Obstlandes früher zum Alltag. Seit man die Deiche nach der verheerenden Sturmflut von 1962 erhöhte, wurden viele kleinere Gräben zugeschüttet. Das veränderte die Landschaft genauso wie der Übergang von hochstämmigen Obstbäumen zu den besser tragenden und pflegeleichteren niedrigen Pflanzen.

Doch die Hanseaten lieben „ihr" Altes Land auch so. Und niemand stört sich daran, daß nur der kleinere Teil dieses

A city of getting on for two million people needs supplies, among other things a daily supply of tons of fruit, vegetables and flowers that reach the market at the crack of dawn. But it also needs a supply of places for outings, places where city pavement-trudgers and office workers can find recreation at weekends. The gigantic orchards and market-gardens just outside Hamburg provide both. To the south of the Elbe and west of the city, stretching for around 25 kilometres between Süderelbe and Schwinge, is the Altes Land, the traditional orchard country for Hamburg and the whole region. To the north of the river and east of the city are Vierland and Marschlande, a fertile lowland area whose market-gardeners have supplied Hamburg with vegetables and flowers for centuries.

## Ditch-jumping beneath apple trees

The Altes Land basks in the glory of being the largest contiguous fruit-growing area in the northern hemisphere. The marshy area along three tributaries of the Elbe, the Este, the Luehe and the Schwinge, still bears the mark of Dutch settlers brought there in the twelfth century by the archbishops of Bremen, the rulers of the day. They dug a right-angled network of drainage ditches through the Altes Land. In those days jumping ditches, now an occasional children's game, was part of everyday life for the people who lived there. After devastating floods in 1962, the dikes were raised and many of the smaller ditches filled in, transforming the landscape. It was further transformed by the switch from tall-growing fruit trees to

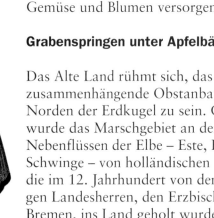

Altländerin in Arbeitstracht beim Kirschensortieren

Woman from the Altlande orchard area in her working clothes sorting cherries

Das Alte Land wurde
von Niederländern kul-
tiviert. Schnurgerade
Gräben prägen das
Landschaftsbild bis
heute.

The Altes Land area
south of the river was
laid out by Dutch farm-
ers. To this day, drain-
age ditches as straight as
a die are characteristic
of the orchard land-
scape.

Gebietes zu Hamburg gehört. Westlich
der Ortschaft Cranz, wo die Este in die
Elbe mündet, beginnt bereits Niedersach-
sen. Doch jedes Jahr im Frühling zur
Kirschblüte und zur Apfelblüte wird das
Alte Land am Wochenende über-
schwemmt von Spaziergängern, Padd-
lern, Radfahrern und Autos mit dem
Kennzeichen HH.

Früher brachten es die Obstbauern
dank der gewinnträchtigen Absatzmög-
lichkeiten im benachbarten Hamburg zu
Wohlstand. Das ist heute nicht mehr so
einfach, und viele alte Gehöfte sind
inzwischen von ihren Besitzern verkauft
worden. Das Land übernahm ein anderer
Hof, das schöne Bauernhaus ein Hamburger als Wochenenddomizil. Von dem
ehemaligen Wohlstand zeugt aber die
gediegene bäuerliche Kultur, die hier
immer noch zu Hause ist. Die Altländer
Trachten, der Festschmuck und die Ausstattung der Häuser sind berühmt. Die
strohgedeckten Fachwerkbauten stehen
zum großen Teil unter Denkmalschutz.
Viele der reichgeschnitzten Prunkpforten
neben den Bauernhäusern wurden in den
vergangenen Jahren restauriert.

low-growing strains which bring a better
yield and are easier to manage.

Be that as it may, Hamburgers still
love "their" Altes Land, regardless of the
fact that only a small part of it actually
belongs to Hamburg. In fact, Lower Sax-
ony starts just to the west of the village
of Cranz, where the Este flows into the
Elbe. Even so, each year in spring, at
cherry- and apple-blossom time, at
weekends the Altes Land is swamped
with walkers, canoeists, cyclists and cars

Wie wohlhabend die
Obstbauern im Alten
Land früher waren, ist
noch heute an der rei-
chen Kultur dieses
Landstrichs abzulesen.

Ornately decorated
farmhouses show how
prosperous fruit-
growers here used to
be.

Die Neuenfelder St. Pankratiuskirche wurde Ende des 17. Jahrhunderts auf einer Düne errichtet. Hier befinden sich das Grab des berühmten Orgelbauers Arp Schnitger und eine seiner Orgeln, auf der noch heute Konzerte gespielt werden.

The Pankratiuskirche, or St Pancras, in Neuenfelde was built on a dune in the late seventeenth century. The church houses the grave of the famous organ-builder Arp Schnitger and one of his organs that is still used for concerts.

## Reiche kleine Dorfkirchen

Zeugen dieser sehr besonderen Bauernkultur sind vor allem die Kirchen, auf die die Deichhufendörfer zu Recht stolz sein dürfen. Das berühmteste Gotteshaus im Alten Land besitzt der Ort Neuenfelde, der von Blankenese aus auch mit der Fähre zu erreichen ist. Die Neuenfelder St. Pankratiuskirche wurde Ende des 17. Jahrhunderts auf einer Düne errichtet. Das reich ausgemalte Tonnengewölbe, die von Engeln getragene Kanzel und das herrliche Gestühl sind eine unendliche Augenlust. Viele Besucher kommen aber auch, um vor allem zu hören. Denn in St. Pankratius ist eine der berühmten

with a Hamburg registration number.

In the old days, thanks to the proximity of the lucrative Hamburg market, the fruit farmers grew prosperous. Nowadays it is not so easy, and many old farmsteads have been sold by their owners, and the region has been taken over by a different kind of farmhouse, one that serves a Hamburger as a weekend retreat. However, the high-class farming culture that is still evident here testifies to this former prosperity. The traditional costumes, jewellery and domestic furnishings of the Altes Land are famous. Many of the thatched, half-timbered buildings are protected monuments, and many of the superb, ornately carved gateways that are a distinctive feature of the region have been restored in recent years.

Arp-Schnitger-Orgeln erhalten. Der große Orgelbaumeister hatte auf einem Hof in Neuenfelde von 1684 bis zu seinem Tod im Jahr 1719 seine Werkstatt. Sein Grab und eine eigens für ihn geschaffene Loge finden sich in der Kirche. Orgelkonzerte in St. Pankratius gehören für viele zu den Höhepunkten eines sommerlichen Ausflugs ins Alte Land.

### Augenfreude und Vitamindepot

Während die Altländer Bauern früher die auflaufende Flut auf der Elbe für den Transport des Obstes in Kähnen nach Hamburg nutzten, brachten die Vierländer Gemüse und Blumen bis in die drei-

### Small but wealthy village churches

Some of the best testimony to this out-of-the-ordinary farming culture is provided by the churches of which the villages in the area can be justly proud. The best-known place of worship in the Altes Land is in the village of Neuenfelde, one way of reaching which is by ferry from Blankenese. Neuenfelde's Pankratiuskirche (St Pancras' Church) was built on a dune in the late seventeenth century. Its richly painted barrel vaulting, a pulpit borne by angels and superb pews are an endless feast for the eyes. But many visitors come there mainly to listen, for the Pankratiuskirche has one of the famous Arp Schnitger organs. The great master organ-builder had his workshop on a farm in Neuenfelde from 1684 until his death in 1719. The church contains his

Die Elbe mit den nördlich gelegenen Vier- und Marschlanden, dem Gemüseanbaugebiet Hamburgs, und der Mündung der Seeve bei Over

The Elbe and, to the north of the river, the Vierlande and Marschlande market garden area of Hamburg and the confluence of the Seeve and the Elbe near Over village

Das Rieck-Haus in Curslack ist heute Museum für die Bauernkultur der Vier- und Marschlande.

The Rieck-Haus in Curslack is now a museum of Vierlande and Marschlande farming culture.

So sahen die Haushalts-gegenstände einer wohl-habenden Bauernfami-lie früher aus.

This is what the interior of a farmhouse owned by a wealthy farming family used to look like.

ßiger Jahre des 20. Jahrhunderts bei ablaufendem Wasser in Ewern mit hohem Segelmast auf die Märkte der Hansestadt. Auch die Vierlande mit den Dörfern Altengamme, Curslack, Kirch-werder und Neuengamme wurden bereits im 12. Jahrhundert besiedelt. Der

grave and a box specially made for him. For many people the organ concerts in St Pankratius are one of the highspots of a summer outing to the Altes Land.

## A delight for the eyes and a vitamin store

While Altes Land farmers used to take advantage of the incoming tide on the Elbe to transport their fruit to Hamburg in barges, until the 1930s the Vierlanders brought vegetables and flowers to the city markets in tall-masted sailing boat on the outgoing tide. Vierlande with its villages of Altengamme, Curslack, Kirch-werder and Neuengamme was settled in the twelfth century. Hamburg's vegetable and flower garden grew in parallel with the city's wealth. Here, too, prosperity was reflected in a farming culture, the best remaining example of which is the Rieck-Haus in Curslack. This magnifi-cent farmhouse is an outpost of the Altona Museum, which as a museum for the North German region keeps alive the memory of the old farming cultures out-side the city gates.

Gemüse- und Blumengarten Hamburgs
wuchs parallel zum Reichtum der Hansestadt. Auch hier schlug sich die Prospe-
rität in einer Bauernkultur nieder, die
heute am besten im Curslacker Rieck-
Haus nachzuvollziehen ist. Das prächtige
Bauernhaus ist eine Nebenstelle des Altonaer Museums, das als Norddeutsches
Landesmuseum die Erinnerung an die
alten Bauernkulturen vor den Toren der
Hansestadt wachhält.

## Maiglöckchen und Blutegel

In den Vierlanden wachsen heute die
meisten Schnittblumen ganz Deutschlands. Viele Bauern haben als sogenannte
Selbsterzeuger ihre Stände auf den zahlreichen Wochenmärkten der Hansestadt.
Ökologisch Angebautes verkauft sich
gut. Doch Wohlstand ist hier wie im
Alten Land schwer erkämpft. Das war
im 19. Jahrhundert anders, als die Vierländer Bauern nahezu ein Monopol im
Handel mit Maiglöckchen bzw. deren
Keimlingen besaßen und das Geschäft
mit Blutegeln blühte. Damals glaubte
man an die Heilkraft der kleinen Blut-
sauger, die gratis aus den Gräben gefan-
gen und in alle Welt exportiert wurden.

Auch in den Vierlanden zeugen reich-
ausgestattete Dorfkirchen von ehemali-
gem Wohlstand. St. Johannis im Orts-
zentrum von Curslack wurde Ende des
16. Jahrhunderts gegründet, St. Severin
in Kirchwerder bereits im 13. Jahrhundert. Beide Kirchen wurden durch die
Jahrhunderte immer wieder vergrößert,
verändert, verschönert. Auf dem Kirchhof von St. Severin finden sich zahlreiche
Grabsteine vom Ende des 16. bis zur
Mitte des 18. Jahrhunderts.

## Lily of the valley and leeches

Vierlande now grows more cut flowers
than anywhere else in Germany. Many
market-gardeners have their own stalls
at Hamburg's numerous weekly markets.
Organic produce sells well. But, as in the
Altes Land, prosperity does not come
easily. Things were different in the nineteenth century, when the Vierlande farmers had a virtual monopoly in lily of the
valley, or rather its seeds, and the leech

Die St. Johanniskirche
in Curslack zählt zu der
herrlichen Kette kleiner
barocker Gotteshäuser
im Osten von Ham-
burg.

The Johanniskirche, or
St John's, in Curslack
forms one of a superb
chain of small Baroque
churches in Hamburg's
eastern suburbs.

St. Severin in Kirchwerder ist die größte unter den Bauernkirchen der Vierlande. Auf dem Kirchhof stehen 90 Sandstein-Grabsteine aus dem 16. bis 19. Jahrhundert.

St Severin in Kirchwerder is the largest church in the rural Vierlande area. Its churchyard features 90 sandstone gravestones dating from the sixteenth to the nineteenth century.

Die vielleicht schönste Dorfkirche im Reigen der Vierländer Gotteshäuser steht in Altengamme. St. Nicolai, ein sakrales Kleinod im riesigen Blumen- und Gemüsegarten der Millionenstadt, ist die bedeutendste Bauernkirche des Barock in Norddeutschland. Sie wurde schon 1250 aus Feldsteinen errichtet. Nach vielfacher Veränderung fällt sie heute durch ihren freistehenden Glockenturm von 1605 auf. In seinem Inneren ertönt die Dom-Glocke Celsa, die die Vierländer beim Abbruch der Hamburger Domkirche erwarben.

Auch die St. Johanniskirche in Neuengamme ist in ihrem Ursprung ein Feldsteinbau aus dem 13. Jahrhundert. Wie in St. Nicolai sind die Männerbänke mit bemalten schmiedeeisernen Hutständern geschmückt.

business was flourishing. In those days people believed in the medicinal powers of the small blood-suckers, which were caught free in the ditches and exported all over the world.

Richly-furnished village churches testify to the former prosperity of the Vierlande area, too. St Johannis in the centre of Curslack was founded at the end of the sixteenth century, St Severin's in Kirchwerder as long ago as the thirteenth century. Over the centuries, both churches were repeatedly enlarged, beautified, altered. St Severin's churchyard has numerous gravestones dating from the late sixteenth to the mid-eighteenth century.

Perhaps the most attractive village church in Vierlande is in Altengamme. St Nicolai, a religious jewel amidst Hamburg's gigantic flower and vegetable garden, is North Germany's finest Baroque village church. The stone church was built before 1250, but was altered many times. Nowadays its most distinctive feature is a freestanding bell-tower dating back to 1605. Inside the church is the

### Eine Stätte des Holocaust

Der Name Neuengamme verbindet sich
aber auch mit einem der dunkelsten
Kapitel der Hansestadt. 1938 richtete die
SS in dem Ort ein Konzentrationslager
ein. Russische, polnische, französische,
ukrainische und jüdische Gefangene
wurden hier inhaftiert und mußten
Zwangsarbeit leisten. Heute weiß man,
daß von den über 135 000 Häftlingen in
Neuengamme und seinen zahlreichen
Außenlagern auf hamburgischem Gebiet
bis 1945 nahezu die Hälfte umkam. Ein
Mahnmal erinnert an die Ermordeten.
Ein Dokumentenhaus informiert über
dieses Kapitel des Holocaust vor den
Toren der Hansestadt.

Celsa cathedral bell which the local people bought when Hamburg's cathedral
was demolished.

St Johannis in Neuengamme was also
originally a thirteenth-century stone
church. As in St Nicolai, the men's pews
are equipped with painted wrought-iron
hat-stands.

### A Holocaust site

The name of Neuengamme is linked with
one of the darkest chapters in Hamburg's history. In 1938 the SS established
a concentration camp there, where Russ-
ian, Polish, French, Ukrainian and Jewish prisoners were held and used as
forced labour. We now know that, of
more than 135,000 prisoners in
Neuengamme and its numerous outposts
in other parts of Hamburg, almost half
died. A memorial recalls those who were
murdered. A document centre provides
information on this chapter of the Holocaust on Hamburg's doorstep.

Die Gedenkstätte in
Neuengamme erinnert
an das Konzentrations-
lager, das hier von den
Nazis eingerichtet
wurde (links).
Häftlinge des KZs Neu-
engamme bei Wasser-
bauarbeiten. Um die
55 000 Menschen
kamen hier und in vie-
len Außenlagern ums
Leben (rechts).

Neuengamme memorial
commemorates the con-
centration camp the
Nazis built here (left).
Neuengamme concen-
tration camp prisoners
are here seen digging
drainage ditches. About
55,000 people died here
and in many camp out-
stations (right).

# Das Alstertal und die Walddörfer
## The Alstertal and the Walddörfer

Idyllisch und einsam ist die Landschaft, durch die die Alster im Oberlauf ihren Weg nimmt. Das Quellgebiet bei Ulzburg liegt 56 km von der Hamburger City entfernt.

The countryside through which the Alster wends its way along its upper reaches is idyllic and isolated. The river's source, near Ulzburg, is 56 kilometres north of Hamburg's city centre.

Wiesen und Felder, Wälder und Moore, Auen- und Heidelandschaft. Wer verbindet diese Zauberworte der Natur mit der Großstadt Hamburg? Selbst viele Hanseaten kennen die ehemaligen Dörfer nicht, die für Liebhaber eines Häuschens im Grünen, eines Domizils mit großem Garten, einer Villa mit Parkanlage längst kein Geheimtip mehr sind. Wie ein grüner Halbkreis runden diese guten Wohnadressen das Stadtgebiet im Norden ab. Wer hier zu Besuch ist, kann sich in den weitläufigen Landschaften, in die diese Ortschaften eingebettet sind, wie verreist fühlen. Wer hier wohnt, liebt „sein Dorf". Und jedes hat denn auch einen ganz eigenen Charakter.

Drei Namen gliedern diesen grünen Wohnbereich im Norden von Hamburg. Im Nordosten liegen die Walddörfer:

Meadows and fields, woods and marshes, water meadows and heathland. Who would associate these magical words of nature with the metropolis of Hamburg? Even many Hamburgers don't know the former villages which have long since ceased to be a little-known haunt of fans of a cottage in the country, a house with a big garden, a mansion set in a park. These exclusive residential areas form a green semicircle rounding off Hamburg's territory to the north. Amid the spacious countryside in which these villages are set, visitors can feel as if they are on holiday. Those who live here love "their village." And each village has is very own character.

Farmsen, Berne, Volksdorf, Wohldorf, Ohlstedt, Großhansdorf und Schmalenbeck. Das Alstertal umfaßt die Ortschaften Hummelsbüttel, Wellingsbüttel, Sasel, Poppenbüttel, Lemsahl-Mellingstedt und Duvenstedt mit dem Duvenstedter Brook. Zu den sogenannten Rühmerdörfern – heute nicht mehr gebräuchliche Landschaftsbezeichnung, die sich vom altsächsischen „rumo" (weit, geräumig) herleitet – zählen die ehemaligen holsteinischen Dörfer Bergstedt, Bramfeld, Alsterdorf, Meiendorf, Oldenfelde, Rahlstedt, Sasel und Steilshoop.

## Durch grüne Tunnel paddeln

Daß der Freizeitwert dieser Wohngemeinden groß ist, versteht sich bei dem Angebot an schönen Landschaften von selbst. Am Oberlauf der Alster finden Paddler Wasserwanderwege, die an manchen Stellen wie grüne Tunnel zugewach-

Three names divide up this green residential area in the north of Hamburg. In the north-east are the Walddörfer (forest villages): Farmsen, Berne, Volksdorf, Wohldorf, Ohlstedt, Grosshansdorf and Schmalenbeck. The Alstertal (Alster valley) comprises the villages of Hummelsbüttel, Wellingsbüttel, Sasel, Poppenbüttel, Lemsahl-Mellingstedt and Duvenstedt with the Duvenstedter Brook. Then there are the so-called Rühmerdörfer, an agricultural term no longer in use which comes from "rumo," an Old Saxon word meaning "broad" or "spacious." They include the former Holstein villages Bergstedt, Bramfeld, Alsterdorf, Meiendorf, Oldenfelde, Rahlstedt, Sasel and Steilshoop.

Die Bewohner der Alsterdörfer – hier bei der Mellingburger Schleuse – lieben ihren Fluß, der von Großstadt noch so gar nichts ahnen läßt.

Residents of the Alster villages through which it passes love the river – here the Mellingburger Schleuse –, which conveys not an inkling of the big city being so close at hand.

Die Alster bei Poppenbüttel, wie sie der Künstler Hermann Carmiencke in der ersten Hälfte des 19. Jahrhunderts malte

The Alster near Poppenbüttel as Hermann Carmiencke painted it in the first half of the nineteenth century

sen sind. Für Radfahrer, Fußgänger, Jogger und Reiter gibt es, abgesehen vom bekannten Alsterwanderweg, auch viele einsame Pfade. Und ein Paradies für Angler ist diese wasserreiche Landschaft sowieso. Allein im Bereich der Walddörfer fließen neun Gewässer von Ost nach West der Alster zu: die Ammersbek und die Drosselbek im Wohldorfer Wald, die Bredenbek in Ohlstedt, die Rodenbek ab der Bergstedter Chaussee, die Lottbek in Volksdorf und Hoisbüttel. Die Lohbek entspringt bei Bergstedt. Die Saselbek markiert die Grenze zwischen Bergstedt und Sasel. Die Gussau fließt in die Saselbek. Der Klosterwiesengraben von Volksdorf schließlich vereinigt sich mit der Berner Aue.

Die grünen Stadtteile im Norden von Hamburg laden aber nicht nur zur Erholung in der Natur ein, sondern auch zu Spaziergängen durch die Wohnarchitektur mehrerer Jahrhunderte. Frühes dörf-

## Paddling through tunnels of greenery

With the amount of attractive scenery on offer, it goes without saying that these residential communities have a high recreational value. Along the upper reaches of the Alster canoers find routes which in many places are overgrown like green tunnels. For cyclists, ramblers, joggers and riders there are many secluded paths in addition to the well-known Alsterwanderweg. And this water-rich landscape is of course a paradise for anglers. In the Walddörfer area alone there are nine stretches of water flowing from east to west toward the Alster – the Ammersbek and the Drosselbek in the Wohldorfer Wald, the Bredenbek in Ohlstedt, the Rodenbek from Bergstedter Chaussee, the Lottbek in Volksdorf and Hoisbüttel. The Lohbek rises in Bergstedt, the Saselbek marks the border between Bergstedt and Sasel. The Gussau flows into the Saselbek. Finally, the Volksdorf Klosterwiesengraben joins the Berner Aue.

In addition to being attractive places to relax in natural surroundings, the green districts in the north of Hamburg

Die Kirche im ehemals sächsischen Runddorf Bergstedt stammt aus dem Mittelalter. Bei Taufen schwebt der Engel an einem Seil von der Decke direkt vor den Altar.

The church in the former Saxon roundling village of Bergstedt is mediaeval in origin. At christenings the angel, suspended on a rope, is lowered from the roof down in front of the altar.

liches Wohnen findet sich neben vornehmer Landhaus- und Villenkultur, neben Siedlungen und auch Hochhausbauten des 20. Jahrhunderts. In Volksdorf, das ab 1914 zur Gartenstadt umgewandelt wurde, ist die bäuerliche Kulturgeschichte der Gegend im Museumsdorf nachzuerleben. In diesem Freilichtmuseum dokumentieren mehrere historische Gebäude ländliches Leben und Arbeiten in der Vergangenheit.

## Hochzeitskirche aus dem 13. Jahrhundert

Der Name Volksdorf taucht erstmals in einer Urkunde von 1296 auf. Das benachbarte Kirchspiel Bergstedt war damals bereits über 100 Jahre alt. Die um 1200 errichtete Bergstedter Pfarrkirche diente den umliegenden Dörfern

offer interesting walks through the residential architecture of several centuries. Early village life can be seen next to exclusive country-house and mansion culture, alongside twentieth-century estates and even tower blocks. In Volksdorf, which was transformed into a garden city from 1914, the history of the

Im Museumsdorf Volksdorf ist die ländliche Kultur der Region zu besichtigen.

The rural lifestyle of the area can be admired in Volksdorf Museum Village.

Im Wellingsbüttler Tor-haus (unten) ist heute das Alstertal-Museum untergebracht. Das schöne Herrenhaus des früheren Gutes Wellingsbüttel (rechts) wurde 1750 erbaut. Beide Gebäude stehen unter Denkmalschutz.

The Torhaus, or Gate-house, in Wellingsbüttel now houses the Alster-tal Museum. The fine manor house of the former Wellingsbüttel estate (right) was built in 1750. Both buildings are now listed monuments.

durch viele Jahrhunderte als geistliches Zentrum. Das ländliche Gotteshaus mit seiner alten bemalten Holzdecke ist heute begehrt als Ort für Hochzeiten, Taufen und Beerdigungen. Und als Raum für stimmungsvolle Konzerte im Kerzen-schein.

area's rural culture can be relived in a museum village. In this open-air museum several historical buildings document rural life and work in day gone by.

### A thirteenth-century wedding church

The name Volksdorf first appears in a document dated 1296, by which time the neighbouring parish of Bergstedt was more than 100 years old. For many centuries Bergstedt parish church, built in around 1200, served as a religious centre for the surrounding villages. The country church with its ancient painted wooden ceiling is now a sought-after venue for weddings, baptisms and funerals – and for idyllic concerts by candlelight.

In general the green northern suburbs have an extremely lively independent cultural life. Take for example the up-market residential suburb of Wellings-büttel. In 1996 residents celebrated the seven hundredth anniversary of the former village's founding. The centre of Wellingsbüttel's cultural life is the gate-house of the former country estate of the von Kurtzrock family. The attractive half-timbered building, which dates back

Überhaupt gibt es in den grünen nördlichen Vororten ein höchst lebendiges, eigenständiges Kulturleben. Zum Beispiel im illustren Villenvorort Wellingsbüttel. 1996 feierte man in dem ehemaligen Dorf das 700jährige Bestehen der Ansiedlung. Zentrum des Wellingsbüttler Kulturlebens ist das Torhaus der ehemaligen Gutsanlage der Herren von Kurtzrock. In dem schönen, 1757 errichteten Fachwerkbau hat das Alstertal-Museum sein hervorragendes Domizil. Hier kann sich jeder über die Schiffahrt auf der Oberalster, über die Heimatkunde der nördlichen Stadtteile und über die Prähistorie des Alsterraums informieren. Außerdem finden im Torhaus Konzerte, Dichterlesungen und Ausstellungen statt.

Die Walddörferschule in Volksdorf hat als kulturelles Zentrum ihre eigene Geschichte. Sie wurde als pädagogische

to 1757, provides an excellent home for the Alstertal Museum. Here you can learn alll about shipping on the upper Alster, the local history of the northern district and about the Alster area in prehistoric times. The gatehouse is also used for concerts, poetry readings and exhibitions.

The Walddörfer School in Volksdorf has its own history as a cultural centre. It was built as a pedagogical reform school between 1929 and 1931 by Fritz Schumacher, Hamburg's famous director of public works. Beneath its roof, school beginners and senior secondary-school students were united, and in the course of the Lebensreform (Life Reform) movement it was dedicated above all to the teaching of art and music. After 1900 there was a secret home of the fine arts in Lemsahl-Mellingstedt, where Gustav Schiefler, 1857– 1935, a patron of the group of Expressionist artists known as Die Brücke, had his summer residence. Schiefler, the author of "Hamburgische Kulturgeschichte 1890–1920"

Die Walddörfer Schule in Volksdorf wurde als Reformschule von Hamburgs berühmtem Baudirektor Fritz Schumacher von 1929 bis 1931 errichtet. Fritz Schumacher (1869–1947) prägt die Hansestadt auch in ihren Randbezirken bis heute.

The Walddörfer Schule in Volksdorf was designed and built between 1929 and 1931 as an educational reform project by Hamburg's famous municipal architect Fritz Schumacher, 1869–1947. To this day, Schumacher's style of building remains widespread in Hamburg and its environs.

Die Kupfermühle in
Wohldorf geht zurück
auf die Mühlen am
Kupferteich, die der
Hamburger Kaufmann
Olde in der zweiten
Hälfte des 18. Jahrhun-
derts mit Gewinn als
Kupferhämmer betrieb.
Auf Oldes Anwesen
waren die Dichter
Klopstock und Clau-
dius zu Gast.

Wohldorf's Kupfermüh-
le dates back to the
mills by the Kupfer-
teich, where a Ham-
burg merchant by the
name of Olde ran a
profitable copper mill
in the second half of the
eighteenth century. Visi-
tors to his estate inclu-
ded the poets Klopstock
and Matthias Claudius.

Reformschule von Hamburgs berühmten Baudirektor Fritz Schumacher in den Jahren 1929 bis 1931 errichtet, vereinte unter ihrem Dach Schulanfänger und Oberrealschüler und widmete sich im Zuge der Lebensreformbewegung vor allem auch der musischen Erziehung.

Ein heimliches Nest der bildenden Kunst gab es nach 1900 in Lemsahl-Mellingstedt, wo der Förderer der Künstlergruppe „Die Brücke" Gustav Schiefler (1857– 1935) seinen Sommersitz hatte. Der Verfasser der „Hamburgischen Kulturgeschichte 1890–1920", die erst 50 Jahre nach dem Tod Schieflers veröffentlicht wurde, lud nicht nur Emil Nolde in sein Sommerhaus ein, sondern auch Erich Heckel, Ernst Ludwig Kirchner und Karl Schmidt-Rottluff. Werke mit entsprechenden Bildmotiven zeugen heute in Museen und Privatsammlungen von den Aufenthalten dieser Maler im Alstertal, zu denen später noch die Künstler Arthur Illies und Ernst Eitner hinzukamen.

### Das alte und das neue Poppenbüttel

Poppenbüttel hat seinen ländlichen Charakter weitgehend verloren und macht von allen Alstertalorten den großstädtischsten Eindruck. Im 18. Jahrhundert sah man sich in dem Dorf noch „am Ende der Welt". Doch erste Anzeichen

– which was not published until 50 years after his death – invited not only Emil Nolde to his home, but also Erich Heckel, Ernst Ludwig Kirchner and Karl Schmidt-Rottluff. The motifs of works in museums and private collections testify to their stays in the Alstertal, where they were later joined by artists Arthur Illies and Ernst Eitner.

### Poppenbüttel old and new

Nowadays Poppenbüttel has largely lost its rural character and is the most urban of all the Alstertal villages. In the eighteenth century, people in the village still felt as if they were "at the world's end." But even in those days there were the first signs of the dawning of the industrial age. The businessman Hinrich Christian Olde ran a profitable copper mill in Poppenbüttel. Visitors to his fine estate included eighteenth-century Hamburg poets Matthias Claudius, Friedrich Hagedorn and Friedrich Gottlieb Klopstock.

In 1981 the Low German Henneberg Theatre was founded in Poppenbüttel. This successful amateur theatre now puts on its performances in the great hall of the Hospital zum Heiligen Geist, a spacious old people's home with 1,200 residents. In the surrounding park there is also an open-air stage.

Incidentally, the Low German amateur theatre takes its name from the Henneberg family, which in the second half of the nineteenth century owned the largest agricultural business in the north of Hamburg, covering 500 hectares in all. "Burg Henneberg" (Henneberg Castle), built from 1884, testifies to the predilection for mediaeval romanticism that was prevalent at the time. Henneberg Park is known for its arboretum, which contains a wide variety of species of trees.

Another centre of upper middle-class life was Wohldorf Manor House. Completed in 1714, it was used by Hamburg senators both as an administrative centre

für den Aufbruch ins Industriezeitalter gab es auch damals schon. Der Unternehmer Hinrich Christian Olde betrieb in Poppenbüttel mit Gewinn eine Kupfermühle. Auf seinem schönen Anwesen besuchten ihn seinerzeit auch die Hamburger Dichter Matthias Claudius, Friedrich von Hagedorn und Friedrich Gottlieb Klopstock.

1981 wurde in Poppenbüttel die niederdeutsche Henneberg-Bühne gegründet. Dieses erfolgreiche Amateurtheater ist heute im großen Saal des Hospitals zum Heiligen Geist zu Hause. Im Park dieser großzügigen Anlage der Altenbetreuung, in der 1200 Menschen leben, findet sich auch eine Freilichtbühne.

Namensgeberin des niederdeutschen Amateurtheaters ist übrigens die Familie Henneberg, die in der zweiten Hälfte des 19. Jahrhunderts mit einem 500 Hektar großen Areal den größten Landwirtschaftsbetrieb im Norden von Hamburg besaß. Die ab 1884 errichtete „Burg Henneberg" zeugt vom Hang zur Mittelalterromantik, der damals herrschte. Der Hennebergsche Park ist für sein artenreiches Arboretum berühmt.

Großbürgerlich ging es auch zu im Wohldorfer Herrenhaus. Das Gebäude wurde 1714 eingeweiht. Es diente den Hamburger Senatoren als Verwaltungssitz bei der Herrschaft über die Walddörfer und als Ort der Erholung. 1969 pachtete die Alfred-Toepfer-Stiftung das Herrenhaus. 1996 ging die noble Immobilie in Privatbesitz über. Wer sich in den grünen Vororten des Hamburger Nordens umsieht, findet solche Anwesen, wenn auch jüngeren Datums, in ungeahnter Fülle. Aber meistens so verborgen in Gärten und Parks gelegen, daß man ihre Schönheit nur ahnen kann.

for governing the Walddörfer and as a place of recreation. In 1969 the manor house was leased by the Alfred Toepfer Foundation, and in 1996 the exclusive property passed into private ownership. Looking around the green suburbs of Hamburg's north you come across an unsuspectedly large number of such estates, albeit of more recent date. Usually, however, they are so well hidden among gardens and parks that one can only guess at their beauty.

Das Herrenhaus in Wohldorf wurde 1714 errichtet und diente den Hamburger Waldherren als Amtssitz.

Wohldorf manor house was built in 1714 and served as the official residence of Hamburg's head foresters.

# Auf nach Harburg!

## Off to Harburg!

A river is a great dividing line. In Harburg, things are still a little different from in Hamburg. A glance at the map makes it clear why the Hanseatic city's southernmost and territorially largest borough, comprising Harburg, Wilhelmsburg and the villages along the Süderelbe, the southern arm of the Elbe, was for centuries an autonomous opposite pole and not a part of Hamburg. The broad floodplain of the Süderelbe and Norderelbe separated the two towns from their very beginnings, not just geographically but politically and economically too.

Horeburg, meaning "castle on the marsh," which stood on an island of sand in the marshes on the south bank of the Elbe, was granted its town charter back in 1297. Part of the Duchy of Brunswick-Lüneburg, in 1642 it fell to the Celle branch of the Guelph dynasty. In 1866 it became part of Prussia. In the nineteenth century Harburg developed into an independent industrial town. In 1927, a merger with Wilhelmsburg made it a city. It was incorporated into Hamburg by official decree when the Greater Hamburg Act of 1937 put an end to the independence of the small industrial metropolis on the southern bank of the Elbe, as it did for Altona on the north bank. Both the economic interest of Hamburg and the ambitions of National Socialist imperial and arms policy lay behind the decision.

## Building bridges between Harburg and Hamburg

Hamburg has long been proud of advantages which Harburg possesses – the international reputation of the Technical University Hamburg-Harburg, founded in 1978, the parks, the nature conservation areas, the Harburger Berge hills with their scenic variety, the Helms Museum (Hamburg Museum for Archaeology and the History of Harburg). In the other direction, Harburgers have no qualms about taking advantage

Dieser Plan des Harburger Hafens und seiner nächsten Umgebung stammt aus dem Jahr 1852. Er zeigt die Schloßinsel (Citadelle).

This map of the Port of Harburg and its environs is dated 1852. It shows the Schlossinsel and citadel.

Ein Fluß ist eine starke Trennungslinie. In Harburg gehen die Uhren immer noch ein bißchen anders als in Hamburg. Ein Blick auf die Landkarte macht klar, warum der südlichste und flächengrößte Bezirk der Hansestadt – Harburg mit Wilhelmsburg und den Süderelbeortschaften – durch Jahrhunderte autarker Gegenpol und nicht Teil von Hamburg war. Die breite Flußniederung von Süder-

und Norderelbe separierte die beiden Städte von ihren Anfängen bis ins 20. Jahrhundert sowohl geographisch als auch politisch und ökonomisch.

Das auf einer Sandinsel in der Südufer-Elbmarsch gegründete „Horeburg" (Sumpfburg), dem bereits 1297 das Stadtrecht verliehen wurde, gehörte zum Herzogtum Braunschweig-Lüneburg, fiel 1642 an die Celler Linie der Welfen und wurde 1866 preußisch. Im 19. Jahrhundert entwickelte sich Harburg zu einer eigenständigen Industriestadt. Durch den Zusammenschluß mit Wilhelmsburg wurde es 1927 Großstadt. Die Eingemeindung nach Hamburg erfolgte auf obrigkeitliche Verfügung: Das Groß-Hamburg-Gesetz von 1937 brachte für die kleine Industriemetropole am Südufer der Elbe, genauso wie für Altona am Nordufer, das Ende der Selbständigkeit. Hinter dem Beschluß standen sowohl wirtschaftliche Interessen der Hansestadt als auch Ambitionen der NS-Reichs- und Rüstungspolitik.

## Brückenschläge zwischen Harburg und Hamburg

Hamburg ist seit langem stolz auf Pluspunkte, die Harburg besitzt: die 1978 gegründete Technische Universität Hamburg-Harburg mit ihrem internationalen Renommee, die Parks und die Naturschutzgebiete, die Harburger Berge mit ihrer landschaftlichen Vielfalt sowie das Helms-Museum (Hamburger Museum für Archäologie und die Geschichte Harburgs). In umgekehrter Richtung nutzen die Harburger ungescheut die Vorzüge der Freien und Hansestadt Hamburg am Nordufer der Elbe.

of the merits of the Free and Hanseatic City of Hamburg on the north bank of the Elbe.

After Hamburg and Harburg had spent centuries being separated from each other by water, it was Napoleon of all people who had the first permanent bridge built across the Elbe. As always, the French military commander and emperor planned generously. In order to ensure that his troops could be transferred quickly from place to place, in 1811 he ordered the building of a military road from Wesel on the Lower Rhine to Hamburg. In the Harburg region, trees were felled in masses. A wooden dam nearly nine kilometres long and several bridges led through the marshes to Grasbrook. The road was officially opened in 1813. However, ferries remained the only way of crossing the Süderelbe and Norderelbe. The first Elbe bridge lasted only a few years and was demolished in 1817. Harburg, which at that time belonged to Hanover, did not want a permanent link across the Elbe because it wanted to be the terminal for north-south traffic.

In 1847, Harburg was connected to the railway line to Hanover. This was a decisive signal for the dawning of the

Napoleon ließ erstmals eine feste Brücke durch das Stromspaltungsgebiet zwischen Harburg und Hamburg bauen.

Napoleon had the first permanent bridge built across the branches of the river between Harburg and Hamburg.

Harburg um 1850. Aus Celle kommend, nähert sich der Zug seinem Endbahnhof, der sich bis 1872 auf der heutigen Bahnhofsinsel befand.

Harburg in about 1850. A train from Celle is nearing the railhead that stood until 1872 on the site of the present Bahnhofsinsel, or railway island.

Nachdem Hamburg und Harburg jahrhundertelang durch das Wasser voneinander getrennt waren, sorgte ausgerechnet Napoleon für einen ersten festen Brückenschlag. Wie immer plante der französische Feldherr und Kaiser auch in diesem Fall weiträumig. Um die schnelle Verschiebung seiner Truppen zu sichern, befahl er 1811 den Bau einer Heerstraße von Wesel am Niederrhein nach Hamburg. In der Harburger Region wurden massenweise Bäume gefällt. Ein fast neun Kilometer langer Holzdamm sowie mehrere Brücken führten durch Sumpf und Marsch bis zum Grasbrook. 1813 konnte die Straße eingeweiht werden. Doch über Süder- und Norderelbe gingen nach wie vor nur Fähren. Die erste Elbbrücke hatte nur wenige Jahre Bestand und wurde bereits 1817 abgerissen. Harburg, das damals zu Hannover gehörte, wünschte keine feste Verbindung über die Elbe, da es selbst Endpunkt des Nord-Süd-Verkehrs sein wollte.

Ein wichtigeres Signal für den Anbruch des mobilen Zeitalters setzte 1847 Harburgs Anschluß an die Eisenbahn-

mobile era. However, it was not until Harburg had passed to Prussia in 1866 that things started happening in rapid succession. In 1872 a bridge was built for the railway. It was followed in 1887 by the official opening of the Neue Elbbrücke, a road bridge across the Norderelbe. Unfortunately, its impressive neo-Gothic arches, for many years a Hamburg hallmark, were demolished in 1957. In 1888 the Billhorn road bridge was extended across the Oberhafen canal. Among the bridges that followed, in chronological order, were the Süderelbebrücke (1899), the Freihafenelbbrücke, the Reichsautobahnbrücke across the Süderelbe (1938), and after World War II the Europabrücke and the Brücke des 17. Juni, which also cross the Süderelbe. Not forgetting the most attractive and elegant bridge of all, the Köhlbrandbrücke, opened in 1974, which links the free port areas of Wal-

Die mächtigen Portale der von 1884 bis 1887 errichteten Neuen Elbbrücke wurden 1957 bei der Erweiterung für den Autoverkehr abgerissen.

The massive portals of the New Elbe Bridge, built between 1884 and 1887, were demolished in 1957 when the bridge was widened to handle more traffic.

linie nach Hannover. Doch erst nachdem Harburg 1866 zu Preußen gekommen war, ging es Schlag auf Schlag: 1872 wurde eine Brücke für die Eisenbahn gebaut. Die Einweihung einer Straßenbrücke, der Neuen Elbbrücke, über die Norderelbe folgte 1887. Ihre eindrucksvollen neugotischen Torbögen – lange ein Wahrzeichen der Hansestadt – wurden 1957 leider abgerissen. 1888 wurde die Billhorner Straßenbrücke über den Oberhafenkanal weitergeführt. In der Chronologie der Brücken folgten unter anderem: 1899 die Süderelbbrücke, 1926 die Freihafen-Elbbrücke, 1938 die Reichsautobahnbrücke über die Süderelbe sowie nach dem Zweiten Weltkrieg die Europabrücke und die Brücke des 17. Juni, die ebenfalls die Süderelbe überqueren. Nicht vergessen sollte man die schönste und eleganteste Brücke von allen, die 1974 eingeweihte Köhlbrandbrücke, die die Freihafenareale Waltershof und Steinwerder verbindet. Unentbehrlich ist natürlich auch der Elbtunnel, der seit 1975 mit drei Röhren den Strom unterquert. Die in den neunziger Jahren in Angriff genommene Erweiterung auf vier Röhren ist aber leider kein Zauber-

tershof and Steinwerder. Another indispensable river crossing is the Elbtunnel, actually three separate tunnels, which has carried traffic beneath the river since 1975. Unfortunately, the fourth tunnel, begun in the 1990s, is not a magical cure

Der Neue Elbtunnel erwies sich bald als zu klein. Modernste Technik kommt beim Bau der vierten Elbröhre zum Einsatz.

The new Elbe Tunnel soon proved too small. State-of-the-art technology at work during construction of the fourth Elbe autobahn tunnel.

Die Harburger Phoenix Werke prägten mit ihrer Weichgummiproduktion die industrielle Arbeitswelt dieser Stadt. Sie sind bis heute der wichtigste Arbeitgeber in Harburg.

The Phoenix works, manufacturing car tyres and rubber products, used to be a cornerstone of Harburg industry and remain to this day the borough's most important employer.

Die Technische Universität Hamburg-Harburg (TUHH) nahm 1980 ihren Forschungs- und Lehrbetrieb auf.

The Technische Universität Hamburg-Harburg (TUHH) started teaching and research in 1980.

mittel gegen die Staus vor und in dem 3,325 Kilometer langen Tunnel. Kluge Pendler zwischen Harburg und Hamburg nehmen längst die S-Bahn.

for the traffic jams on the approaches to and inside the 3.325-kilometre-long tunnel. Shrewd commuters between Harburg and Hamburg have long travelled by suburban train.

**Tradition and progress**

Two firms in particular were responsible for the advent of the industrial age in what had been rural Harburg. The Harburger Gummi-Kamm Compagnie, founded in 1856, is still a major employer. The hard-rubber combs and hairbrushes made by the company were much prized in the nineteenth century. The Phoenix works started up in Harburg in the same year. In its case soft rubber was the material from which products were made for export worldwide. In the twentieth century, rubber was joined by plastics.

It may have been said in former times that the Unterelbe region was lacking in technical innovation and creativity, but in the nineteenth century these two rubberware manufacturers proved that as far as Harburg was concerned the judgement was wrong. That having been said,

## Tradition und Fortschritt

Der Aufbruch ins Industriezeitalter wurde im bis dato ländlichen Harburg vor allem von zwei Firmen getragen. Die Harburger Gummi-Kamm Companie, 1856 gegründet, ist bis heute ein wichtiger Arbeitgeber. Die Hartgummiprodukte der Firma – Haarkämme und -bürsten – wurden im 19. Jahrhundert hochgeschätzt. Im selben Jahr nahmen die Phoenix-Werke in Harburg ihre Arbeit auf. Hier war Weichgummi der Stoff, aus dem die weltweit exportierten Produkte gefertigt wurden. Im 20. Jahrhundert kamen neuere Kunststoffe hinzu.

Wenn es früher einmal hieß, daß der Unterelberaum arm sei an technischer Innovation und Kreativität, so widerlegen dieses Urteil für Harburg im 19. Jahrhundert vor allem diese beiden Gummiwaren-Produzenten. In der zweiten Hälfte des 20. Jahrhunderts ging am Technik-Himmel dieser oft übersehenen Großstadt im Schatten der Freien und Hansestadt jedoch ein Stern auf, der heute wahrhaftig globalen Glanz verbreitet. Die Technische Universität Hamburg-Harburg (TUHH) nahm 1980 ihren Forschungsbetrieb auf. Auf dem Campus mit seinem modernen Ensemble von Backsteingebäuden gibt es keinen Muff

Das Harburger Rathaus mit dem Vorplatz entstand gegen Ende des 19. Jahrhunderts im Stil der Neorenaissance (links).
Die Windmühle an der Schönenfelder Straße ist das Wahrzeichen von Wilhelmsburg (rechts).

Harburg's Rathaus, or City Hall, and its forecourt were designed and built in the neo-Renaissance style at the end of the nineteenth century (left).
The windmill on Schönenfelder Strasse is a well-known Wilhelmsburg landmark (right).

in the second half of the twentieth century a star rose in the technological firmament of this often-overlooked city in the shadow of Hamburg which now sheds a truly global light. The Technical University Hamburg-Harburg (TUHH) began its research operation in 1980. There is no thousand-year dust on the campus with its modern ensemble of brick buildings. People appear young and dynamic. They are innovative, keen to experiment and very successful. The latter is evident from two facts. Each year about 30 patents are registered. The proportion of research funds awarded is well above average. TUHH's youngest offspring is the Northern Institute of Technology (NIT). Privately financed by business sponsors, the NIT awards scholarships to foreign students. Its goal is on the one hand to provide outstanding training and on the other to build an international network of students, university and business.

## Harburg for day-trippers

Die Harburger Berge laden ein zu Wanderungen durch eine weite Waldlandschaft (links). Am Wilhelmsburger Reiherstiegdeich ist nichts zu ahnen von den sozialen Problemen dieses Stadtteils.

The Harburg Hills invite you to talk a walk through the extensive woods (left). To look at Reiherstiegdeich in Wilhelmsburg (right), you would not for one moment suspect the social problems that beset this area.

von tausend Jahren. Man gibt sich jung und dynamisch. Man ist innovativ, experimentierfreudig und sehr erfolgreich. Letzteres läßt sich gut an zwei Fakten ablesen. Jährlich werden hier rund 30 Patente angemeldet. Der Anteil eingeworbener Forschungsgelder ist überdurchschnittlich hoch. Das jüngste Kind der TUHH ist das Northern Institute of Technology (NIT). Privat finanziert von Sponsoren aus der Wirtschaft, vergibt das NIT Stipendien an ausländische Studenten. Ziel ist eine hervorragende Ausbildung einerseits und ein internationales Netzwerk aus Studierenden, Universität und Wirtschaft andererseits.

## Ausflugsziel Harburg

Mit allen Mitteln moderner Didaktik wird im neueingerichteten Hamburger Museum für Archäologie und die Geschichte Harburgs (Helms-Museum) am Harburger Rathausplatz Menschheitsgeschichte anschaulich gemacht. Man kann das Schädelfragment eines Neandertalers bewundern, der vor etwa 36 000 Jahren in Norddeutschland lebte. Der Knochen wurde in der Nähe von Cranz gefunden, das heute zum Bezirk Harburg gehört. Zu sehen ist, wie Men-

The history of mankind is brought to life with all the methods of modern didactics in the newly refurbished Hamburg Museum of Archaeology and the History of Harburg. Visitors to the museum on Harburg's town hall square can admire a fragment of the skull of a Neandertal man who lived in northern Germany about 36,000 years ago. The fragment of bone was found not far from the village of Cranz, now part of the borough of Harburg. They can also see how people were buried in northern Germany not long after the birth of Christ, and much more besides. The museum, founded in 1898, was named after its founder, the Harburg mill-owner August Helms. Further insights into local history are conveyed by the Museum of the Elbe Island of Wilhelmsburg and by the Wilhelmsburg Windmill, the emblem of the island linked to Harburg.

Shaped by the Ice Age, the countryside just outside Harburg is very varied. Woods, fens and heathland, broken by broad expanses of field, are favourite destinations for day-trippers. One special attraction is the 126-metre Kiekeberg in Ehestorf, where a group of reconstructed

schen in Norddeutschland kurz nach
Christi Geburt beerdigt wurden, und vie-
les mehr. Das seit 1898 bestehende
Museum wurde nach seinem Begründer,
dem Harburger Mühlenbesitzer August
Helms, benannt.

Heimatkundliche Kulturgeschichte
vermitteln auch das Museum der Elbinsel Wilhelmsburg und die Wilhelmsburger Windmühle, die das Wahrzeichen der
an Harburg angeschlossenen Elbinsel ist.

Die von der Eiszeit geformte Land-
schaft vor den Toren der Stadt ist
äußerst vielfältig. Wälder, Moore und
Heide, unterbrochen durch weitläufige
Felder, sind beliebte Ziele für Ausflügler.
Eine besondere Attraktion ist der 126
Meter hohe Ehestorfer Kiekeberg, wo ein
Ensemble wiederaufgebauter historischer
Bauernhäuser veranschaulicht, wie unse-
re Vorfahren im 17., 18. und 19. Jahr-
hundert auf dem Lande lebten.

So schön ist Harburg? Nicht ganz.
Denn in der Stadt selbst ist viel historische Bausubstanz durch die Bombenan-
griffe während des Zweiten Weltkriegs
vernichtet worden. Abrißaktionen und
architektonisch mißlungene Neubauten
haben das Gesicht von Harburg nach
1945 zusätzlich lädiert. Erst allmählich
hat man sich in den vergangenen zwei
Jahrzehnten darauf besonnen, daß die
Stadt eine uralte Geschichte besitzt,
deren Spuren noch nicht ganz verloren
sind. Auch die Tatsache, daß Harburg
ebenso wie Hamburg am Wasser liegt, ist
inzwischen wieder ins Bewußtsein
gerückt. Der Harburger Binnenhafen
war in der Vergangenheit die Keimzelle
der Kommune. Eben hier, zu beiden Seiten des westlichen Bahnhofkanals, der
das Gelände des Binnenhafens erschließt,
hat sich in den vergangenen Jahren ein
Netzwerk von Hightech-Unternehmen
und Forschungseinrichtungen angesiedelt. Das junge Hightech-Zentrum weist
mit seinem Namen „channel Harburg"
auf die Lage am Kanal hin.

Auf nach Harburg!

historic farmhouses show how our fore-
fathers lived in the countryside in the
seventeenth, eighteenth and nineteenth
centuries.

Lovely Harburg? Not entirely. Many
historic buildings in the town itself were
destroyed in World War II air raids.
Demolition campaigns and architecturally unsuccessful modern buildings have
added further blemishes. Only gradually
have people begun to recall in the last
two decades that the town has an
ancient history the traces of which have
not completely been lost. They have also
become aware that Harburg, like Hamburg, is a waterside town. Meanwhile,
awareness has grown that Harburg, like
Hamburg, is situated by the water. In the
past, Harburg's inland port was the core
of the community. And in this very
place, a network of high-tech companies
and research establishments has settled
in recent years on both sides of the west
Bahnhofkanal that opens up the inland
port area. The name of this young high-
tech centre, "channel Harburg," is a ref-
erence to its location on the canal.

So off to Harburg it is!

Blick in den Harburger
Lotsekanal südlich der
Süderelbe

A view of the Harburg
Lotsekanal (Pilots'
Canal), south of the
Süderelbe

# Schöne Aussichten für die Metropole am Wasser

A bright outlook for the riverside metropolis

Moderne Bürobauten der westlichen Speicherstadt sind die Vorreiter der geplanten Hafen-City auf dem Grasbrook.

Modern office buildings in the west of the Warehouse City are the forerunners of the planned HafenCity (Port City) on Grasbrook.

Die Chance ist einmalig. Wenn sich alle Träume erfüllen, kann Hamburg zu Beginn des 21. Jahrhunderts mit dem Bau der HafenCity eine Stadterneuerung ohnegleichen gelingen. Meßbar an dem Großprojekt Ende des 20. Jahrhunderts in London. Dort wurde das Nordufer der Themse mit seinen Docklands erfolgreich zu einem urbanen Quartier umgemünzt. Auch am Südufer des Flusses entstand ein neugeschaffenes weltstädtisches Milieu, sein Zentrum, das Museum Tate Modern, ist heute Ziel eines Millionenpublikums.

   Die Meßlatte liegt hoch. Die Ausgangssituation für das derzeit größte Städtebauprojekt Europas ist grandios. Die 155 Hektar umfassende Industriebrache auf einer Elbinsel nur 800 Meter südlich des Rathauses bietet beste Voraussetzungen, der Stadt ein neues Viertel mit neuer Urbanität zu entwickeln. Wohnen und Arbeiten am Wasser in engster Nachbarschaft zum Herzen der Stadt,

The opportunity is unique. If all the dreams come true, Hamburg will in the early years of the 21st century embark on an unparalleled programme of urban renewal, successfully implementing the HafenCity (PortCity), a project comparable only with London's large-scale late 20th century programme. In London, Docklands on the north bank of the Thames was successfully transformed into an urbane district. On the south bank too, a new cosmopolitan neighbourhood took shape. Its centre, the Tate Modern, is an art gallery that attracts visitors by the million.

   Standards are high. The starting position for what is currently Europe's largest town planning project is grandiose. The 155-hectare industrial wasteland site on an island in the River Elbe just 800 metres south of Hamburg's City Hall offers the best development prospects for a new district with a fresh level of urbanity. With the prospect of living and working by the riverside in closest proximity to the city centre, imagination is required. The new BoBo (short for bourgeois Bohemian) trendsetter must feel just as at home here as the

Das Hanseatic Trade Center an der Kehrwiederspitze bietet in seinen oberen Etagen einen faszinierenden Blick über den Hamburger Hafen.

The upper floors of the Hanseatic Trade Center on Kehrwiederspitze command a fascinating view of the Port of Hamburg.

Phantasie ist gefragt. Der neue Typ des BoBo (des bourgeoisen Bohemiens) muß sich hier genauso wohl fühlen können wie der kleine Laden- und Restaurantbesitzer, der Unternehmer im New Economy Business, die Mutter mit Kind, die Internet-Künstlerin, der leidenschaftliche Großstadtflaneur, der klassische Hanseat im Im- und Exporthandel, die Designerin, der Medienexperte.

Ein Ort nicht nur für die hedonistischen Spitzen der Gesellschaft. Ein amphibischer Stadtteil mit exzellenter neuer Architektur, der nicht nur den Reichen vorbehalten ist. Das ist das Ziel. Die Hafencity – ein weltstädtisches Quartier im Wassernetz der Elbverzweigungen, das in Europa nicht seinesgleichen hat. Das ist der Traum. Eine Vision, die vielen Gefahren ausgesetzt ist: dem puren Gewinnstreben der Investoren,

small shopkeeper or restaurant owner, the New Economy businessperson, the mother with children, the Internet artist, the passionate city stroller, the classic Hamburg businessman and importer or exporter, the designer and the media expert.

This must be a part of town that is not just designed for hedonists at the summit of society. It must be a waterside district

Die Fleete zwischen den noblen Geschäften am Neuen Wall und Große Bleichen wurden für Flaneure neu erschlossen.

The canals between the exclusive shops on Neuer Wall and Grosse Bleichen were redeveloped for strollers and coffee-house aficionados.

Das Medienzentrum
von Gruner + Jahr,
Architekten Steidle und
Kiessler, beherbergt gut
dreitausend Mitarbeiter.
In seiner Architektur
wurden gleich mehrere
Motive aus der
Geschichte des Ortes
und seinem heutigen
Ambiente aufgenom-
men: das ehemalige
Gängeviertel, die Stahl-
architektur der Schiffe
sowie das Hochbahn-
viadukt. In den benach-
barten engen Straßen
am Baumwall haben
sich neue Kneipen,
Restaurants, Herbergen
und Schiffsausrüster
etabliert. Mit ihnen ist
die alte Atmosphäre des
hafennahen Quartiers
wieder entstanden.

The Gruner + Jahr
media centre, designed
by architects Steidle
and Kiessler, accommo-
dates well over 3,000
workers. Its architec-
ture incorporates sever-
al motifs from the his-
tory of the area and its
present ambience: the
former district of nar-
row alleys, steel ships
and the elevated rail-
way. New bars, restau-
rants, inns and ship's
outfitters have estab-
lished themselves in the
adjacent narrow streets
on Baumwall, restoring
the traditional atmos-
phere of the district
around the port.

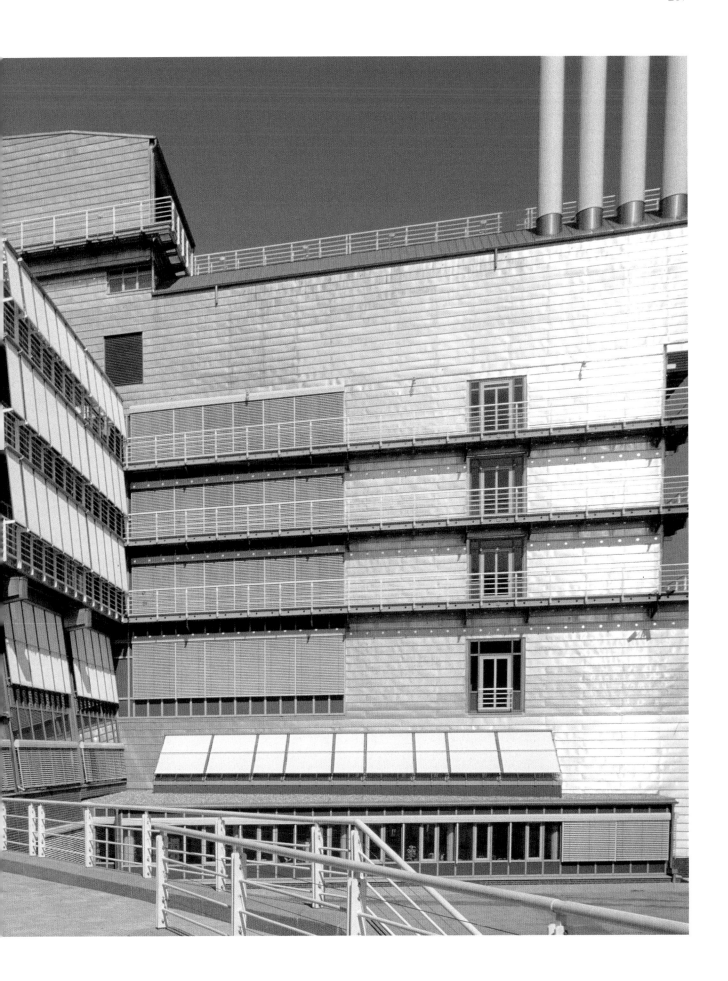

In einer modernen Architektur spannt sich der gläserne neue Kontorhauskomplex am Anckelmannplatz über das Hochwasserbassin in Hammerbrook. Den Architekten Bothe, Richter, Teherani ist es gelungen, hier, an der Stadteinfahrt zur Hamburger City, ein ganz ungewöhnliches Bauwerk zu schaffen, das nicht nur funktional hohe Qualitäten hat, sondern auch eine energiesparende Bauweise aufweist.

The modern architecture of the new glass office complex on Anckelmannplatz extends across the Hammerbrook high-water basin. Architects Bothe, Richter and Teherani have succeeded in producing a really unusual work of architecture here at the entrance to downtown Hamburg. It is both highly functional and of energy-saving construction.

Der durch Jahrzehnte vernachlässigte Hafenrand glänzt heute mit zeitgenössischer Bebauung (oben), gleiches gilt für die Neue ABC-Straße.

After decades of neglect, areas on the outskirts of the port now boast some superb contemporary buildings (above). The same applies to Neue ABC-Strasse.

dem Kleinmut und der Phantasielosigkeit der Politiker, der Ausgrenzung neuer wagemutiger Ideengeber. 1999 schrieb die Hamburger Kultursenatorin Christina Weiss in ihrem Buch mit dem Titel „Stadt ist Bühne – Kulturpolitik heute" (ein Titel, der auch zu lesen war als „Stadt ist Kulturpolitik heute") einen Satz, der wie eine Warnung an die

with first-class modern architecture that is not an exclusive preserve of the rich. That is the objective: the HafenCity, a cosmopolitan district amid the network of waterways that characterise the River Elbe at this point and an area unrivalled in Europe. That is the dream, a vision that is exposed to many risks: the unbridled profit motivation of investors, the faintheartedness and lack of imagination of politicians and the exclusion of people with bold new ideas. In 1999 Christina Weiss, Hamburg's Arts Senator, wrote in her book The City as a Stage – Arts Policy Today (a title that could also be read as meaning that the city is arts policy today) a sentence that could be taken as a warning to the people behind the new HafenCity project. "Where politics forgets the intellectual anchoring of society and its individual members in the arts, it neglects what politics really is."

The HafenCity as a grand design can only succeed if architecture is not made the handmaiden of investors, if sellers of

Macher der neuen HafenCity gelesen werden kann: „Wo Politik die geistige Verankerung der Gesellschaft und ihrer einzelnen Mitglieder in der Kultur vergißt, vernachlässigt sie das eigentlich Politische."

Die HafenCity als großer Wurf kann nur gelingen, wenn die Architektur nicht zum Knecht der Investoren gemacht wird, wenn Seelenverkäufer keine Chance haben, wenn behördliche Auflagen nicht der große Hemmschuh für neue Ideen sind. Die Feststellung eines Stadtplanungsexperten, daß Hamburgs ganzer architektonischer Stolz, das in den 1920er Jahren von Fritz Höger errichtete Chilehaus, heute wegen der Vielzahl behördlicher Auflagen nicht mehr gebaut werden könnte, stimmt nachdenklich. Das Chilehaus ist neben den Bauten von Fritz Schumacher die Krone der Hamburger Backsteinarchitektur.

Die Metropole an Alster und Elbe hat sich immer schneller gemausert, verändert als andere Städte. Hat alte Schalen abgeworfen und neue angesetzt. Mit den traditionellen Backsteinfassaden konkurriert seit einigen Jahren eine Vielzahl exzellenter Glas-Stahl-Bauten, die das Gesicht der Stadt aktuell geprägt haben. Weltweit agierende Architekturbüros haben hier Zeichen gesetzt. Der neue Flughafen, die luftige Glasbebauung am Elbberg in Altona und an der ABC-Straße, die Fleetinsel. Das sind vehemente Auffrischungen des Stadtbildes. Hinzu kommt die Umwidmung historischer Gebäude zu neuen Aufgaben. Das Stilwerk am Altonaer Fischereihafen ist zum Mekka aller Designliebhaber geworden. In dem ehemaligen Industriegebäude gegenüber hat Greenpeace seinen Platz

souls stand no chance and if planning procedures do not prove a major obstacle to new ideas. It is alarming to note a town planning expert's comment that Hamburg's architectural pride and joy, the Chilehaus office block, built by Fritz Höger in the 1920s, could today no longer be built because of the plethora of building regulations. The Chilehaus ranks alongside Fritz Schumacher's work as the crowning achievement of the Hamburg redbrick style of architecture.

Hamburg has always changed faster than other cities, casting off old guises and donning new ones. For a number of years a large number of excellent glass and steel buildings have competed with Hamburg's traditional redbrick exteriors, giving the city its current appearance. Architectural partnerships that do business all over the world have set trends. The new airport terminal, light and airy glass-clad buildings on Elbberg in Altona, on ABC-Strasse in the city centre and on the Fleetinsel. They all go to make up a decided freshening-up of the cityscape and have been accompanied by conversion of historic buildings for use in a new function. The Stilwerk down by the Fischereihafen, or fish docks, in Altona has come to be seen as a Mecca for all lovers of design. In a for-

Das Medienzentrum an der Rothenbaumchaussee plante Lord Norman Foster.

The media centre on Rothenbaumchaussee was planned by Lord Norman Foster.

Der Architekt Bernhard
Winking entwarf den
eleganten Bau des Fleet-
hofes zwischen Stadt-
hausbrücke und Her-
rengrabenfleet. Seine
Arkaden und der
öffentliche Durchgang
durch die interne Halle
schaffen viele Verbin-
dungswege zwischen
dem Wohngebiet am
Großneumarkt und den
eleganten Einkaufsstra-
ßen und Passagen zum
Jungfernstieg.

Architect Bernhard
Winking designed the
elegant Fleethof build-
ing between Stadthaus-
brücke and Herren-
grabenfleet. His arcades
and the public pathway
through the interior
hall create many links
between the residential
area on Grossneumarkt
and the elegant shop-
ping streets and arcades
toward Jungfernstieg.

Zu der Neubesinnung
auf die Schönheit der
Stadt am Ende des 20.
Jahrhunderts gehörte
die Restaurierung histo-
rischer Gebäude – wie
hier an der Ecke Post-
straße/Neuer Wall.

The new urban con-
sciousness at the end of
the twentieth century
led to the restoration of
historic buildings like
this one on the corner
of Poststrasse and
Neuer Wall.

Bei der Umnutzung ehemaliger Industriegebäude ist Hamburg seit den 1970er Jahren vorbildlich. Die Lagerhäuser an der Elbkante wurden phantasievoll zu Kontoren, Lofts und Wohnungen umgebaut wie hier der Komplex des Altonaer Stadtlagerhauses.

Hamburg has since the 1970s served as a model in converting former industrial buildings to other uses. The warehouses by the Elbe imaginatively turned into offices, lofts and apartments, like the Altona Stadtlager building complex seen here.

Das ehemalige Gaswerk in Bahrenfeld bildet mit dem „Gastwerk", einem Designhotel, und umgebauten Maschinenhallen einen neuen Stadtteilmittelpunkt.

The former gasworks in Bahrenfeld is now a new centre for the district, incorporating Gastwerk, a designer hotel.

gefunden. Ein 1950 stillgelegtes E-Werk an der Altonaer Straße Beim Alten Gaswerk wurde unter dem Namen „Gastwerk" zum extravaganten Hotel, neue Büros und Restaurants beleben die ehemalige Industriebrache.

Bei der Modernisierung trauern viele dem alten Zustand nach. Kampnagel ist nicht mehr, was es mal war. Die maroden Fabrikhallen, die seit Anfang der achtzi-

mer industrial building opposite the Stilwerk, Greenpeace is now housed. A power station in Altona that was shut down in 1950 and is located on a street by the name of Beim Alten Gaswerk (At the Old Gasworks) was transformed into an extravagant hotel by the name of Gastwerk (Guestworks), plus offices and restaurants that have given this former industrial wasteland a fresh lease of life.

In the process of modernisation there are many who lament the passing of the old. Kampnagel, for instance, is no longer what it was. The dilapidated factory and workshops that from the early 1980s proved an enormous source of inspiration for artists of all kinds were ironed smooth into an ordinary venue. A city that lays claim to a soul needs its unsightly but creative corners. No-one was as keenly aware of that than the composer Rolf Liebermann. When the cosmopolitan bid Hamburg farewell as manager and artistic director of the

ger Jahre Künstler aller Art ganz außer-
ordentlich inspiriert hatten, wurden
glattgebügelt zu einem gewöhnlichen
Spielort. Eine Großstadt, die eine „Seele"
haben will, braucht kreative Schmuddel-
ecken. Niemand hat das so gut gewußt
wie der Komponist Rolf Liebermann. Als
dieser Weltbürger 1988 seiner Intendan-
tenzeit an der Hamburgischen Staatsoper
ade sagte, verlegte er sein Abschiedsge-
schenk für die Hansestadt nach Kampnagel. Seine von dem Amerikaner Robert
Wilson inszenierten „Cosmopolitan
Greetings" wird niemand vergessen, der
damals dabei war. „Kosmopolitische
Grüße" sind für eine Großstadt das Salz
an der Suppe. Gut, daß sowohl das
Deutsche Schauspielhaus als auch das
Thalia Theater, die Staatsoper und
Kampnagel den heute schon legendären
Inszenierungen von Bob Wilson ein Dach
über dem Kopf gaben.

Bei diesen immer teuren Unternehmungen wurde eingeübt, was heute aus
dem Kulturleben gar nicht mehr wegzudenken ist: die Partnerschaft zwischen
Kultur und Wirtschaftsunternehmen.
Dem Kultursponsoring gehört die
Zukunft. Das Engagement des Staates ist
sowieso Ehrensache. Was den hanseatischen Politikern allerdings immer wieder
hinter die Ohren geschrieben werden
muß. Wenn Wirtschaft und Politik sich
in der schönsten und reichsten Stadt
Deutschlands für die Kultur stark
machen, winken am Horizont der
Zukunft mit Sicherheit SCHÖNE AUS-
SICHTEN AN ALSTER UND ELBE.

Um das Kulturzentrum
auf dem Gelände der
ehemaligen Kranfabrik
„Kampnagel" zu retten,
mußte der Komplex mit
Neubauten für die Me-
dienbranche ergänzt
werden. Zweifellos kon-
trastieren diese stark
mit dem Reiz der
improvisierten Spiel-
stätten.

To save the arts centre
on the site of the for-
mer Kampnagel crane
factory, the complex
had to be complement-
ed by new buildings for
the media industry. Un-
doubtedly, they form a
stark contrast with the
charm of improvised
venues.

Staatsoper in 1988, he transferred his
parting gift to the city to Kampnagel.
No-one who saw his Cosmopolitan
Greetings, directed by Robert Wilson,
will ever forget the event. Cosmopolitan
greetings are the salt in a city's soup. It is
good to feel that both the Deutsches
Schauspielhaus and the Thalia Theater,
the Staatsoper and Kampnagel staged
Bob Wilson's legendary productions.

They were always expensive ventures,
but they practised something that is now
a mainstay of the arts: partnership
between the arts and business. Cultural
sponsorship is the shape of things to
come. The public sector's commitment is
a point of honour, of course, although
Hamburg's politicians constantly need to
be reminded of the fact. If business and
politics join forces to promote the arts in
Germany's richest and most beautiful
city, the prospect on the horizon of the
future must surely be A BRIGHT OUT-
LOOK ON THE ALSTER AND THE
ELBE.

Dee Dee Bridgewater
bei Rolf Liebermanns
legendärem Abschied
von seiner Operninten-
danz auf Kampnagel
mit „Cosmopolitan
Greetings" 1988.

Dee Dee Brigdewater
conveying "Cosmopoli-
tan Greetings" at Rolf
Liebermann's legendary
farewell as director of
the Hamburg Opera
House at Kampnagel in
1988.

Der Hamburger Hafen als Tor zur Welt ist noch immer eine der faszinierendsten Visitenkarten der Stadt.

As a gateway to the world, the Port of Hamburg is still one of the city's most fascinating visiting cards.

Die Deutsche Bibliothek – CIP-Einheitsaufnahme

Hamburg : Metropole an Alster und Elbe / Anna Brenken (Text). Egbert Kossak (Fotos). – Hamburg : Ellert und Richter, 2001
ISBN 3-8919-0011-6

© Ellert & Richter Verlag GmbH, Hamburg 2001

Text und Bildlegenden/Text and captions: Anna Brenken, Hamburg
Übertragung ins Englische/English translation: Paul Bewicke, Hamburg
Lektorat/Edited by: D. Kanzelberger
Gestaltung/Design: Büro Brückner + Partner, Bremen
Satz/Typesetting: KCS GmbH, Buchholz
Lithographie/Lithography: ORC, Offset-Repro im Centrum, Hamburg
Druck/Print: Girzig + Gottschalk, Bremen
Bindung/Binding: Buchbinderei S. R. Büge GmbH, Celle

**Titelabbildung:** Binnenalster mit Blick auf Jungfernstieg/ Inner Alster with a view of the Jungfernstieg